GEORGIA HARKNESS

Georgia Harkness

For Such a Time as This

ROSEMARY SKINNER KELLER

Abingdon Press / Nashville

GEORGIA HARKNESS: FOR SUCH A TIME AS THIS

Library of Congress Cataloging-in-Publication Data

KELLER, ROSEMARY SKINNER.
    Georgia Harkness : for such a time as this / Rosemary Skinner Keller.
        p.   cm.
    Includes index.
    ISBN 0-687-13276-2 (alkaline/hard cover)
    1. Harkness, Georgia Elma, 1891-1974.   2. Theologians—United States—Biography.   I. Title.
    BX8495.H255K45   1992
    230'.76'092—dc20
    [B]   92-5777
                                                                                      CIP

The author gratefully acknowledges the following for permission to reprint:

Abingdon Press for excerpts from Georgia Harkness's books: *The Dark Night of the Soul,* copyright renewal © 1972 Georgia Harkness; *The Glory of God,* copyright renewal © 1974 Georgia Harkness; *Understanding the Christian Faith,* copyright renewal © 1974 Georgia Harkness.

Henry Holt and Co., Inc. for excerpts from Georgia Harkness, *The Resources of Religion.* Copyright 1936 by Holt, Rinehart, and Winston.

Hope Publishing Company for "Hope of the World." Words copyright © 1954. Renewal 1982 by The Hymn Society, Texas Christian University, Fort Worth, TX 76129. All rights reserved.

TO THOSE
WOMEN IN THEIR RED COATS:

MY FEMALE COLLEAGUES ON THE FACULTY OF
GARRETT-EVANGELICAL THEOLOGICAL SEMINARY, 1992:

PHYLLIS BIRD
RUTH DUCK
LALLENE RECTOR
ROSEMARY RUETHER
BARBARA TROXELL
LINDA VOGEL

AND DOROTHY JEAN FURNISH: EMERITUS

*

AND TO THE MEMORY
OF MY MOTHER
MARY MORLEY SKINNER
OCTOBER 2, 1899–MARCH 5, 1992

Acknowledgments

Murray and Dorothy Leiffer are foremost among the host of individuals and institutions whom I wish to thank for the support given to me in the research and writing of this biography of Georgia Harkness. Murray died on February 1, 1992, and Dorothy remains in serious medical condition in La Jolla, California. Several years ago, they catalogued and indexed the fourteen-box collection of Georgia Harkness Papers in the archives of Garrett-Evangelical Theological Seminary. This collection will remain the major source of Harkness's primary and secondary source materials. Without this service for a colleague and friend whom they loved, a biography of Georgia Harkness could not have been written. Too, my interview with them in 1990, during their retirement in La Jolla, was one of the most valuable and delightful experiences of this entire project.

Final resources and grants of time were made available through Garrett-Evangelical Theological Seminary, with my thanks to President Neal Fisher and Vice-President of Academic Affairs Richard Tholin, and the Methodist Educational Funds. A further financial grant was received from the General Board of Higher Education and Ministry of The United Methodist Church, with my appreciation to Dr. Thomas Trotter, formerly executive general secretary of the Board. During his administration, and immediately after

Harkness's death, the Board also instituted the Georgia Harkness Scholarship Fund for women preparing for ordained ministry in The United Methodist Church.

My special thanks for the private archival sources of the Harkness Family Collection, made available by Georgia's niece and her husband, Peg and John Overholt of Kilmarnock, Virginia; the Harkness United Methodist Church, Harkness, New York, provided through the graciousness of its pastor, the Reverend Marion Moore-Colgan; and the private papers of George Arnold, whose family has lived on the property adjoining the Harkness homestead for several generations.

Two manuscript resources invaluable to this study were the Harkness Collection in the United Library at Garrett-Evangelical Theological Seminary, with special thanks to Al Caldwell, head librarian, and David Himrod, research librarian; and the two hundred letters exchanged between Edgar Brightman and Georgia Harkness in the Brightman Collection deposited in the Department of Special Collections of the Mugar Memorial Library, Boston University, with thanks to W. Perry Barton, senior manuscript technician. My appreciation, too, for manuscript collections and library resources at the Claremont School of Theology, Cornell University, Elmira College, Mount Holyoke College, and The State University of New York at Plattsburgh. Thanks to Celia Goodale for her work in the Mount Holyoke Collection.

Interviews were held throughout the country with relatives, friends, students, and colleagues who knew Harkness from her childhood to her death. My thanks to John Bennett; John, Jean, and Theodora Cobb; Mary Durham; Durwood Foster; Dorothy Jean Furnish; Harland Hogue; Paul and Georgina Irwin; Pierce Johnson; Florence Lerrigo; Charles McCoy; Charles Marks; Walter Muelder; Harry Pak; Louise Proskine; Wayne Rood; Harvey and Lois Seifert; Jan Shipps; and John and Helen Von Rohr, as well as to others who have already been mentioned: George Arnold, Marion Moore-Colgan, and Murray and Dorothy Leiffer. Lynette Danskin and Jane Borden also provided interview resources.

Three Ph.D. dissertations provided highly significant background: Martha Lynne Scott, "The Theology and Social

Thought of Georgia Harkness" (Northwestern University, 1984); Paula Elizabeth Gilbert, "Choice of the Greater Good: The Christian Witness of Georgia Harkness Arising from the Interplay of Spiritual Life and Theological Perspective" (Duke University, 1984); and Dianne Evelyn Carpenter, "Georgia Harkness's Distinctive Personalistic Synthesis" (Boston University, 1988). Helpful published essays on Harkness were written by Martha Scott and Joan Englesman, along with unpublished essays by Dianne Grier, Mary Hunt, and Mary Elizabeth Moore.

Over the past two years, I have presented papers related to this project at the American Academy of Religion, the American Society of Church Historians, and the Canadian Methodist Historical Society. Lectureships at the Iliff School of Theology, St. Paul School of Theology, and the Pastors and Laity School of the Pacific Northwest Area of The United Methodist Church also provided opportunities for me to present my work in progress.

My sincere appreciation for the research assistantship provided by Koby Lee-Forman, Chris Evans, and Eleanor Stebner in the Joint Ph.D. Program of Northwestern University/Garrett-Evangelical Theological Seminary. I am equally grateful to Rosalyn Dryer-Scott, a Master of Divinity student at Garrett-Evangelical, who transcribed from tapes the many interviews that I have used in this study.

My husband, Bob Keller, read and critiqued this manuscript from beginning to end. I am grateful beyond words for his keen editorial eye, his involvement in the several research trips we took together, and his day-to-day support and endurance. Further, several of my female colleagues—Ruth Duck, Lallene Rector, Rosemary Ruether, Barbara Troxell, and Linda Vogel—read all or parts of this manuscript and gave me encouragement and support beyond measure.

Finally, my sincere thanks to Mary Catherine Dean, my editor at Abingdon Press, for her editorial skill as well as her patience and grace in relating to me as we worked together on the life journey of Georgia Harkness, for such a time as this.

Rosemary Keller

Contents

Foreword

F. THOMAS TROTTER

Our generation takes for granted the presence of women in theological schools. It was not always so. Women now make up more than 50 percent of the students of the theological seminaries related to the Association of Theological Schools. Although gains are modest in faculty positions, women are taking their places in distinguished chairs. Given the slowness of change, it is all the more surprising that Georgia Harkness should have been a leading theologian in distinguished faculties of higher education as early as the 1920s!

Harkness was an exceptional woman by any standard. She was one of the most respected theologians of her period. The time is right for a major study of her life and work.

She retired to Claremont, California, after leaving her chair at the Pacific School of Religion in Berkeley. Before P.S.R. she had been at Garrett Biblical Institute, later Garrett-Evangelical Theological Seminary. I was the Dean at Claremont and invited her to participate in the seminary. I enjoyed her stimulating conversation, the intensity of her spirit, and her friendship. We even survived a rear-end collision together on a Los Angeles freeway.

Harkness had been a student of Edgar Sheffield Brightman at Boston University and inherited his notorious passion for precision and disciplined work. She was enormously productive as a writer with thirty-seven titles to her name. At her death, she had a half-finished manuscript in the typewriter. She met deadlines without fail. She had the capacity for focusing on her work in spite of distractions, which in her declining years included discomfiting health.

The three women who studied for their Ph.D.s with Brightman at Boston in the 1920s ended their careers as neighbors. Mildred Cranston, Pearl Winans, and Georgia Harkness, classmates a half-century earlier, lived their last years in Claremont. Each was remarkable in her own way.

Her companion for thirty-three years was a sparkling woman named Verna Miller. Harkness and Verna were brought together by Ernest Fremont Tittle when each was being counseled by him for loneliness and depression. The two women were wonderful together. Harkness was amused by Miller's sharp tongue and somewhat more conservative posture. Miller saw to it that Harkness had what she needed to be a scholar.

Harkness's books were very popular with several generations of pastors. It is ironic that she was criticized by some for writing for working pastors. This was carelessly thought to be something of a weakness in her theological equipment. In fact, as she demonstrated, her eye was on the pastor in the church who had to face daily the direct questions of belief and moral existence with the people.

It is not surprising that Harkness was a faithful and active member of her church. She took seriously the responsibility of a Christian life. That included serving on committees and being one of the most generous givers in the congregation. She patiently instructed her pastors in Claremont from time to time. The several pastors at the Claremont United Methodist Church during those years had developed special ways of dealing with a congregation that included, in addition to Harkness, a dozen other world-class theologians. James Dallas once observed, "There is at least one person in this congregation who is the world's expert on any subject I may mention in a sermon. So I just go ahead and do my best." Harkness appreciated her pastors, and they loved her.

Her career spanned several great movements in the church. She participated actively in the various branches of the ecumenical movement that flowered in the post–World War II period. She was a pacifist long before that was an acceptable position even in the churches. She was an outspoken advocate of human rights.

She was a delegate to several General Conferences of the Church and always outspoken when she could get recognized by the chair. Her ecumenism was so consistent that she tried to get the Pacific School of Religion included in the new United Methodist Ministerial Education Fund at the General Conference of 1968. She resisted the notion that funds should support denominational institutions and urged that funds follow individual students into non-UMC schools. She and I never settled that argument.

Georgia Harkness was a feminist in terms that many may have some difficulty understanding today. As Rosemary Keller notes in this biography, Harkness was assertive about her right to be accepted in the male-dominated world of theological education. But she was not militant. Some commentary about her younger and more militant feminist friends reflected the perspective of a woman who had made it in a man's world without special access. One younger female colleague called her the "queen bee," an uncomplimentary allusion to the lack of females in her rather wide circle of male admirers.

She had a personal and confident view of the contributions women would make in theology. After all, she had paid her duties in a landscape without many female colleagues. But she always attended the bright new women in theology with a mixture of appreciation and reservation. In that understandable mode, she seemed to some to be out of touch with feminist movements.

Hundreds of pastors of the last generation owe the vitality of their preaching to Georgia Harkness. She was a pastor's theologian. She wrote with an eye to the issues of faith as she understood them. She was always pushing against the rim of that circle of faith. She resisted being distracted to pursue faddish themes because of her conviction about the persistence of the central questions of belief and action.

When she died, there was a rush of special interests to claim her legacy. Georgia would have understood that. She never ducked, but always maintained her personal poise and grace, preferring to be remembered as a theologian.

She was a complex and remarkable woman. Her writings have no trace of bitterness or party passion. She was at home in theology and comfortable being a faithful member of the household of God. She was a remarkable theologian in her time.

Rosemary Keller stands in the tradition of Harkness. She too has the scholarly impulse and the discipline to bend it to useful purpose. Her studies in Harkness remind a new generation of the character of this woman and will help establish her as one of the premier figures in American religious thought in our century. For that we all owe Keller appreciation and thanks.

F. Thomas Trotter
President
Alaska Pacific University,
Anchorage, Alaska

Preface

ON VOCATIONAL JOURNEY WITH
GEORGIA HARKNESS

ROSEMARY SKINNER KELLER

I began my vocational journey with Georgia Harkness several years ago. Initially, it was an academic pilgrimage. On the faculty of Garrett-Evangelical Theological Seminary throughout the 1980s and today, I became aware of the legend of Georgia Harkness, the first professional female theologian in the United States, who had spent a significant portion of her teaching career at Garrett Bible Institute. As a historian of Religion and American Culture, with special fields of research and teaching in Women and Religion and Biographical Studies, I became increasingly curious about who this woman was.

Living from 1891 until 1974, Harkness's life spanned the turn of the century and the first three quarters of the twentieth century. She was a pioneer Professor of Applied Theology first, for eleven years, 1939 until 1950, at Garrett Biblical Institute, and then for eleven more, 1950 until 1961, at Pacific School of Religion. Throughout her adulthood, she was one of the most distinguished persons, prophetic critics, and hardest workers in the ecumenical church and her own Methodist denomination.

Realizing that Harkness would have been one hundred years old in 1991, I believed that her life needed to be recovered before she was lost to history. Further, she had given to Garrett-Evangelical Seminary a vast amount of private and public papers that were indexed and organized by her former colleagues and close friends, Murray and Dorothy Leiffer. In 1976, the Georgia Harkness Chair was inaugurated through the vision of President Merlyn Northfelt and women students on campus. Rosemary Radford Ruether was selected as the most appropriate person to fill that chair, and she holds the distinction today as The Georgia Harkness Professor of Applied Theology.

Based on Harkness's significance, my academic interests, and the presence of her papers only steps from my office, I decided that I should write her biography. My initial question, which relates to the recovery of all women's history in the late twentieth century, was "who was Georgia Harkness and why don't we know anything about her?"

In the 1970s, after my marriage and the birth of our two children, I had returned to graduate school and gained a Ph.D. in American and Women's History at the University of Illinois in Chicago. Years before, I had entered Yale Divinity School in 1956 and received a Master of Religious Education degree there. That was the same year women were granted full clergy rights in The Methodist Church, with Georgia Harkness being a prime mover in that long struggle. Further, she was a full professor at Pacific School of Religion and had been serving on seminary faculties for more than fifteen years by that time. In 1956, however, I had never heard of Georgia Harkness. Her reality simply had not penetrated the Yale Divinity School curriculum.

In the 1980s, the need was obvious to recover the life and thought of Georgia Harkness "for such a time as this" in the history of women and religion. Beginning this outward and academic vocational journey as her biographer, I did the things that a historian should do. I delved into her papers in the Garrett-Evangelical archives and into her books, which amounted to a staggering thirty-seven and which were almost all out of print by that time. I learned from three dissertations that had already been written on Georgia Harkness by Martha Scott (on whose dissertation committee I served in the Joint Northwestern/Garrett-Evangelical Graduate Program, 1984; Paula Gilbert (Duke University, 1984); and Dianne Carpenter (Boston University, 1988).

Then I began to travel the United States, my husband often going with me, to retrace Georgia's steps and to gain the flavor of her life. These wonderful trips began in the far northeast, in the vicinity of her beautiful home country of Harkness, in far up-state New York. Then I went to the central part of the state to Ithaca, where she attended Cornell University, and to Elmira, where she had her first and most lengthy teaching tenure of fifteen years at Elmira College.

In Massachusetts, I visited Mount Holyoke College, where Georgia taught for two years after Elmira, and Boston University, where she earned her Master's and Ph.D. The Mugar Library at Boston University brought one of the most significant finds of this geographical pilgrimage. Two hundred letters, exchanged between Harkness and her mentor, Edgar Sheffield Brightman, were deposited in the archival collection of Brightman papers. Their use in this biography brings richness to the "inner" Georgia that no other source provided.

I traveled as far west in the continental United States as did Georgia, visiting and gaining valuable interviews with persons who knew her well in her later years at Pacific School of Religion in Berkeley and in Claremont, California, where she retired. In the midst of these trips, I spend wonderful time with Peg and John Overholt, her closest living relatives today, in Kilmarnock, Virginia. They shared the extraordinary collection of family papers and pictures with me. In between all the trips, I spent most of my time on the Garrett-Evangelical campus, where Harkness lived during the most crucial and formative part of her life as she descended into her "dark night of the soul" and recovered from it.

"On vocational journey with Georgia Harkness" increasingly became more than an academic and geographical pilgrimage to me, as exciting as all that was. I was drawn to her inward journey and to the way in which she, as a pioneer woman in a man's professional world, lived out her calling and career. In this biography, I have tried to bring together, interweave, and be faithful to her inward and outward vocational journeys.

The story begins with her deep rootage in the beautiful rural, isolated foothills of the Adirondack Mountains in the far northeastern corner of up-state New York. There she was grounded in evangelical Christianity, an inheritance she never forsook but expanded on throughout her eighty-three years of life. She cherished the wholesome values of her "goodly heritage," but her intellectual and spiritual precociousness as a child soon gave evidence that she would venture on to a heretofore uncharted life pilgrimage.

On her own, though with family support, this "shy, green, and countrified" girl stepped into another world when she entered Cornell University as a very young adult of seventeen years old. Soon after graduation, she went on to Boston University for advanced studies and responded to the exciting intellectual challenge of the philosophy department and its academic giants of the day, Edgar Brightman, Albert Knudsen, and others. Her young adult dreams were to become a teacher and a writer. She worked hard, and she soared during those years.

By her mid-years, Harkness's career escalated and she was described as "famed female theologian." She brought together her evangelical Christianity with her philosophical idealism to gain prominence in the academic disciplines of both theology and philosophy. She also became a fearless social prophet, challenging the ecumenical church and her Methodist denomination to stand against the destructive "isms" of the day—including militarism, racism, sexism, and classism—out of their commitment to Christ. Further, she began to practice a deep, inward spiritual life in the train of the great mystics of the past and present, through the reading of devotional classics and her writing of poetry and prayers.

Later mid-life brought conflicts and crises, in both her inner and outer worlds, which led Georgia into a prolonged "dark night of the soul" over several years. Coming to grips with her calling, in greater depth than ever before, she was released from spiritual depression and gained new and fruitful life as she moved into older adulthood. Her companionship with Verna Miller, with whom she shared her home for the last thirty years of her life, began during these years and contributed new happiness and meaning to both their lives.

An inner spiritual maturity characterized Georgia's later years and brought a balance to her personal and professional life that was a fruit of her generativity. John Cobb's judgment that Georgia Harkness would have fit well into a "Department of Wholistic Living" sums up the witness—and the legacy—of her life.

I have long been taken by Dorothy Day's expression that the spiritual life is the greatest adventure of the modern age. Traveling with Georgia Harkness on her inner and outer journey, I have come to understand the profundity of Day's words and to experience their meaning more deeply in my own life.

In the very moments that I was writing the final few pages of this book and drawing Georgia Harkness's life to a close, my own mother, Mary Morley Skinner, died on March 5, 1992. She was ninety-two years old, was happy about my venture, and was trying to help me through to its completion. She stayed until she knew that I was through. She helped me.

My interpretation of Georgia Harkness's life develops the theme of her lifetime vocational journey, in terms of both her work and her larger vision of responding to God and living in partnership with God with the wholeness of her life. There are other emphases that writers could take, and I hope that my venture will encourage others to step forth and be moved by her life, as I have been.

Introduction

GEORGIA HARKNESS:
THEOLOGIAN FOR ALL SEASONS

ROSEMARY RADFORD RUETHER

*F*or American Christian women, seeking their rightful place in the ministry and the teaching profession in churches and seminaries, Georgia Harkness stands as both forerunner and role model. Born in 1891 and dying in August of 1974, Georgia Harkness stands in the middle distance behind the current reality of American women in the church. Her childhood lies in the Victorian era at the end of the nineteenth century. Her first social involvements coincide with the end of the First World War and the culmination of the first feminist movement, which finally won women's suffrage in 1921.

The last years of her life in the late 1960s and early 1970s overlap with the events that shaped the current feminist movement. Alert and socially involved to her last days, Harkness was deeply concerned with the civil rights movement and supported the opposition to the Vietnam War. Her book *Women in Church and Society* was published in 1972, when she was eighty-one years old. In its opening chapter she surveys the phenomenology of the Women's Liberation Movement of the late 1960s, ranging from WITCH (Women's International Terrorist Conspiracy from Hell) to the National Organization for Women and the National Women's Party. While clearly on the moderate and practical side of this specrum, she refers to the radical feminists with gentle humor, rather than condemnation.

In June of 1974 I gave a talk on feminist theology at the Community Church in Claremont, California, the university town where I had received my undergraduate and graduate education. A bright-eyed elderly woman approached me after the talk to tell me how much she had enjoyed the presentation. It was Georgia Harkness, who, at that time, I knew only by her 1931 book on Calvin's life and ethics. Georgia Harkness would die a little over two months later. Little did either of us imagine that two years later I would be invited to Garrett-Evangelical Theological Seminary, where Harkness had taught from 1939 to 1950, to be the first holder of the Georgia Harkness Chair in Applied Theology.

Georgia Harkness remained all her life very much a product of the Social Gospel of the 1920s and early 1930s. Trained more in philosophy than theology in the school of Boston personalism, she grew into becoming a Christian theologian very much in tandemn with the growth of her recognition of her need for a living, personal faith to support her own active life as a teacher, writer, world traveler in ecumenical circles and social critic. In her forties and fifties, Georgia Harkness became increasingly clear that a purely academic or intellectual mode of thought could not sustain her. She needed a deeply affective faith, nurtured by prayer, poetry, and worship. In turn, she would nurture the spiritual lives of many others with her own religious poetry, hymns and devotional writings.

In an article on her spiritual pilgrimage, published in *The Christian Century* in 1939, Harkness would forthrightly declare, "I was a pacifist and a socialist ten years ago and still am." Like many other Christian socialists of that era, Harkness saw economic justice as integral to Christian faith. The capitalist system, with its impersonalism, inequity, and primacy of profit over people, was intrinsically contrary to Christian ethics. Capitalism on an international level was expressed in economic imperialism, the root of world wars. Advocacy of economic justice, as a central message of the church's social teachings, continue to be stressed in Harkness's writings throughout her life.

Harkness also was an intrepid critic of racism in American life. Although she saw racism expressed in economic injustice, Harkness also recognized that racial prejudice goes beyond economics and manifests a deeper pathology that refuses to recognize other groups as our neighbors. While most Americans ignored injustice to Japanese-Americans during the Second World War, Harkness denounced this unjust treatment. "The internment of 110,000 Japanese on the Pacific Coast, including more than 70,000 American citizens, will, I am sure, long remain a blot on our democracy," she wrote.

Harkness was particularly disturbed when racism was condoned within the church, including the church body she held most dear, The Methodist Church. This concern led her to oppose the merger of The Methodist and Evangelical United Brethren churches in 1968 until such time as the segregated Central Jurisdiction of The Methodist Church had been abolished. Harkness described her revulsion against this racist structure in the church in the strongest terms: "The segregated Central Jurisdiction, which has existed in Methodism since 1939, is a clear contradiction of Christian morality. . . . This injustice I cannot stomach, and I hope my church cannot" ("Letter to the Editor," *The Christian Century*, March 7, 1967, p. 2).

For Harkness the encompassing manifestation of evil in human life was war. She became a committed pacifist in the 1920s and remained so all her life. Already in 1919 Harkness would criticize the injustice of the punitive measures heaped on the defeated Germans by the victorious allies. With prophetic insight, she discerned that such treatment of that defeated nation would not make the First World War the "war to end all wars," but would fuel a thirst for vengeance and lead to new war.

Harkness continued to maintain her pacifism during World War II, when such a stance was hardly popular, even among her colleagues in the church. She was one of two theologians, in a committee of experts called by the National

Council of Churches in 1950 to evaluate the ethics of obliteration bombing, who rejected the use of nuclear weapons as inherently evil, opposing such eminent divines as John Bennett and Reinhold Niebuhr. In the late 1960s Harkness readily sided with those who denounced the war in Vietnam as "so unjust and immoral that its continuance cannot be justified." She believed that this war had polarized the nation more deeply than at any time since the Civil War.

Harkness also recognized that a major arena of warfare was the Middle East. Here American Christians often found themselves confused by their biblical lenses for viewing this area as the Jewish "promised land" and their contemporary concern to redress the injustices against the Jews, which culminated in the Nazi Holocaust. These dispositions to side with Israel were fed by anti-Arab prejudices and ignorance of the recent history of the area. Impelled by the 1973 Middle East conflict, Harkness set to work in last year of her life to write a comprehensive study of the biblical roots and recent history that fueled war in this region.

Harkness made clear in the introduction that she was equally concerned about mutual understanding and justice for both peoples, Jews and Palestinians. But, for Western Christians, this entailed learning the Palestinian story and being as critical of anti-Semitism toward Arabs as toward Jews. Anti-Semitism toward Jews should be abhorrent to all Christians, she wrote. "Yet, if one is unable to feel any sympathy for the dispossessed Palestinians or see some justice in their yearning for an independent state on the West Bank of the Jordan, one falls into another kind of anti-semitism" (Georgia Harkness and Charles F. Kraft, *Biblical Backgrounds of the Middle East Conflict* [Nashville: Abingdon Press, 1976], p. 11). Harkness died before she could complete this book. It was finished by her former colleague at Garrett-Evangelical, Charles F. Kraft, and published in 1976.

Harkness also was deeply concerned all her life about women's rights in the church and in society. As a young academic in the 1930s, she had experienced the difficulties a woman had in finding college-level teaching jobs. Harkness also supported the ordination of women and their full rights as lay and clerical officers in the church. She was herself ordained to local deacon's and elder's orders, although she did not seek full Conference membership when that became available in 1956. Yet she was almost eighty before she put together a major book on issues of women in the church and society.

Like many single professional women of her generation, Harkness was ambivalent about being identified as a feminist. She accepted the implicit double bind of her cultural milieu, which required that she be simultaneously "fully feminine," and yet "the same" as any male in her field. Almost all her life she was the only woman among male colleagues on theological faculties or in national and international church assemblies. She prided herself on being fully accepted as an equal by her male colleagues and not being seen in any way as special because she was a woman. Yet she was also acutely aware that, in all these settings, she was seen as representing women.

In 1969 she gave two addresses to the Association of Women Ministers, one on the history of women in ministry and one on how to achieve their full inclusion in ministry. The principles she laid down in this second talk epitomized her acceptance of this double bind as the "rules of the game" for women: women ministers should (1) always maintain their femininity and never forget that they are women; (2) cooperate with men on all suitable occasions; (3) trust their men friends—sometime they can speak for us better than we can for ourselves; (4) choose their priorities; the gospel is more important than women's rights; (5) be faithful to their calling (Georgia Harkness, *Women in Church and Society: A Historical and Theological Inquiry* [Nashville: Abingdon Press, 1972]).

While such a set of principles may have been practical as an accomodation to a highly sexist environment, it gave these women little handle on how to analyze this sexist environment itself as unjust. During the 1956 debate on the ordination of women, Harkness herself followed her third principle by sitting silently, allowing the men to speak for the women's issue, since she decided that they could be more persuasive than she could be. Yet it was clear to most people at the Conference that she was the leading spirit behind the victory. Her major role in the struggle for women's full clergy rights in The Methodist Church was recognized that evening, when, after the vote, the whole assembly rose to applaud her.

In her 1972 book *Women in Church and Society*, Harkness not only surveys women's exclusion from and inclusion in leadership in the church and in society from biblical times to the twentieth century, but she also attempts a theological anthropology to defend women's full participation in such roles. Here Harkness's theology of continuous creation plays a key role. She argues that creation is not static and completed in the past, and therefore one cannot argue from past social roles of men and women to either their "nature" or God's intention.

Rather, creation continues as an expanding process. Thus, though women seem to be specialists in the maternal aspects of psychic development and social activity (and Harkness is at pains to support these roles), nevertheless women are showing that they are also equally capable of capacities and roles traditionally associated with men, and they should be allowed to do them. Men too should not be seen as static. They need to develop the affective and caring sides of humanity that they have hitherto left to women. Thus Harkness suggests a developmental anthropology that would mandate a growing androgyny for both men and women.

Harkness's theology in her later years remained in continuity with her progressive Christian socialism of the 1930s, although she accepted the critique of neo-orthodoxy that stressed the power of human sin. She became a "chastened" progressive, revising the optimistic and triumphalistic aspects of progressivism to accommodate not only a realism about power of evil, but also the realities of depression and despair, feelings that very much gripped her own life in her middle years.

Yet Harkness never fully adopted the neo-orthodox model of theology. In her maintenance of the social commitments of Christian pacifism and socialism, she was perhaps more able to respond to the new social gospel movements that arose in the 1960s, with the civil rights and peace movements, than many Christian theologians who had jettisoned these ideals in the late 1930s to 1950s. This helps to account for the remarkable fact that this woman, in her late seventies and eighties, seemed so at home in the issues of young people in the 1960s.

In addition to a lifetime as a professional academic, first teaching philosophy to undergraduates and then teaching theology to seminarians in two major theological faculties (Garrett Biblical Institute in Evanston, Illinois, and the Pacific School of Religion in Berkeley, California), Harkness was a dedicated churchwoman. She was active as a lecturer in local and national church gatherings. She also was the first major woman theologian to be part of the Protestant world ecumenical circle. Her world travels and lectures in such countries as India, Japan, the Philippines, the Middle East, as well as Europe, gave her a global perspective. She was frequently asked to serve on special commissions for the World Council of Churches.

Harkness considered herself a systematic theologian and wrote numerous books on aspects of Christian faith and doctrine. Although she wished to speak to her academic colleagues as a peer, she was also concerned to write on Christian faith in a manner accessible to the educated laity. She sought to bridge the academic and lay worlds and to provide a theology for the whole church, not simply for an elite cadre of scholars. Perhaps her own decision not to seek full Conference membership in 1956 was part of her desire to remain a part of the laity, able to make the theological tradition of the church meaningful to ordinary Christians.

As mentioned at the outset of this preface, Harkness wrote not only as an academic, but also as a religious poet, liturgist, hymnist, and mystic. Her own experiences of depression and despair led her to study the traditions of the "dark night of the soul" of the great mystics, such as John of the Cross. For Harkness, mysticism was not an esoteric discipline accessible only to monastics, but was the practice of prayer, of putting oneself in the presence of God, which should be integral to the life of every Christian.

Harkness sought to make mystical prayer and communion with God accessible through several works on mysticism, as well as popular devotional books that provided guidance for Christians in their daily lives. Harkness developed the affective side of her own nature by meditation and religious poetry. Her famous hymn "Hope of the World" was the theme hymn for the meeting of the World Council of Churches in Evanston in 1954 and has remained a favorite in the United Methodist Hymnal.

The concluding word that sums up Georgia Harkness's life and work is *wholeness*. She is remarkable for the many-sidedness of her life and writings that constantly sought integration of realities so often split apart from one another. In the language of liberation theology, her life and thought were an integration of theory and practice. Her ethical and theological reflection was rooted in concrete commitments to justice—justice for working people, for women, and for discriminated against racial and ethnic groups—and, above all, in her dedication to peace.

Her life and work show a constant integration of spirituality and social responsibility; of rational, intellectual discourse complemented by mystical and poetic discourse. Christian faith was, for her, something to be understood intellectually, reflected upon with the most careful tools of history and theology, but always in the context of a faith to be lived. Daily living of Christianity meant regular prayer and devotions, at times leading to ecstatic depths of communion with God, and also active commitment to justice and peace in society.

Yet these many dimensions of her thought were always expressed in simple language accessible to the layperson in the pew, language that did not set Harkness apart from lay Christians, but showed these concerns to be the expressions of the common life to which all Christians are called. Thus I salute Georgia Harkness as a theologian for all seasons. I commend the work of my colleague at Garrett-Evangelical, Rosemary Skinner Keller, in bringing the fullness of the vocational journey of this remarkable woman compellingly into our presence. This book stands as a tribute to Georgia Harkness's life.

I. "These *Were* and *Are* My Roots"

CHAPTER ONE

"The Woman in the Red Coat" *1710–1852*

Georgia Harkness loved to tell the story of her great-grandmother, Abigail, whom the religiously proper villagers branded "the woman in the red coat."[1]

Abigail Cochran came to the northeastern frontier of New York state in 1801 to visit her brother, Daniel, already a settler in the AuSable hamlet. Soon after her arrival, she met Daniel Harkness, a good Quaker who had recently picked up his stakes in Adams County, Massachusetts, to "go west" and homestead with other family members on the New York frontier.

As Georgia told the story, "Abigail was not only *not* a Quaker but was known as a 'worldly woman,' who affronted her neighbors by 'appearing out of plainness' and was referred to scornfully as 'the woman in the red coat.' Whether because of the red coat or more abiding charms, she won the heart of Daniel Harkness and they were married in November, 1802."

In response, the Society of Friends presented Daniel Harkness with a letter of dismissal for marrying out of the meeting. "To 'make satisfaction to the meeting' he would only have had to say he was sorry he married her. But he was not sorry, and he would not say it!" Georgia stated flatly—and proudly. The Quakers wrote Daniel out of the fold and, in Georgia's words, "Through this combination of feminine charm, masculine stubbornness and ecclesiastical stupidity, Providence thus decreed, a hundred fifty years ago, that I should be born a Methodist."

Georgia Harkness cherished Abigail, her great-grandmother, for standing up for her right to be her own person. And she esteemed Daniel, her great-grandfather, because he affirmed his wife's decision and put their relationship above loyalty to institutional religious affiliation. Though Georgia always had the highest regard for the Quakers, and believed that she would have been happy in that fold, she deeply treasured two documents in her family archives. "One is a letter from Daniel's father, the devout Quaker Adam Harkness, solemnly abjuring his son 'to hartedly Give up In Full Obedence,' " to the Quaker Discipline. The other is "the dismissal paper by which Daniel Harkness was disowned from the Society of Friends for marrying out of the Meeting."

In her mature years, Harkness shared her story of "the woman in the red coat" with widely diverse gatherings. She included it in one of her few personal reminiscences, a twenty-nine page autobiographical sketch that was written for the Pacific Coast Theological Group in 1953 when she was sixty-two years old. As Professor of Applied Theology at Pacific School of Religion in Berkeley, California, from 1950 to 1961, and previously at Garrett Biblical Institute in Evanston, Illinois, from 1939 to 1950, she was the only woman among these professional theologians who met twice a year to read professional papers and share their life journeys.

The year before, Georgia also told the story in what she described as one of the most important sermons she had ever delivered, when she preached at the one hundred year celebration of the founding of her small home church in Harkness and West Peru, New York. "I have no better friends anywhere on earth," she wrote.

When Abigail died in 1848 and Daniel in 1859, they were buried in the cemetery in Harkness, New York, a part of the original town of AuSable that was named after their son and Georgia's grandfather, Nehemiah Harkness. The burial ground is owned today by the Harkness United

Methodist Church, and grave sites are free for the burial of all residents of the town when they pass away.

Georgia designated that when she died her ashes were to be placed in the family plot, just a few yards from the bodies of Daniel and Abigail. Her gravestone reads simply: "Georgia Harkness—Ph.D., 1891–1974," a fitting epitaph for the first woman theologian in a profession dominated by men. A life-long resident of the town surmised that the inscription was her family's choice, an expression of their pride in having in their line the only Ph.D., and a woman at that, to be buried in the town cemetery.[2]

———

The two nearby grave plots of Abigail Cochran Harkness, "the woman in the red coat," and "Georgia Harkness—Ph.D." speak volumes about the right and independence of a woman to be her own person. Both were exceptional women of their times who defied social and church conventions of a "woman's place." Edgar Brightman, the distinguished profes-sor of philosophy at Boston University and Georgia's mentor in her doctoral program in the early 1920s, initially ques-tioned whether she was that exceptional and whether he should take her as a Ph.D. candidate. He judged "that I had the preparation, probably the brains, but that I lacked the stick-to-itiveness." Clear in her own mind, Georgia "told him that if that was all, I would see to that." And she did.[3]

Like Abigail Cochran, Georgia Harkness was a red-coated woman seeking to be a person in her own right. She was of a similar stripe to such women of her day as Margaret Mead, Pauli Murray, Hulda Niebuhr, Georgia O'Keeffe, Mary McLeod Bethune, Eleanor Roosevelt, and Thelma Stevens. All excelled individually in professions dominated by men and forged new ground for their sex. But some shied away from the word *feminist*, feeling that it applied to a more rad-ical countercultural type of woman than they represented.

However, Harkness, like these exceptional women of her day, stands in what American historian Mary Ryan describes as "a tortuous and long path toward the continuing feminist critique of the American family and American society."[3] During her professional career, which spanned the second and third quarters of the twentieth century, she charged the church to confront social oppression within its own institution and to lead society in envisioning a new reign of God. Her prophetic witness to mainstream Christianity on the rights of women may be dated from 1924, when she wrote her first article in a religious journal, until 1972, when she made her last statement on the floor of the General Conference of The United Methodist Church. These first and last words were on the same subject: the ordination and equality of women alongside men in the church.

Active in mainline Christianity from the local congregation to the World Council of Churches for over fifty years, Harkness was a forerunner of liberation theology and the liberation of women and racial minorities. Like other women of this pre-feminist generation, she did not work out of a consciously developed analysis of systemic social oppression. Whether she realized it or not, however, she was developing a structural analysis to combat the interrelated evils of sexism, racism, and militarism, along with classism and clericalism, in the institutions of church and society.

Harkness's ministry of the Word, applied in her teaching, writing, and speaking, extended from immediately after World War I through World War II and the conflicts in Korea and Vietnam. It embraced the early years of the freedom revolutions for women, for blacks and other racial and ethnic minorities, for youth, and for the elderly in society and the church. During this period, too, the leadership of laypersons, alongside clergy, came to the forefront in the church. Georgia was a lone woman who often went out in front of her male colleagues in her advocacy of social justice issues, pointing the way for the larger hosts who would follow in the late twentieth century and beyond. It took such a woman as Georgia Harkness to witness prophetically "in such a time as this."

Her academic title of Professor of Applied Theology expresses the commitment to human rights that was at the heart of Harkness's professional career for over fifty years.

She sought to apply theology, to keep it from being abstract, and to make faith responsible to the everyday lives and needs of persons, individually and corporately. Whether deepening laypersons spiritually and theologically, preparing pastors to minister to local church congregations, or challenging national and international leaders, she spared no words in critiquing the daily life of mainline Protestant Christianity from the vantage point of a loyal protagonist from within.

This is the story of Georgia Harkness, the "woman in the red coat." Her story begins with the fascinating journey of a community of faith at the roots of her heritage: the movement of a people, at first set apart and over against the dominant culture, who then sought to live fully in its midst and to bring new life to their society.

===

Other people's lives are not in themselves models for our own, states Carolyn Heilbrun, the contemporary scholar of women's biography. Rather, it is the stories we are told about persons that enable us to identify with them, to enter into their world of daring and achievement, and to launch forth on a "quest" plot for our own lives.[5]

This world of inner adventure must have opened for Georgia Harkness when she heard the rich stories of her own ancestors and their neighbors. The family trunks of Harkness's genealogical records are filled with treasures that were recorded and preserved, in large part, by J. Warren Harkness, Georgia's father, a local historian of credibility and repute. He published in area newspapers almost fifty articles on regional, local, and family history, and he compiled and duplicated in booklet form even more essays, from the genealogies of nearby families to the origins of rural roads. Georgia and later family members inherited his love of genealogy, carefully maintaining the family records and digging more deeply into their heritage.[6]

The Harkness archives provide an invaluable source of the "goodly heritage" that was passed on to Georgia through her ancestors. However, the primary limitation of the collection is predictable. Virtually no material is included that relates to women of the family. Further, the entire collection comes from the Harkness side, with no information, other than a picture of Georgia's mother's parents, of the Merrill line.

Georgia Harkness's roots can be traced back seven generations on her father's side to the Harkness families in Glasgow and Aberdeen, Scotland. Two branches of the Harkness line left Scotland in the same year, 1710. One strain of ancestors came straight to the American colonies, began making money, and became generous benefactors of Yale, Harvard, and other colleges. The other strain, Georgia's direct ancestry, was represented in the children of John Harkness and his wife, whose name is not known. Their offspring moved to northern Ireland in 1710, resulting in the intertwining of Scottish and Irish roots in her family heritage. One of John's sons, Adam, emigrated to the American colonies twenty years later. He settled in Smithfield, Rhode Island, and with his family established the lineage through which Georgia would be born.

Adam Harkness's son, Adam, Jr., married a woman named Mary, and they bought a farm in Adams, Berkshire County, Massachusetts. Adam, Jr., and Mary, the great-great grandparents of Georgia Harkness, bore at least six children and gained considerable wealth. While Georgia surmised that her earlier Scotch-Irish ancestors were of Presbyterian descent, the Quaker roots of the family were set by the generation of Mary and Adam, Jr., said to be a solid man who "feared God and eschewed evil."

Four of Adam, Jr., and Mary's children left the family homestead in Massachusetts and were among the early white pioneers to settle in northeastern New York in the early nineteenth century. David and one of his sisters, Thankful, traveled by horseback from Massachusetts in 1797 to establish a new family home in the AuSable/Peru area, just south of Plattsburgh on the New York frontier. Not long after the arrival of a second sister, Deborah, both women were united in marriage to young men within the Quaker fold.

The Quakers in the AuSable area gathered for their first service in 1789, and ten years later the first monthly meeting was held. Of the two sons, David and Daniel, who came from Massachusetts, David Harkness was an eminent Quaker preacher of whom it was said "that when the Spirit moved him to speak it was with great power." David traveled extensively, establishing Friends meetings throughout a broad area.

He also had a mind for business, multiplying his original fifty acres of land to five hundred. David built a sandstone house on his property in 1804, just two years after the first Quaker meetinghouse was constructed at the Peru Union, designating both the village of Friends and their place of worship. However, the New York climate did not agree with him and finally in 1834 he packed up his wife and ten children and moved to Michigan.

Georgia esteemed her Quaker heritage, proud that six of her father's eight great-grandparents were Quakers and that enough of her ancestors had "served with distinction in the Revolutionary War so that joining the D.A.R. would have been a very simple matter had I ever wished to do so."[7] She also cherished the Friends' underlying belief in the mutuality of men and women in the Quaker ministry, as stated unequivocally by Warren Harkness: "They knew that the 'inner light' could shine as brightly in woman as in man, that is the spirit of Christ could move one sex as powerfully as the other, so they claimed it was perfectly proper for a woman to accept a call to the work of the ministry and many of their most gifted preachers were women."[8]

However, not only was her direct lineage of Quakers broken by 1802, with the marriage of Daniel and Abigail, but also the membership of Friends in the AuSable/Peru vicinity became greatly reduced by the first decade of the nineteenth century. One cause of the decline was the settlement of territories and the founding of new states west and south of New York. After 1810, the number of departures greatly exceeded the new arrivals settling in the northeastern region of the state.

Warren Harkness's concern was not with this natural attrition of pioneers but with a second reason for decline: the large numbers of persons who were disowned by the

Friends. By 1810, only twenty years after the first meetings were held, sixty-four persons had been expelled from the Society.

The strictness of principles and practices demanded of its members was questionable to Georgia's father. The Quakers "objected strongly to balls, gambling-places, horse-races, and theatres, as being 'nurseries of debauchery and wickedness,' and their members who attended such 'places of diversion' were promptly disowned unless they acknowledged and condemned the offense and promised to do better in the future." They also objected to reading novels, plays, and other "pernicious books." Warren Harkness himself was a devoutly religious man and a pillar of the Methodist Church. Such rigidity seemed inappropriate to him in terms of his faith and the changing times, a liberal leaning that his daughter would inherit. "It does not seem strange that such young people, brought up among those who were not Friends, should frequently be tempted 'to appear out of plainness' and sometimes to 'attend places of diversion,' " he wrote.

In his "History of Peru," which included much material on the Quakers, Warren sought not to judge whether "any member was ever disowned by the Society without sufficient cause," but rather to "mention some of the more common offenses and let the reader judge for himself." One man and woman were disowned for having their marriage performed by a magistrate instead of according to the established rules of the Society. Another young man was removed for "appearing out of plainness" and attending the wedding of an acquaintance who married outside the Friends, while many others were also dismissed for "appearing out of plainness and attending places of diversions."

If anybody had a right to talk about the Friends, Warren Harkness believed it was he. With his strong Quaker lineage of six great-grandparents who were respected members of the Society, he would have had a birthright among them if his grandfather had not been disowned. It wore hard on him that his ancestor was one of twenty-six Friends who had been dismissed for marrying outside the fold.

In the final analysis, Warren could not help stating direct-ly his evaluation of the unyielding spirit of the Quakers, that went to the roots of his family, religious, and community heritage: They were "so plain spoken and even bitter in their denunciation of everything which seemed to them sinful and immoral that they made many enemies."

The decline of the Friends in the AuSable area was not caused by the westward movement and the narrowness of disciplinary requirements for membership alone. Finally, the deepest cause of division lay within the Quaker Union itself. The Friends worshiped together in the Quaker meet-inghouse thousands of times on Sundays and in Thursday meetings during their thirty years together. However, response to the preaching of Elias Hicks on Long Island cre-ated such dissension within the Peru Union that more than half the members left to become Hicksites.

The split that occurred within the Quaker Union in the AuSable/Peru area was a manifestation of a wider division created by Hicks throughout the Society of Friends in the East and Midwest. One of the most prominent and widely traveled Quaker ministers, Elias Hicks became suspect by regular Quakers in the Philadelphia area by 1819. They were alarmed by his claim that the immediate presence of Christ's divine light received by the Friends made Christ's atonement unnecessary to them. Orthodox Quakers under-stood themselves to stand within the Protestant evangelical fold and saw Hicks's formulations to be a denial of funda-mental Christian doctrine.

A forceful personality of striking appearance, Hicks reminded many of his Quaker forebear, George Fox. So great was his appeal that by 1827 orthodox and Hicksite Quakers began disowning one another in yearly meetings in Philadel-phia, New York, Baltimore, Indiana, and Ohio.

The followers of Hicks were either more numerous or more obstinate than the orthodox Quakers in the AuSable area, for the Hicksites retained possession of the meeting-house. By 1832, the "Regulars" built a new house on the same three-acre lot directly south of the one occupied by the Hicksites. The orthodox and liberal wings continued to worship side by side on the same land, if not in the same building, despite their irreconcilable differences.

The split also led to the closing of the Union Academy for boys and girls from the families of AuSable residents. Opened in 1812, the school had provided offerings in a variety of basic courses, including reading, writing, arithmetic, English grammar, and geography. The names of almost all the children on the class lists in its early years were found on the adult membership rolls of either the Regular or the Hicksite meetings by the 1830s.

In the early years of the academy, children of non-Quaker families were admitted alongside the Friends. One boy who attended the Quaker school was Georgia Harkness's grandfather, Nehemiah. Even though Nehemiah's father, Daniel, had been dismissed from the Society after his marriage to Abigail Cochran, the Union Academy was open to the young boy. During these early school years, Nehemiah walked each morning and evening from his home on Hallock Hill to the Quaker Academy, a distance of two and one-half miles.

By 1836, the Academy was vacant. Never again was it used as a schoolhouse, because the Quaker Union was fast becoming a deserted village. During the ensuing years that it remained empty and unused, the building acquired the reputation of being haunted, "its spectors being a number of young men who used to meet in its upper rooms to play cards and eat melons."

━━━━━

Despite the dissension, division, and sense of superior holiness that marked the journey of the Society of Friends in the AuSable/Peru area, Georgia Harkness knew that she could have been as happy in the Quaker fold as in the Methodist, had it not been for the fateful "combination of feminine charm, masculine stubbornness and ecclesiastical stupidity" that brought Daniel and Abigail together. She was guided throughout her life by the fundamentals of the Quaker faith. A strong belief in communion with God and the mystical presence of Christ, close to the Friends' experience of the inner light of the Spirit, characterized Georgia's personal spiritual understanding by her mid-years.

However, Methodism was Georgia Harkness's direct religious heritage, and "the Methodist Church in the old schoolhouse" on Hallock Hill provided the deepest roots of her intertwining heritage of church, family, and neighbors. She attended her first service of worship there when she was one week old, became a member of the church when she was fourteen, and, as she wrote at age sixty-two, expected to remain a member until called to the church triumphant.[9]

By 1836, the year in which the Quaker Academy closed, the Methodist society was thriving in the AuSable/Peru area. And fifty years earlier, at almost the same time the Friends began to meet in the 1780s, Methodist-ordained preachers were sent to ride the circuits in northeastern New York state.

The New York colony was a strong initial center for the spread of the Methodist movement in America. One of the two earliest societies in the American colonies had been founded in New York City in 1766 by laypersons, including Barbara Heck, "the mother of American Methodism," and her cousin, Philip Embury.

The first Methodist Meeting House in the northeastern corner of the state was built in Peru, adjacent to AuSable, in 1807, only a few years after construction of the Quaker Meeting House of the Friends at the Peru Union. The log church built by the Methodists was heated by a "huge potash kettle turned upside down upon a foundation of brickwork in the center of the church." When the next edifice was constructed in 1811, Bishop Asbury wrote that he preached to one thousand souls in the new chapel and that it was a "gracious time."[10]

Methodism came to the western part of the town of Peru and to AuSable about 1825, when the schism was deepening between orthodox and Hicksite Quakers. Its bearer was a local, or unordained, preacher from England, Robert York, who brought his family to settle there. Both he and a son, Robert, began to hold regular services in the old schoolhouse on Hallock Hill.[11]

The Methodists were no more sanctified against inner rifts than were the Quakers. When the Yorks and Benjamin Pomeroy sought to construct a church building in west Peru in 1852, dissension arose over the site of the structure. The people of Hallock Hill were "not pleased with the decision to locate it a half mile farther from them."

It is not known how Georgia Harkness's ancestors stood on the issue. However, the congregation had worshiped in the schoolhouse for over twenty-five years, and the majority of members were of no mind to give up their turf. The Hallock Hill Methodists seceded from the West Peru congregation and continued holding their own services in the school for fifty-five more years. Though determined to keep their separate property, the West Peru and Hallock Hill congregations maintained cordial relations and later merged, to the apparent satisfaction of all concerned.[12]

═══

Methodism received a hearty reception from the frontier families throughout the nineteenth century. Camp meetings and the revivalistic spirit became a hallmark of the movement on the expanding frontier from New York state to the far west. Whether in local congregations or at camp meetings, salvation of individual souls was the American Wesleyans' means of "spreading gospel holiness and reforming the continent."

Wesleyan Perfectionism, the belief that the individual could be converted from worldly ways and grow in spiritual goodness to become closely attuned to the way of Christ, was at the heart of Methodist theology. Arminianism, emphasizing that the individual could exert freedom of the will to respond to God's call upon his or her life, went hand-in-hand with Wesleyan Perfectionism in forming the revivalistic spirit. Many evangelists in the New York area, including Methodist Freeborn Garrettson and Presbyterian Charles Grandison Finney, took it further, contending that society also needed to be transformed. They believed that as countless numbers of individual wills are changed inwardly,

44

the spirit also would lead these persons to address the evil in social conditions.[13] Georgia Harkness was raised in this school of individualistic evangelicalism, one foundation that she and others of the avant garde, within and outside the Methodist fold, would balance with a liberal social evangelicalism.

Warren Harkness's papers contain an extraordinary description from a letter of the Reverend Buel Goodsell of an early spirited camp meeting in the AuSable/Peru area in 1825. Between three hundred and four hundred tents were raised at the meeting, even though there were only three Methodist churches on the western, or New York side, of Lake Champlain.[14]

The little church in the Hallock Hill schoolhouse was one of those vital Methodist gatherings! Georgia's roots were planted there, and they intertwined with those of her own family and community.

CHAPTER TWO

"A Goodly Heritage"
1802–1903

*T*he men of the Harkness line, particularly Georgia's father, Warren, and grandfather, Nehemiah, were builders of the AuSable/Peru communities. A reporter summed up Warren Harkness's identity in his obituary: "a fine patriarch"—a designation that still would have been considered a compliment when he died in 1937. And an elderly man in an adjoining county shared with Georgia the esteem in which her father was held: "I never met your father, but I've always heard say that if there was something you wanted to know, you went and asked Mr. Harkness." So cherished was the vision and hard labor that Nehemiah put into the life of the town that in the late 1860s the grateful citizenry named the hamlet of Harkness, New York, after him.[1]

The heritage transmitted through Georgia's male relatives on New York soil was laid by her great-grandfather, Daniel, who joined his brother, David, and sisters, Thankful and Deborah, in AuSable in 1801. Daniel's distinctive contribution to the family and community lay in his identification with the land.

When Georgia was more than sixty years old and a permanent West Coast resident, she described the family homestead that Daniel built as "the big, rambling old farm house, which is still home to me."[2] Daniel and Abigail Cochran Harkness began their married life in 1802 in a small house of logs that was on the property when he bought it. In 1820 Daniel built the more spacious home, and he and Abigail raised their family there.

He set up a farm on fifty acres deeded to him by Stephen Starks in 1801, and his brother, David, sold him twenty more acres the following year. On this plot, Daniel began to cultivate the soil and construct the homes and barns that became the farmstead of subsequent Harkness generations: Georgia's grandparents, Nehemiah and Deborah; her parents, Warren and Lillie; her brother Charlie and his family; and her great-nieces and nephews even today.[3]

However, Daniel did not inherit from his father the measure of business sense that David demonstrated in his land investments. When Adam Harkness came from Massachusetts to visit his children, he found Daniel living on his original landholding and offered to buy an additional one hundred adjoining acres for him. Daniel declined his father's offer, saying that he did not care to have the one hundred acres because they were covered with overgrown pine trees. The years did not bear out his decision, for the land was purchased by another owner who cut down the trees and sold them for more than enough to pay for the farm. The land became "worth a fortune to the man who bought it," Warren Harkness reported.[4]

The business acumen of Nehemiah Harkness, Daniel and Abigail's oldest son, exceeded that of his father. As he grew to young manhood and established himself and his family in the AuSable area, Nehemiah acquired large landholdings and expanded the family property to 175 acres. Besides managing the family farm, he also owned and ran a sawmill with a neighbor in West Peru, surveyed land, and dug roads.[5]

Nehemiah's enterprising nature enabled him to see the need to diversify occupationally and expand beyond farming, both for his own business needs and those of the community. AuSable was not a great agricultural center, for at least half of its thirty-eight square miles was unfit for cultivation. As Georgia's father, Warren, described it in his local history, one would "need more dynamite than the DuPont Power Company can furnish to make good, mellow soil."

However, the area contained rich deposits of iron ore, and during the mid-years of the nineteenth century it was the leading mining and iron-making town of Clinton County. Three miles to the south lay the great Arnold ore bed, one of the richest and oldest in the Champlain Valley, and the Ketchum and Etna iron blast furnaces already were in operation.

"Colonel N'miar," as Georgia's grandfather was known in the community because of his commission in the New York state militia in 1837, saw that better means were needed to transport the valuable deposits of iron ore to commercial centers. Nehemiah used his influence to have a branch of the railroad being built from Albany to Montreal run through the community. He sought to put the locale on the map in a period of expanding commercial enterprise in New York state.

A large share of the supervision and actual work of constructing the tracks also fell upon him. "Unable to get men who would work in the hot sun to drive their oxen to pull stumps for making the road-bed, and determined that the railroad should go through at all costs, he did it himself," Georgia wrote.[6]

Overworked by the strenuous labor of clearing a right-of-way for the railroad, Nehemiah suffered a sun stroke in the summer of 1868. The illness developed into apoplexy, and he died a year and a half later at age sixty-seven. The railroad went through, and the grateful community honored its "favorite son" by selecting the name of Harkness for the station and the hamlet lying within AuSable and adjacent to West Peru.

However, Georgia's legacy from her grandfather was more than a town bearing the family name. At his funeral, Colonel N'miar was memorialized with the biblical injunction, "Blessed are the peacemakers" (Matt. 5:9). The tribute was fitting for a man of strong Quaker lineage who would pass on to his granddaughter the Friends' commitment to pacifism. Nehemiah's reputation as a peacemaker grew out of his daily round of work as a land surveyor, an occupation that often provided him the opportunity to settle boundary disputes regarding fences and roads between neighbors.[7]

He also passed on to Georgia a wider vision of peace, embracing racial justice, beyond the local community. The family papers contain a remarkable letter written by Nehemiah Harkness in which he broods over the impending doom of a civil war. Fearing that "much blood will be shed between the North and the South," he hoped that the old Democratic Party would be "annihilated and a Republican party established in lieu of it." Although he dreaded the possibility of an overcentralized national government, his greater fear was the curse of slavery. "I for one am willing to come under a Monarchy for the sake of getting rid of Slavery," he wrote, "for I think it is a great National evil and had ought to be done away with."

━━━━━━

By the time Georgia was born in 1891, twenty-two years after her grandfather's death, Harkness, New York, had changed very little. "When I say 'rural' I mean rural," she wrote, for Harkness was not even a village—"rather a hamlet or four-corners with some houses clustered about but with most of its post-office-address population living on outlying farms." She remembered from her childhood that a country store housing the post office stood at the four corners. The men of the community rendezvoused inside around the box-stove and cracker barrel. A sawmill and a butter factory were close by. "As time moved on, the saw-mill burned; the milk was shipped away to some mysterious place known as 'the city'; a saloon for a brief—but only a brief—period rivaled the store as a lounging-place; and the church and parish house were built." By 1925, the post office was closed and the community was placed on the R.F.D. route of the neighboring village of Peru. "But the church, parish house and a modernized successor to the store still stand at the four corners."[8]

Harkness was a substantial rural farming community in which most of the people "were not rich, but comfortably well-to-do farmers living out from the four corners either on Hallock Hill, where we lived, or in the other direction in West Peru." She remembered wholesome moral standards, a warm sense of neighborliness, and good feelings between the Protestant community and Roman Catholic brothers and sisters, some of whom were in her own family. The community and church of Harkness were simply an extended family to Georgia.[9]

Quite naturally for Georgia, her own family lay at the heart of this closely knit community, and she received her most direct legacy from its members. She always identified her father as more influential on her life than any other person. The role J. Warren Harkness played in the local community and the church became the example that Georgia would emulate on the national and international scenes.

The overt expressions of her father's Christian life were readily identifiable in his church activities. He was "easily the leading figure in our church," Georgia wrote. He taught Sunday school from age sixteen until he was in his eighties, except for a brief absence from home while attending Oswego Normal School, and he was a longtime member of the Board of Trustees. When he died at age eighty-eight, his obituary identified the Harkness Methodist Episcopal Church as the interest nearest his heart.

However, Georgia understood the tie between her father's religious faith and his social responsibility to be at the core of his identity. As his own father had done, Warren brought new and better life to Harkness, New York, by introducing the advantages of modern secular life to the rural countryside. He was the moving spirit in bringing the Normal School, now a State Teacher's College, to the county seat of Plattsburgh, fifteen miles away. Further, he organized and was the chief officer of the Peru Grange, initiated rural free mail delivery, inaugurated and was secretary of the farmers' cooperative fire insurance company, started the local telephone company and ran lines throughout the county, surveyed land and roads, and was a notary public who drew land deeds and other legal papers for area residents.

Warren Harkness was a trusted counselor to whom neighbors came for advice in legal tangles rather than seeking a lawyer. He was deeply valued as the most knowledgeable person for miles around and for his availability to share himself and his wisdom with others. The neighbors said that there were "few subjects of general human interest on which he did not have something significant to say in conversation."

As far as the public was aware, this long list of contributions to his church and community told the story of Warren Harkness. An area newspaper described him in these words: He was "a prosperous and successful farmer (an 'old fashioned' farmer he likes to be called) and he lives on the farm which his grandfather bought in 1801 and where his father was born in 1803. He has shown no disposition to move to the city or to 'go west and grow up with the country.' With rural mail delivery, and the telephone, both of which he has been instrumental in obtaining for himself and his neighbors, he considers the old farm the best place on earth for himself and his family."

Georgia saw the truth in the rural reporter's evaluation of her father's life and his close tie to the style of life and the inheritance of his ancestors. However, she knew more of his vocational dreams and of the legacy that he had left to her.

Going through his accumulations of eighty-eight years after his death in 1937, she discovered an entry in his diary dated January 4, 1871. At age twenty-three, exactly one year after his own father had died, Warren Harkness speculated on his future in these words:

> I am sitting at the old table, near the old stove, in the old room where I have sat for so many, many times and the old home seems dear to me tonight though I often think that I had rather be away, out in the world fighting life's battles and winning life's victories. Here I was born; here I have grown to be a man, and here one year ago today my father died, and here I should love to live and die if I thought that I could here be as useful to God, to the world and to my fellowmen as anywhere else.

Warren had graduated from Oswego State Normal School, north of Syracuse on Lake Ontario, the preceding year. To go beyond high school was "unusual for a country boy in those days, and he longed to be a teacher," Georgia wrote. "When his father died, about the time of his graduation, he surrendered his ambitions to come home, look after his mother and sisters, and run the farm. Though he taught country schools in the winter term for many years when the farm work was slack, he remained a farmer all his days."

As she grew up, Georgia experienced her father as a "quietly content, 'well-adjusted' personality," who had lived as useful a life conceivable "within the sphere to which his influence reached." Warren had the incentive to be a teacher and a scholar, though. He opened opportunities for himself which were possible within the boundaries of his life and responsibilities as a farmer, teaching in nearby schools for a while and writing for local papers. However, Georgia sensed that his intellectual curiosity and drive were not satisfied. He enjoyed figuring out in his head intricate mathematical problems "which I couldn't do on paper," she wrote. Had he been able to achieve his vocational dream, she believed that he would have become a historian, attested by his great flair for local and family history.

Georgia's descriptions of her mother, Lillie Merrill Harkness, reveal that her father held this same role within the home. "Having spoken at such length of my father, I should say something of my mother. There is much less to say. Due to a fall and ensuing illness, she did not go to school beyond the eighth grade. She married my father at the age of eighteen, and adapted her life to his."[10]

Warren Harkness was almost thirty and Lillie Merrill eighteen years old when they wed, an age difference that is enough, in most relationships, to result in a highly dominant position of the older spouse. However, Warren and Lillie personified the marital relationship of the man and woman in modern middle-class, mainline American society during the late nineteenth and early twentieth centuries. Warren was the public figure representing the family on the public scene and doing it admirably. And from the time of her marriage, Lillie gained her identity through her family, her "life was centered on him and the children," in Georgia's memory.

Georgia probably took for granted this kind of relationship between her parents when she was growing up, having no living model of an alternative. She recalled their having a happy marriage and seldom exchanging cross words with each other. They were blessed with fifty years of life together on the old homestead. However, Georgia saw the patriarch in her father in identifying the one negative characteristic that she ever wrote about him: "I am afraid her husband did not praise her as much as he should have—he took her fidelity for granted."

Significantly, when Georgia lifted up the positive characteristics that ennobled her father to her, they were his actions on the public scene in the Harkness community and church. And when she remembered the qualities that she associated with her mother, they were all demonstrated in relationship to her family: her simple goodness, loving self-giving, and patient endurance. But these virtues, synonymous with true womanhood, would not be enough to contain the identity of a woman like Georgia. In adulthood she came to understand and appreciate the sacrifices her mother had made for the family. However, her father's life was the primary model that Georgia emulated.

Georgia, the youngest of four children, might have been the favored one simply because of her place in the family line. In a picture of the Harkness children taken shortly after her birth, Georgia is sitting on the lap of Hattie, her twelve-year-old sister, and standing next to them are Everett and Charles, eight and six respectively. The resemblance of the four is striking, all tall, dark-haired with deeply set eyes, and well-groomed. Hattie, Everett, and Charles are properly posed, erect and straight-faced. Too young to be fully posed, Georgia is chubby and bright-eyed with her mouth open and her hands and feet relaxed in a naturally crossed position. Alert and interested in the special happenings, she is truly an adorable baby.[11]

In the next picture of the children contained in the family collection, Georgia, probably seven, is standing beside her two tall brothers, now handsome young teenagers. Her baby fat is gone, and with long, flowing, curly hair she is growing into an attractive young girl.

With the two pictures side-by-side, Hattie's absence tells the tragic story. Hattie died when she was seventeen, her life cut short prematurely by measles that rapidly turned into diphtheria. Georgia had looked with great admiration to her smart sister, whom all believed had inherited her father's intelligence. The family held high expectations for Hattie. At the time of her death, she had taught a term in the country school and was preparing to go to a state teachers' college. The faces of the children are serious, but surely not solely because the picture is posed. They must have felt the loss of their sister at such a special time as this, when their picture was being taken. In later years, when Georgia looked back on her first experience with death, she remembered that the family considered it providential that no one else in the family had contracted diphtheria. The horror of Hattie's death left a picture that remained a vivid memory: "When I first discovered that a man could weep, and when she who had been alive at 10:00 A.M. was in her grave at 1:00 for fear of contagion . . . what usefulness was lost to the world through lack of medical care that might have saved her life, only God knows."[12]

———

Georgia greeted her second experience of death "with very different emotional accompaniments. . . . Grandma was old, and it seemed all right that she should die." Her tale of the death of her paternal grandmother, Deborah, sounds like that of a typically impish seven year old. "When asked by my other grandmother, with a hushed voice, if I knew that Grandma had passed away the night before, I replied nonchalantly that since everybody had said she was going to die, I supposed she had!" And at the funeral service she found something more interesting to occupy her thoughts: a fat cousin arrived late and was seated with "the mourners" on a two-hundred-year-old antique chair resting on a small base, "and my grief was swallowed up partly in amusement, partly in mild apprehension."

Not only was Georgia's sense of humor blossoming by the time she was seven, but her spiritual conscience was also dawning. At about six or seven she began to say her prayers. She was not taught at her mother's knee, "contrary to the usual custom," and she did not know whether her mother ever prayed vocally. The only family prayers came at meal-time when her father said the grace, and there was no corporate Bible reading. "Who then taught me to pray? A hired girl, who soon after we summarily dismissed for adultery." The moment of revelation came as a blow to Georgia, and she always remembered it. "I did not know what had happened, but I can still see the blaze in my father's eyes and hear the tones of decision with which he told her to pack her satchel while he hitched the horse to the buggy, *and not come back.* I was sorry, for I liked her, and it was a bit lonesome to have to say my prayers alone."

Georgia was beginning to think and feel deeply, and the questions of faith were opening all around. Her experience at age six or seven, when the hired girl who taught her to pray was "summarily dismissed by her father," had to be one of those times. Being so young, she was told none of the details. In her idolization of her father, however, she always credited him with almost ultimate wisdom and goodness.

Georgia held this story close to her throughout her adult life, confirmed by its inclusion in her autobiographical sketch for the Pacific Coast Theological Group. Without openly challenging her father's verdict, she seems to be expressing her care and appreciation of the hired girl—and her belief in God's love and forgiveness, an attitude that she could not ascribe to her father in this situation.

"I was a religiously sensitive child and had loved the church for as long as I can remember," Georgia recalled of herself. Going to church was as natural and unquestioned a part of the family life as was eating and sleeping. However, from the time she was six or seven, she excitedly anticipated the revivals every winter and eagerly "undertook the nightly long drive involved in these 'special meetings' for the love of the Lord and the desire to win souls for his Kingdom. As often as the revival came I got converted," Georgia recalled with humor. "Then I backslid during the summer, and was ready for conversion again the next winter. I do not know how many times this happened, but I recall that when I wanted to join the church at the age of seven, my mother, to my considerable disappointment, thought I ought to wait till I was a little older." So she waited until high school to become a member of the church, an age that all agreed was right for her to make her own decision of faith.

Religious questions captivated the young Georgia's mind. If faith and reason ever journeyed together in a child's life, they did in hers. Georgia's words tell the story of a pre-teen experience that must have left her parents wondering what sort of daughter they had born. She described an experience that occurred when she was nine or ten, and which convinced her of the "reality of child religion."

One Sunday after church I asked my father, "Pa, what are angels?" His answer touched off a chain reaction. "Some people say that when folks die they go to heaven and become angels, but I don't know how they know it." I am sure he had no doubt of personal immortality, and this did not immediately trouble me. What got hold of me were the words, "I don't know how they know it." How did anybody know that the things we heard in church were true? In the Bible, yes, but the Bible might be a made-up book, like the many I was reading by this time. And if so, why might not Jesus be like a man in a story-book? And if Jesus did not really live, how could we know that God existed? The awful possibility seized my mind that He did not exist. And if He did not, it was foolish to pray. In fact, without being sure, one could not pray. So with full consistency, I stopped saying my prayers. But this did not solve the problem. I felt alone, bereft, queer. I knew of nobody else who did not believe in God, and was too appalled at myself to talk to anybody about it. I clearly remember lying awake alone at night, sobbing because I could not pray and could have no certainty that God existed.

It was during this period that the annual revival came along. I went, but the services brought no answer. They did not touch my problem. One night, the minister said that if anybody had any questions, we might stay after the meeting and ask him. My heart leaped with hope! The minister, if anybody, should know. I sat on the front school bench, a-quiver with eagerness while Gertie Baker talked to him about something. Just as I thought Gertie was about through and my redemption nigh, my mother came and said it was getting late and we had better be starting home. Obediently, I climbed into the cutter and carried my problem home.

How did I escape from my theological dilemma? By accident—or Providence—I came upon a book entitled *Donovan* by Edna Lyell, which I have not seen from that day to this. It was the story of a young man named Donovan who went to college and came there to question the existence of God. On a right-hand page about two-thirds of the way down I came upon a word which I had never seen before, but which I pronounced "ath-eist." Yes, that was what I was! But Donovan was one also. So there were at least two of us! With an eagerness I have seldom, if ever, experienced since, I read on to see what happened to him. He went to a wise teacher, who told him nobody could prove the existence of God, but who showed him that there were many more reasons for belief than disbelief, and who assured him that the greatest and best people of all ages had lived by this faith. Donovan's troubles cleared up, and with them mine. I began again to say my prayers, and to sleep nights. The connection between this painful experience and my present profession I leave you to trace.

From early years, the religiously and intellectually precocious Georgia Harkness subjected her most difficult questions to the test of reason. And by the time she was ten, she had gained a liberating religious answer: Faith provides reasonable assurance, though not absolute certainty. In her professional writings throughout her career, Georgia returned countless times to the relationship between faith and reason, but she never stated it more persuasively than in this story of a childhood religious experience.

"We are not called upon to live in the past. It would be a serious mistake to try to do so. Yet it is essential that we let the past speak to the present and that we be gratefully mindful always of a goodly heritage," Harkness wrote in her devotional autobiography, *Grace Abounding*, in 1969.[13]

She applied this perspective of the past and present to her own inheritance from Harkness, New York—family, church, and community—in these significant words: "I have no better friends anywhere on earth. These *were* and *are* my roots—and for these roots I humbly thank God. If in some measure He has been able to use my words to speak in plain language to common folks, the reason is not hard to find. It is simply this—that I am one myself."[14]

Harkness pointed to her distinctive professional talent over a fifty-year career that extended through her retirement: "to make theology understandable to people."[15] She was gifted with the ability to communicate through the spoken and written word in nonacademic language without watering down the content of her message. Georgia Harkness was a "folk theologian," a theologian of the people. A primary reason for this definitive ability was her strong identification with her heritage, the extended family of Harkness, New York, and the little Methodist Episcopal Church. She understood the people, their needs, and the importance of communicating with them in ordinary words.

However, Georgia's own identification of herself with the "common folks" because "I am one myself" tells only a part of her story. Harkness became a "theologian of the people," but such a vocational center to her life did not blossom simply out of the natural sprouting of her roots. A wider and deeper understanding of the people, and of their spiritual and physical needs, manifested itself as Georgia Harkness journeyed vocationally far from home during her adult years. She took the first steps away from home when she entered high school five miles away from the Harkness homestead.

II. "I Stood Number One"

CHAPTER THREE

"To Be as Smart as Hattie Harkness"
1903–1908

*T*he Spring I was twelve, I started to high school at Kee-seville, five miles away. My brothers had been going for two or three years, and I had dabbled enough in their text-books to be very eager to begin," Georgia reminisced fifty years later in her autobiographical sketch.[1]

Georgia and Everett, her older brother who was still in high school, had commuted from the Harkness farmhouse during her first year of high school. They drove a horse daily for a round trip of two hours. However, the trip was time-consuming and tiring, and the horse was needed at home. So the second year Georgia and Everett roomed in Keeseville during each week with "old Aunt Sallie—no relation, but a kind of 'universal aunt' at whose home many generations of country kids attending high school stayed."

Starting to school when she was five years old, Georgia took the short walk daily to the Hallock Hill country school, which still doubled on Sundays as the Methodist Episcopal Church. Lessons came easily and enjoyable for her, a child who read voraciously and rapidly inside and outside of school. She experienced herself as large and awkward, never being good at sports, and lacking "the key to success on the playground. Nevertheless, I got along fairly well with my school-mates, who accepted the fact that I was better at diagramming sentences or spelling down than at throwing or hitting a ball." She remembered herself as neither a very bad nor a very virtuous girl, who had a typical childhood that held a few minor flurries and was neither a particularly happy nor unhappy time in life.

There were memorable occasions, however, related to new worlds that began to open for Georgia even when she was in elementary school on Hallock Hill. When she was eleven and unable to see the stars that enraptured everyone else, she was taken by her parents to a nearby town to be fitted for glasses. Warren and Lillie had been convinced for some time that Georgia's nearsightedness was not so serious that she needed glasses. "In the midst of the examination," Georgia recalled, "somebody called out to say that there was an automobile out on the street! We all rushed out, and I had my first view of a puffing, wheezing horseless carriage!" This was in 1910, and her father predicted that the time was coming when "you would see more of those things than of horses on the roads." Some of the viewers were skeptical of his prediction, but all probably agreed that cars would be dangerous if they weren't fixed so that they couldn't go over fifteen miles per hour.

A new world of nature unfolded to young Georgia when she received her glasses. "I have never had—and do not expect to have—a mystical vision which gave me as much ecstasy as the discovery that when I looked down I could see, not simply a patch of green, but blades of grass," she remembered in wonderment. The mature Georgia was awe struck by the mystery of God's created order that was revealed in the ordinariness of life. The illumination of God's presence in nature, which pervaded her devotional poetry and scholarly prose in later years, may have been born for her in this simple experience.

When Georgia began high school, however, "another new world was opened, vastly more challenging than anything I had found in the country school, and I count my five high school years as among my happiest." Her budding joy came from the intellectual challenge of the bigger school, the freedom of living away from home a few days of the week, and the expansiveness of mixing with new friends.

Georgia soared during high school. Under the New York Regents system at that time, a student got credit for whatever among the uniform state examinations she or he could pass, regardless of whether the person had ever taken a class in the subject. After two and one-half years, Georgia took the Regents exams—and had enough credits to graduate when she was fourteen years old! Nobody, including her family, teachers, and herself, thought she was old enough to go to college, realizing that at fourteen years of age she would be a social misfit. So she "post-graduated" in high school for another two and one-half years.

Warren and Lillie Harkness must have wondered what to do with their brilliant daughter. They were willing to let her graduate at the end of four years but were relieved that of her own volition, and perhaps timidity, she decided to stay at Keeseville for another year. As a result, Georgia was given a graduation certificate with a "purple seal" for having accomplished the equivalent of eight years of high school work! "Needless to say, I did not know eight years' worth," she added wryly to her Pacific Coast colleagues.

Georgia's parents appear to have been sensitive to the particular aptitudes and interests of each of their children. Charlie became the farmer of the family and a skilled carpenter. He followed his father as the caretaker of the property, living and dying on the Harkness land as Warren, Nehemiah, and David had in past generations. Warren and Lillie saw potential mechanical skills in Everett and helped him attend Union College in Schenectady, where he graduated in civil engineering. He worked for many years for the New Jersey Zinc Company in eastern Pennsylvania and was a beloved vestryman of the Episcopal Church, before dying of a heart attack in the fall of 1950, when Georgia was moving to Berkeley, California.

The family soon recognized that not only Hattie, but Georgia as well, had inherited Warren's special intellectual curiosity and abilities. Had Hattie lived, the primary expectation of intellectual advancement and achievement undoubtedly would have been vested in her. But her sudden death when she was seventeen caused the mantle from both

Warren and Hattie to lay with greater weight on Georgia's shoulders. Only five when her sister died, Georgia grew up on the adage to be "as smart as Hattie Harkness."

"As far back as I can remember, I expected when I grew up to be a teacher. No other vocational possibility ever crossed my mind," Georgia wrote in reflection on her professional journey. At this early date, she undoubtedly anticipated becoming a high school teacher in a nearby rural school or perhaps in one of the major cities of New York state. This was one of the few career options open to women of her day, and it perfectly suited her aptitude and interest.

The realistic possibility for any young woman of northeastern New York who sought teacher training was to attend Plattsburgh Normal School, relatively inexpensive and located only fifteen miles from Georgia's home. This was her expectation, too, and she took pride in the fact that her father had a guiding hand in seeing that the school was brought to Plattsburgh. But Warren and Lillie Harkness wanted their youngest and smartest child to receive the best education available from one of the distinguished institutions of the nation.

"It was a great day, therefore, when my father told me that if I wanted to go to college he thought he could manage it, particularly if I could win a Cornell scholarship. One per county was awarded by competitive examination, and I straightway began to prepare for it. It was a stiff all-day examination, preceded by a 3-hour ride to Plattsburgh behind a horse, and I thought I had failed it." In due time she received her official notification. Returning home after picking blueberries in their pasture one day, Georgia found a letter that announced that she "stood Number One. That settled the matter."

Georgia Harkness always stood number one, or very close to the top in her academic work. This was the pattern in elementary and high school, and throughout her undergraduate experience at Cornell University and her Master's and doctoral work at Boston University.

═══

On January 1, 1904, during Georgia's second year at Keeseville High School, she came down to breakfast in the big rambling Harkness farmhouse to find a New Year's present awaiting her. Under her plate was a small, leather-bound diary given to her by her parents in which to record the happenings of her daily life in high school while she was living at Aunt Sallie's. Her first words in the diary were these: "I found this diary under my plate this morning and so I suppose now I must write in it."[2] Georgia's initial entry sounds refreshingly typical of any twelve year old, rather than of a precocious young woman of extraordinary religious sensibility and intellectual promise!

Her diary, from the first of January to the fifteenth of June, 1904, is one of three such journals extant in the private papers still preserved by her Harkness descendants. A special family treasure exists in the three journals that detail the ordinary events in the day-to-day life of Harkness family members during their school days.

The second diary is from the hand of J. Warren Harkness and covers a seven-month period from May 25 until December 22, 1867, when he was nineteen years old and a student at Oswego Normal School in Oswego, New York. His small journal, which would fit easily into a pocket or a purse, is almost identical to the one given to Georgia thirty-seven years later, when she attended Keeseville High School.[3]

The third diary was written by Hattie Harkness when she was in her mid-teens, attending Keeseville High School, and living at Aunt Sallie's. She recorded her diary in 1896, eight years before twelve-year-old Georgia followed in her footsteps at Keeseville. Whether Hattie also had a palm-size journal will never be known, for the diary in the family papers is a copy of the original, rewritten on a medium-sized tablet with a red cover and an eagle on the front. After their eldest daughter's death, the journal was recopied by her mother to preserve Hattie's comments on her high school experience.[4]

The immediate perception gained from reading the three diaries is that Georgia, her father, and her sister wrote for private use only with no expectation that their words would ever be read by anyone outside the family. The straightforward reporting constitutes their great worth. Taken together, the three diaries convey the values underlying the everyday world of the Harkness family.

━━━━

Warren Harkness was older than his two daughters had been and was a college student at the time he wrote in his diary.[5] At nineteen, he had gone away to school to Oswego Normal School, on the southern shore of Lake Ontario in north central New York. It was an uncommon step for a farm boy of his day to go halfway across New York state to attend college.

He vested a bountiful vocational dream in being a high school teacher. The pages of his diary are filled with the daily preparations of a young man seeking to excel in preparation for that profession. Being in college and committed to a vocational goal, Warren was more self-reflective than his daughters were in writing their journals.

The first two entries in his journal present something of Warren's philosophy of life as a young adult. He was well-indoctrinated in the Ben Franklin school of hard work and self-knowledge, and Georgia received its full inheritance. Perhaps Warren believed that his words would someday be good food for thought for his children. The initial entry of May 25, 1867, reads:

> There are many things which I hear and see every day that I desire to remember for the reason that each little straw that I can glean from the great field of knowledge is well worth preserving for it helps to make the bundle which I hope to collect as my share of the great harvest. But the grainery of my mind is not as safe as it should be for there are many things which leak out and are lost forever. Perhaps there is no one who needs this knowledge more than myself and if I can retain it by writing in this book each day an account of what I have learned, if I can learn anything, and I hope that I shall, for no one can afford to lose even an hour, for life is short and there are many things to learn.

What have I learned today? I have studied my lessons nearly all day and hope that it was not in vain but I have learned a lesson of more importance than those of Chemistry and Geology. I have tried to learn something of myself and I found out that which others have always known, that I am a very ignorant boy. It does not seem that this lesson would be a hard one, for it is plainly shown by my writing as well as my composition yet I have been a long time learning it. I have been to the library and there found my friend Henry Douglass reading to increase his store of knowledge. If I had always made as good use of my time as he has, I should not have so much to regret but there is no use of mourning for time which has gone. I will try to lose none in the future.

Warren's journal gave him the space to learn about himself as well as to record the numerous specific pieces of information before they "leak out and are lost forever." The next day he recorded a wider vocational purpose, even more important than his professional dream of being a teacher. These specific words were written in a letter to his sister. Because he was a deeply spiritual man, Warren also must have transmitted this vocational ideal to his children in a host of different forms. Further, Georgia's spiritual meditations were often written in poetry, and Warren occasionally wrote poetry of his own, as demonstrated in this entry:

I live for those who love me.
For my friends so kind and true.
For the Heaven that smiles above me,
And awaits my spirit too.

For the human ties that bind me
For the task which God assigned me
For those I leave behind me
And the good that I can do.

The above lines express all that is worth living in this world of sin and sorrow. All of our selfish thoughts and actions will amount to nothing in the end, for if [we] obtain wealth or power we cannot take it with us when we die.

When Georgia wrote of her father and his deep influence on her life, she remembered the qualities found in these entries. First was his attention to the details of daily life and his good stewardship of time. But more important was the care and concern he expressed for her and his ability to accept with grace his lot in life.

The bulk of Warren Harkness's diary is not given to philosophizing or theologizing, but simply to recording the day-to-day happenings inside and outside the classroom. His response to life's daily round reflects a healthy and happy young man, juggling and balancing coursework in geology, chemistry, philosophy, rhetoric, and ancient history with playing ball, going swimming, taking boat rides, attending church, and taking part in "sociables."

He recorded at one point some "excellent remarks" and good advice for a teacher of any day from Miss Rice, his instructor in rhetoric. "She told us that the Teacher should always leave the cares of the school in the school room and never take them home. She told us that she hoped that she should never have a house large enough to contain her school house and she should never try as some do to carry the school house around with her when she went anywhere."

Warren Harkness "stood Number One" at the end of his spring term of 1867. His grades, recorded in his diary on July 5, read: rhetoric, 99 percent; philosophy, 98 percent; chemistry, 96 percent; geology, 97 percent; and spelling, 100 percent. After the closing exercises, when the reports of scholarship were made, he wrote: "I am well satisfied with mine. I find that my scholarship is as good as any in my class."

However, it is refreshing to realize that Warren was not quite perfect. His final diary entry of December 17 states that he "did not have my lessons very well though the teachers did not find it out." Worth noting, too, is the fact that autographs of several girls appeared in the back of his diary!

———

Hattie Harkness's diary from 1896 covers a portion of the last year of her life during a term at Keeseville High School.[6]

She stayed at Aunt Sallie's during the week and took the horse and buggy back and forth from the Harkness farm on weekends, the same arrangement under which her brothers and sister would later attend the school.

On weekends Hattie spent all day Saturday helping with housework, particularly cooking for Sunday and preparing food to take back to the rooming house for the upcoming week. Baking cakes, pies, and cookies was the order of the day on Saturdays. She often spoke of Charlie helping her "or I should never have got through." Typical, too, was considerable family entertaining of neighbors and relatives from nearby towns. In its own way, the Harkness home was a town center.

Hattie was often the woman in charge when her mother was away visiting her own relatives and caring for her nearby parents. She came to sympathize with Lillie's hard work and lot in life, but Hattie's frustration with the domestic tasks indicates that she envisioned a different existence for herself.

After expressing appreciation in her diary one Saturday for Charlie's help in making the cake and molasses puffs, Hattie continued: "As it was I made my pies after supper and it was near bed time before I got them baked. This afternoon nothing special happened but it does seem as if there never was so much to do." The burden mounted on Sunday: "I don't wonder Ma don't feel like going to Sunday school by the time she is ready. I hurried like fury to get the work done so that I could leave at all but managed to get there in time though I don't know how I did it. I made out the bread after 9:40 and then got ready and got there in time." The observance of a sabbath time of rest and no work on Sunday had to be put aside, Hattie concluded, acknowledging: "I expect it is wicked to work on Sunday especially such work as baking and so forth but it had to be done sometime."

Social time during the week in Keeseville was spent mostly with girl friends in the same rooming house or in ones nearby, leading to close sisterly relationships. A typical evening of ups and downs might have been one that Hattie recorded in which the band began to play a few blocks from the rooming house and the girls left their lessons to go down the street to hear it. "They never played a bit while we were down there but began again after we got home!"

Another evening in the village occurred when several girls met after school to go to an evening church service. While taking a walk, "when we got down quite a piece we looked back and there was Miss Parsons coming. We spoke about how we never could go down street without meeting some of the teachers and how they would think we don't study much. When we were coming back we had got nearly up to Mrs. Beadlestons and who should we meet but Miss Hallock going down." Undoubtedly with a wink in her eye, Hattie continued that the next morning about 7:00 A.M. some girls went out to get some bread and "we did not meet any teacher this time."

Hattie's purpose in school was to excel in her work, and she was pushed by her teachers to meet her high goals. She sought consolation one day from her geometry instructor, Mr. Sanders, for not getting her homework done because she could not understand it, and his only response was that it was explained in pretty plain language and he guessed she could understand it "if [she] gave it enough study."

Hattie put herself to the grindstone, as testified by her examination marks: 99 percent in geometry, 95 percent in drawing, 100 percent in English history, and 93 percent in algebra. "I don't feel very bad," she wrote in her diary. "It is quite good to feel that I was the head in the two classes and that only one got more than one credit above me in anything else." After examining the grade reports tacked up on the cupboard door at school "so that everyone could see what their marks were and everybody elses too," Hattie admitted proudly, "I can't help feeling a little elated at my marks."

Hattie, too, "stood Number One," and she was proud of the reputation and esteem she gained among her classmates. She cherished the story of an incident that occurred when she and her girl friends listened to a band serenade a wedding couple near the shirt factory. "They played finely," Hattie wrote, and then she shifted to the main event of the evening for her. "Mabel Clark, Jessie Thomas and Maud stood near.

Though we were in the shadows of a tree, I heard Maud ask Mabel who had the highest mark in English history. Mabel turned and merely said 'I would have you know Hattie Harkness is in that class' as though that was enough to tell who got the highest mark." Then Hattie concluded, "I mean to keep my standings as good next month as they were this." If she could not fulfill that aim in the years to come, surely Georgia would.

———

The small black, leather-bound diary that Georgia received as a New Year's present on January 1, 1904, is a striking symbol of the intellectual and vocational expectations passed from Warren to Hattie to Georgia.[7] During that week when she began her diary, Georgia was home in Harkness between terms at Keeseville High School. It was a cold week, typical of winters in upstate New York, with temperatures ranging from 12 to 18 degrees below zero. The activities of the week for Georgia were similar to those many weekends that she spent back home.

Warren and Lillie, as well as Everett and a neighbor, Norris Cochran, went to Willsboro, twenty miles away, on New Year's Day for the morning celebration at which Warren installed new officers of the Grange. Georgia's responsibility, like Hattie's in years past, was to take charge of the housekeeping and cooking during her mother's absences. At least one neighbor, Henry Stafford, ate the New Year's Day dinner that Georgia prepared for them. "I wished Mamma was at home to help get supper but I got along the best I could. I think I have got along pretty well today at keeping house. I don't know how it will be tomorrow," wrote the twelve-year-old Georgia, proud of her accomplishment but glad not to be doing it regularly.

In later years, Georgia's colleagues who were entertained in her home were surprised that it was not just Verna Miller, her housemate of thirty years, who did the cooking and prepared the house for company. Georgia was adept at gourmet cooking and loved to host dinner parties. It is doubtful that much gourmet cooking was done on the Harkness farm, but hearty meals topped off with delicious desserts were the order of the day.

Growing up in the Harkness home, Georgia must have fulfilled well the functions expected of the surviving daughter. Countless entries tell of Papa and the boys working in the woods on Saturdays while Georgia helped her mother with the domestic chores. Her words on one occasion were typical of many: "[I] worked about as hard as I could today. Papa, Mamma, and I cleaned the whole upper part of the house, except the hall, and the boys room."

Georgia's heart lay in other pursuits, however. When home, she spent much of her free time reading. She entered in her diary the names of her current books, from *The Lively Adventures of Gavin Hamilton, The Lion's Mouth*, and *The Isle of the Lake*, to *The Transformation of Job* and *Ivanhoe*, "a splendid story." She could admit that she hadn't "done much today but help Mamma a little and sit around and read." Another time, in which she hadn't "done hardly anything today except sit around and play the organ," she queried of herself: "Perhaps I ought to help Mamma more than I do."

The daily accounts in her diary confirm that the neighbors related as an extended family to Georgia and other members of the Harkness household. When she was at home on weekends or for holidays, friends came for an evening together or dropped in unannounced—and stayed for dinner. Frank Felio came by often to play "Pit" or "Flinch" with the family. Georgia described one evening of playing "Pit" with neighbors in these words: "It was a pile of fun. I haven't played a game I like so well in a long time."

Neighbors often joined with the Harknesses to go to ball games or band concerts in other towns. Georgia wrote of one special Decoration Day when she had no school and a major excursion was planned to the circus. Their close friend from the adjacent farm, Edith Arnold, joined Papa, Mamma, Everett, and herself for an evening performance. "But there wasn't one so we didn't see it." The day was good anyway, and she concluded her entry, "I had a lovely time." These words well sum up Georgia's reaction to her high school day as gained through her diary. They were satisfying years. She enjoyed them and felt good about herself while at Keeseville High School.

————

Reflections from Georgia's adult life add another dimension to the diary accounts of her high school experience, particularly regarding her growing spiritual understanding. In 1969, when Georgia published *Grace Abounding,* she wrote that she owed "much to those high school years, but two things in particular have 'left their residue,' " her relationship with the village church in Keeseville and the support and training given by her teachers.[8]

During the week, while staying at Aunt Sallie's, Georgia and her roommate got their homework done early on Wednesday evenings so they could attend the weekly prayer meeting. "It sounds archaic to say it!" she added in 1943, when prayer meetings were no longer held in more liberal Methodist churches. However, the mid-week prayer meetings and the evangelistic services led by traveling preachers during the winter months were a special part of the week to Georgia and her friends when they were in high school.

At one of these meetings "midway in high school occurred my definitive conversion" and "I made my basic commitment to Christ." Here lay the seeds of what Harkness described in later years as her lifelong theological stance as an evangelical liberal. "Whether it should be called conversion," in the evangelical tradition, "depends on the meaning given to the term. I felt no great upheaval of soul, but I did feel that from then on I must be a Christian." She knew that she "had been a religiously sensitive child and had loved the Church since before I can remember." But to "be a Christian," in bringing together an evangelical with a liberal perspective, meant "that the time had come to take a definite stand and join the Church."

She wrote in her diary of going to her home church in Harkness on a Sunday in January and her pastor, Mr.

LaGrange, gave her "a little book entitled *The Probationer's Hand Book*" to study in preparation for church membership. Nothing could better confirm the religiously precocious nature of Georgia Harkness during her teen years than her description to the Pacific Coast Theological Group of the way in which she joined the church and the events leading up to it.

> Under the preaching of a traveling evangelist, whose name I cannot remember, I decided that the time had come to take a definite stand and join the Church. I so informed my home minister, who set a day for me to be taken into the Church. Had I not taken the initiative, I might have got into the Church without being baptized, for he erroneously assumed that I had been baptized in infancy. However, I studied the *Discipline,* learned that baptism is supposed to precede church membership, and told him the situation. This meant postponement in order to procure a bowl of water, but two weeks later he baptized me and I took my solemn vows of church membership standing alone before the front school bench in the presence of my family and neighbors. I was a timid adolescent, and I felt self-conscious. Yet in spite of this, the sacredness of that hour and the gentle, reverent, dignity of that country minister make that Sunday afternoon in the old school-house one of my richest memories.[9]

When Georgia remembered the experience of conversion she had at a younger age, she described herself as anticipating a radical inner change, through which she as a child of six or seven years would put behind her sinful ways and walk in the perfected life. As a teenager, however, she did not associate conversion with evangelicalism in this revivalistic tone; her "definitive conversion" now referred to her own decision to be a Christian and a member of the church, rather than participate in the church through her parents' commitment. Evangelicalism meant that she was able to accept the "good news of Jesus Christ" for her own life because of the Christian nurture received from her parents over many years.

In a newspaper interview given later in life, Harkness captured the essence of the Christian faith as it was practiced within her home: "My parents weren't the narrow bigoted kind of Christians usual in those days. . . . Smoking, playing golf on Sundays and wearing makeup were much less important sins to them than to many of their contemporaries. They were just ordinary faithful church-going people and instilled in our family basic Christian values for everyday living."[10]

An earlier account in the nearby Plattsburgh newspaper, describing the fifteenth wedding anniversary of her parents in 1893, when Georgia was only two years old, confirms her understanding of her parents as "just ordinary faithful church-going people." The celebration was festive, with the home of Warren and Lillie "besieged and taken without resistance" by over eighty guests. The Sunday afternoon and evening were "spent in the most social manner, each visiting with the other to make it enjoyable in the best possible way. At supper time the tables were spread, and well supplied with the essentials for such an occasion." All eighty people feasted bountifully, "and several baskets were left over." The celebration was capped with the singing of several gospel hymns and the presentation of a full set of 113 pieces of china, a beautiful lamp, and other gifts to Lillie and Warren. The reporter summed up his point: the Harknesses and people of the vicinity "are good livers, and can supply the need of the hungry or the taste of the epicure."[11]

The Harknesses were thankful for life and the good things they were graced to receive. They were frugal spenders but not particularly pious in the religious upbringing and daily life within Georgia's home. By the standards of rural and small-town farm communities of the time and place, the Harknesses lived well. They gave and received love graciously within their immediate circle of family and friends.

Training in basic Christian values, practiced in relationships with family members, neighbors, and the community, formed the essence of Christian upbringing in Georgia's life. Building upon this foundation, she was prepared to step forth on her own to join the church as a teenager.

When Georgia turned seventeen in 1908, she put behind her childhood days and began to venture in the "big sophisticated, urban university" of Cornell. But when she looked back after many years on her early Christian upbringing, she also remembered with humor, appreciation, and tenderness other aspects of her "varieties of religious experience." She told the Pacific Coast Theological Group about her "school-house religion," the Sunday school classes in the Methodist Episcopal Church on Hallock Hill:

> of Myron Baker who taught the young people's class, who lived in a hovel but had the soul of a Christian gentleman, and who discoursed on the prophets and Jesus with prophetic fire and Christian insight as strange crawling things went up and down his black Sunday coat; of Horatio Baker who was the Sunday School Superintendent for all those years, never varying once his Sunday prayer that we be delivered from the wiles of "the Evil One who goeth about like a roaring lion seeking whom he may devour," and who whenever he called on me to substitute at the wheezy organ always announced the same hymn for fear I might not know any other. It bade us to
>
> "Trust and obey,
> For there's no other way
> To be happy in Jesus
> But to trust and obey."
>
> Incidentally, I still believe those sentiments to be good Christian advice! It was he also who devised the plan of having all of us when I was about ten or eleven learn to repeat the books of the Bible. I was soon repeating the Old Testament sequences so volubly that my father advised me when we got to the New Testament to keep still and give others a chance, with the result that I can now find any book in the Old Testament with relative ease, while in the New I flounder beyond Corinthians.

In due course, she added, "We moved into the lovely new church at Harkness and things became gradually more modernized, though for years we still used the David C. Cook lesson materials. But I am not aware of any element in my sixteen years of school-house religion that did me any harm, and there was much in it for which I can profoundly thank God."[12]

Georgia might also have enjoyed sharing with her colleagues one final incident from her childhood religious experiences that she recorded in her diary as a budding teenager. For whatever reason, she wanted the Methodist Episcopal bishop to appoint a different pastor to the Harkness circuit in 1905. After attending church on Sunday, March 20, she wrote: "Mr. LaGrange will be here only one Sunday more before conference. I hope he won't come back." She, like many others undoubtedly, was anxious for the new pastor to come, and she reacted on May 1 in this way: "I went and heard the new preacher, James Cass. He is young and good looking and I like him very much!"

━━━━━━

Besides her rich experience as a child and teenager in the Keeseville and Hallock Hill churches, Georgia also expressed indebtedness in *Grace Abounding* to the support and training she received from her high school teachers. Only in looking back, after many years as a professor and scholar in higher education, did she evaluate the high caliber of her high school training. She especially remembered her teachers' kindling her interest in the subjects they taught and taking pains to see that she had the courses she needed, "even when I was the only one in the class," in her post-graduate high school years. "The teachers encouraged my love of learning, made what I studied come alive, and saw to it that I was prepared for college." The college-preparatory students were few, and Georgia and her teachers took pride in her accomplishments and potential. In considering the values of excellence in teaching, Georgia referred throughout her life to the highly individualized attention she received in high school and in her graduate work at Boston University.[13]

However, when Georgia was a teenager, her primary concern was to excel at Keeseville High School. In describing her academic experience at age twelve, she recorded her good grades, which placed her among the top students in her small freshman class. She fulfilled well her parents' expectations and her own.

Georgia thrived on the scholastic competition, evidenced by her reaction to the success of her team on the Latin word list: "I seem to be beating the other side quite badly and I hope it will continue." It did continue, and Georgia won the pin as the team's leader. When her father took her to Keeseville on a Monday morning in mid-June to get her Regents' scores, she and her parents were well satisfied: Algebra, 100 percent; Latin, 97 percent; Advanced Drawing, 94 percent; English, 91 percent. Like her father and her sister, Georgia "stood Number One."[14]

CHAPTER FOUR

"I Was Shy, Green, and Countrified"
1908–1912

Almost one century before Georgia Harkness entered Cornell University in 1908, New York state took the lead in expanding higher education for women. It responded to the rising demand for professional teachers, and especially for women, who could be hired for lower wages than men.

Emma Willard's Female Academy in Troy, the first institution to challenge the accepted belief that women could learn only domestic accomplishments, began to train women in college-level work in 1821. Mary Lyon's Mt. Holyoke in Massachusetts, often considered the first women's college in the United States, was founded in 1837, but did not gain college status until 1893, long after the opening of two New York women's colleges, Elmira in 1855, and Vassar in 1865.

Notably, for almost one-half of Harkness's professional career, she taught at two of these educational institutions for women, Elmira and Mt. Holyoke. And her years as a seminary professor were spent at two other schools, Garrett Biblical Institute and Pacific School of Religion, which historically have been among the vanguard in advocating equal opportunities for women alongside men for training in professions of the church.

Not surprisingly, Georgia began her academic training in a university that was among the earliest coeducational institutions. Opened in 1868 in "a few grim, unfinished buildings set in a cornfield of Ezra Cornell's hilltop farm" overlooking Ithaca, Cornell's initial purpose was to educate farmers and industrial workers, persons not served by most existing institutions of higher education. Four hundred twelve students, the largest entering class of any contemporary American college, made up the first "Cornellians." Though the school was not opened to women until 1872, its three male founders, Cornell, Andrew White, and Henry Sage, were radical for the time in their advocacy of women. Significant women in their family lines, including their wives, mothers, and daughters, encouraged the men's pioneering outlook.[1]

The founders envisioned a new type of education, leading to individual perfection, increased options for economic independence, and societal improvement. Their goals related broadly to the purposes of evangelical Christianity, Enlightenment liberalism, and social reform. A commitment to equality—an opportunity for an education should be open to any person regardless of sex who was intellectually worthy—ranked Cornell in the vanguard of the movement for the education of males and females together.

Ezra Cornell wrote to his daughter, Eunice, in 1867: "I want to have girls educated in the university as well as boys, so that they may have the same opportunity to become wise and useful to society that boys have." In a similar vein, Andrew White, who would become Cornell's first president, stated in a letter to abolitionist Gerrit Smith in 1862: "To admit women and colored persons into a petty college would do no good to the individuals concerned; but to admit them to a great university would be a blessing to the whole colored race and the whole female sex—for the weaker colleges would be finally compelled to adopt the system."[2]

However, White feared that conservative New York legislators' support would be lost if "the provocative issue of coeducation" was introduced into the debate on the university's charter. "Therefore, he laid the groundwork for future action by deliberately selecting the word 'person' instead of 'man' for all legislation pertaining to Cornell University." The charter was approved in 1865.[3]

Henry Sage's major contribution came in 1872. Though women had not been barred from admission at the founding of the school, neither had the proper inducements been present. The tide turned with the official announcement that Sage would give the university $250,000 on the condition that "instruction shall be afforded to young women . . . as broad and as thorough as that now afforded to young men." Sage Hall, a dormitory to accommodate up to 120 women, was opened and Cornell officially became coeducational.[4]

Despite the early advocacy of women by its founders and the outstanding women who graduated from Cornell during its early years, discrimination by male students resulted in a highly oppressive atmosphere for their women peers. An editorial in the first issue of *The Cornellian*, published in 1869 by the fraternities on campus, set the tone: "The Woman's Rights monomaniacs are attempting to mislead the public into the belief that women students are to be admitted here. The foundation of the rumor probably exists only in the imagination of some enthusiast, who, thinking that the thing ought to be so, unhesitatingly sets up the cry that it is so. . . . We sincerely trust that Cornell University will never come to be ranked and classed among the Oberlins of America," Oberlin being the first college to allow women to study alongside men in 1837.[5]

Anna Botsford was told by a male student when she entered Cornell in 1874 that she wouldn't have fun because "the boys won't pay any attention to the college girls," leading her to conclude that "Cornell must be a good place for a girl to get an education; it has all the advantages of a university and a convent combined." In fact, Botsford blossomed both academically and socially, being a pioneer in the field of nature study and marrying her professor.[6]

Her experience was much more the exception than the rule, however. As Victorian society bifurcated the roles of men to the public sphere and women to the domestic in the late nineteenth century, "so did the college campus, where the social chasm between men and women became wider and more rigidly structured." By unwritten law, women were out of place at Cornell. They were discouraged from participating in campus organizations and excluded from the social activities of fraternities which set the tone of social life. Members were punished by penalties that ranged from fines to removal from membership for speaking to women students on campus, inside or outside of class, inviting them to parties, or giving them their fraternity pins.[7]

During Harkness's years on campus from 1908 until 1912, discrimination against women was particularly intense. In her annual report of 1912, Gertrude Martin, the Adviser of Women, challenged the university forthrightly, noting "an unwillingness to admit that the institution is really and permanently committed to the policy of coeducation; the feeling that the presence of women somehow renders it inferior to the other great eastern universities . . . a determination to keep it in curriculum and atmosphere as distinctly a man's institution as possible."[8]

A classroom photograph taken in 1910 portrays the academic atmosphere in terms of male-female relationships during Harkness's student days. Approximately sixty men are pictured in one large lecture hall, while three women are seated in the first three desks in the right-hand corner of the first row. The photograph captures the established seating pattern that had been practiced for thirty years.[9]

The report of a Cornell woman student in the 1930s, whose father graduated in 1913, verifies the predominant social attitude toward women when Georgia was on campus:

> [My father] was horrified about my coming to Cornell. I had applied on my own. When I was accepted, my father said he could never go back and face his friends, now that his daughter was a coed. When he was here, [the coeds] were dirt under their feet. The men in his fraternity were fined for even speaking to a coed and they had their fraternity pins taken away if they dated a coed.[10]

Georgia's experience at Cornell must have been similar to that of many women, causing her to conclude years later that "Cornell University was not the right place for me, academically or personally. I diligently did my assignments, got middling good grades, and eventually a Phi Beta Kappa." By any standards, her grades were excellent, primarily clustered from the high eighties to the mid and upper nineties. Her highest marks came in psychology, philosophy, American history, and home economics, as well as the ancient and modern languages of Greek, Hebrew, and German. Evaluating her transcripts in 1990, a member of the Cornell Registrar's staff described Harkness as an exceptional student in a day when professors graded much more rigorously than in the late twentieth century.[11]

Harkness pointed to the words of William Temple to express her standard for academic training: "The essence of all education, mental or spiritual, is the intercourse of less mature with more mature minds." By this standard, "I did not get much education. The big lecture courses never thrilled me as did either my high school or later my graduate work, and personal contacts with the faculty were few. My adviser perfunctorily signed my registration card twice a year, but I doubt that he knew me by sight."

Her social experience fit the pattern of most women students of the day. Whether her adjustment was worse than that of most coeds, Georgia described her situation as precarious. "I was shy, green and countrified, and when I left for college I had never been more than 20 miles away from home. To be plunged abruptly into a big, sophisticated, urban university was a radical change."

The pain of her college years left a deep mark on Harkness, as she remembered forty years later: "My clothes were queer; I had no social graces; and I did not come within gunshot of being asked to join a sorority. I never, in my four years, held a campus office. In fact, I was the utter antithesis of a Big Shot on the Campus."

———

Despite her well-taken, largely negative experience of the Cornell campus and her academic and social life there, Cornell was the right place for Georgia in significant ways.

83

Three areas of her experience there were particularly influential in the molding of her vocational purpose during this formative period: her study of philosophy under Professor James E. Creighton, dormitory life in Sage College, and her "real home and greatest satisfactions" in the Student Volunteer Movement.

In the preface to *Recovery of Ideals,* one of Harkness's definitive books written during the earlier period of her career, she acknowledged her primary indebtedness to her "first teacher of philosophy, Professor James Edwin Creighton." She had only two classes with him, both basic courses, probably of the large lecture style, taken during her second and fourth years. Georgia may have had little direct contact with Creighton; however, she corresponded with him professionally while working on her doctorate, asking him to suggest readings related to her dissertation and to write letters of recommendation for early teaching positions she sought.[12]

Harkness wrote little directly about Creighton during her professional career, but he introduced her to the academic discipline in a profoundly meaningful way, providing the grounding of her own understanding of the task of philosophy and the nature of the truth the philosopher seeks. She never forsook these roots, and their flowering is evident in her later distinctive contribution as an applied theologian.

By the time Georgia took classes under Creighton in 1910 and 1912, he was one of the most distinguished philosophers in American academic circles, elected president of the American Philosophical Association at its founding in 1902. In his presidential address given at the society's first annual meeting, he challenged his fellow professors in the field to fulfill this basic purpose: "The history of philosophy is only intelligible when read in the light of present-day problems." All thought of the past must be a means "to the better comprehension of the problems of the present time." Philosophy should never be understood as an abstract science, but serve the most practical, even spiritual, goal, Creighton stated. "Philosophy must bake *some* bread; it must, like the other sciences, minister to human life . . . we cannot divorce the intellectual and the practical, or say that one is for the sake of the other. Intelligence, when it is complete intelligence, is itself practical."[13]

Speaking at the Eastern Branch of the American Philosophical Association at Vassar College almost ten years later, he reminded his colleagues that "when philosophy is carried on largely by schools and schoolmen it may become artificial through too great an emphasis upon formal completeness and the requirements of technical demonstration." The philosopher is not set apart for "some precious but obscure inquiry," rather the "important matter is to rid thought of abstractions that are not instrumental to concrete knowledge."[14]

Creighton opened the doors for his students to the classical systems of philosophy as a means to help persons relate to their world. But he especially prodded both colleagues and students to begin with concrete experience:

> The kind of insight that constitutes philosophy may be drawn from the understanding that we have of that part of the world with which we are most familiar, such as the circle of the home, or the life of a small community whose members have known each other long and intimately. In such situations the spirit of the whole is comprehended as the common life of which all the individuals partake, and in terms of which their relations to each other seem natural and reasonable.[15]

The individual, the subject of philosophy, is the only real entity, Creighton insisted. However, philosophy must be "occupied with the relations of concrete individuals and systems of individuals," in order to find the wisdom for "a common basis for life in society."[16]

He advanced his own system of speculative idealism as the best guide for a system of relations and values for living in the world. As speculative, it posited that the nature of the mind is to know, that "the mind can go on knowing." As idealistic, it held that the mind can "progressively overcome its onesidedness, can penetrate through the continuity of experience more and more deeply into the nature of reality." This does not mean that the mind of any particular individual can penetrate to the deeper meaning of life at any one moment. But "the mind as the free and comprehensive principle of intelligence . . . manifests itself as the principle of criticism," enabling the individual to correct and complete any given experience. This progression led Creighton to his basic point: "It is just this free and unlimited spirit of critical inquiry that constitutes the ideal of philosophical experience."[17]

Creighton was not a philosopher of religion, and he was not concerned with an understanding of divinity in the Christian view of an eternal being to whom the individual looked for power and goodness. For him, the world of nature constituted the larger, eternal principle.

The three dynamic coordinates of experience to which Creighton appealed were the self, other selves, and nature. Together, they formed a process of intelligence that makes possible a social dialectic. The world of nature "as a uniform and permanent system of natural laws" was "a necessary element in a rational experience. I am unable to conceive how there could be a rational life without an apprehension of an objective order, unmoved by our clamor, indifferent to our moods." A steady and dependable world could be termed the ultimate reality for Creighton as a philosophical or speculative idealist. Belief in a sane world, in which individuals, other selves and social systems, and the natural order functioned together harmoniously furnished the "only possible basis for rationality."[18]

James Creighton introduced Georgia to an approach to the study of philosophy that she would embrace throughout her scholarly career as a philosopher and as an applied theologian. His emphasis on the necessity of philosophy to minister and bring deeper meaning to everyday life situations and present-day problems within the home, school, and work setting describes her life-long academic approach.

Further, Creighton's speculative idealism provided her a natural entry into Boston Personalism. The two philosophical systems shared common optimistic liberal tenets of the centrality of the individual and personality, the ability of the mind to bring truth and freedom to any given situation, and confidence in a steady and dependable natural and social world. The philosophical map that Creighton provided for Georgia enabled her to venture forth on her academic journey and, in time, to move in her own distinctive direction.

———

Resilience characterized Georgia's response to countless obstacles throughout her life, and at Cornell this personal quality enabled her to find a more positive side to her social, as well as her academic, life. The lack of social contact between men and women on a campus dominated by a fraternity caste system created a vacuum, leading Georgia and countless other women students to experience a deep feeling of social inferiority. However, a community of support generated among the women students living in Sage Hall notably offset the sense of ostracism by male peers and created a deeper alternative bonding among the women.

"By that alchemy of dormitory life which welds together even the most disparate personalities, I soon knew many of the other women students, and formed among my classmates some warm and life-long friendships," Georgia recalled. Unable to gain access into the dominant social world of the Cornell campus, she noted that her acceptance of her "inferior social status as being in the natural course of events, kept me from having an unhappy four years."[19] This fellowship became an essential outlet, enabling her to gain companionship and a sense of worth at a time in her life when her sense of inferior social status could have been crushing.

The bonding among women living in Sage College contributed immeasurably to their academic excellence as a group. Equality of educational opportunities appears to have prevailed in the classroom, and men faculty members often must have been dismayed at the higher caliber of work by their women students. The report on the state of education for women, made with pride by Sage College alumnae in 1895, could have applied when Harkness was a student fifteen years later. Though women constituted a small proportion of the total enrollment, they won more than their share of academic honors. Only about 14 percent of the students were women, but one-half of the most recently elected Phi Beta Kappas were women. Recent women graduates were studying for advanced degrees at Cornell and at a host of other United States and foreign universities, several being the first women admitted to these institutions. Others were pioneering in professions previously reserved for men, including medicine, scientific research, and business.[20]

Time was required to build the presence of women at Cornell. They did not flock to the doors when Sage College opened. In the fall of 1875, only twenty-nine women were in residence there, scarcely enough "to keep the ghosts out of the corners," while twenty others were living at home, with other relatives, or in boarding houses. Twenty years later, in 1895, the dormitory was filled to capacity, with 104 students, and a total of 224 women were enrolled in the university.[21]

The founders and officials of Cornell always had intended that young women should have an education that was as broad and thorough as that open to men. However, they had never proposed that public careers should be an alternative to marriage and motherhood, the assumed natural state of womanhood. Women students were to be prepared to work in the public world "so that in case of adversity, they may be sure of a good self-support." Adversity referred to the loss of a husband through death: divorce likely would not be mentioned. To be able to work in case of unforeseen need was the spoken intention of higher education of college women, even though some consciously chose not to marry.[22]

The attitude toward women held by officials and male students at Cornell was paralleled at universities throughout the country. Harkness was part of the second generation of college women who entered from 1890 to 1920. Widespread popular perception held that they were more interested in marriage than in scholarship, wanting a social, rather than an academic, degree. Women students of this generation have been depicted traditionally as "frivolous and socially preoccupied," contrasting "unfavorably with the serious and dedicated pioneer generation of 1865 through 1890."[23]

First-generation university women students traditionally have been considered the pioneers for women's rights in education and professions; they were committed to careers and rarely talked of combining careers and marriage. Recent revisionist studies demonstrate that the large number of women students of Harkness's generation, however, were not seeking marriage rather than careers, but that they hoped to combine the two. Lynn Gordon, in her *Gender and Higher Education in the Progressive Era*, contends that "what truly distinguished the second generation from its predecessor (and its successors) was the linking of gender consciousness to campus life and to postgraduate plans for social activism, a growing commitment to egalitarian rather than separatist feminism, and a simultaneous interest in marriage."[24]

Though Georgia did not write in detail about dorm life at Cornell, the broader strokes of her experience fit into the revised view of second-generation university women. Growing out of the close bond she experienced with other women of Sage Hall, the women developed their own student governance system and set the rules for women students on campus.[25] They also sought entrance into campus activities on an egalitarian basis with men. Integration was denied to Georgia and contributed in large measure to her feeling of social ostracism. Throughout her entire life, however, the goal of full and equal participation with men in professional and social life, as a natural right of humanity, continued to be her personal goal and her aim for other women.

Georgia also probably hoped to combine marriage with a public career. She dated young men while she was in her twenties and thirties, though no relationship led to marriage. Georgia broke off at least one romance at Cornell with a young man whose last name was Appleton. She may have met him through the Student Volunteer Movement because he was planning to be a preacher. He was "a meek and mild" kind of person and her friends kidded about him, calling him "little green apple." Understandably, "this bothered Aunt Georgia," her niece, Peg Overholt, recalled from family remembrances, "and we always thought this had something to do with her stopping the romance."[26]

═══

Despite this awkward and unpleasant situation, Georgia found her self-described "real home and greatest satisfactions" at Cornell in the Student Christian Association and the Student Volunteer Band. Joining the Movement during the spring of her freshman year was not a sudden decision, she remembered, "for back in high school I had thought about being a missionary though I told nobody. I am one of the many thousands who signed the Student Volunteer pledge, 'It is my purpose, if God permits, to become a foreign missionary.' "[27]

Not to articulate this vocational dream during high school was perfectly natural. Such a life's purpose would have been so radically different from the course of all young women in the Harkness community that even her parents, good Christian laypersons who prodded and supported her in different ways, would have had difficulty in taking her dream seriously.

As one of the thousands who took the pledge to become a foreign missionary, Georgia stood in a line of college students dating back to 1888, when John R. Mott organized the Student Volunteer Movement (SVM). Also the future world leader of the Young Men's Christian Association, Mott himself graduated from Cornell in the same year that he formed the student volunteers. His vision for the SVM originated through his leadership of the Christian Association while on campus.[28]

However, the original impetus for the SVM came from the First International Christian Student Conference, brought together at Mt. Hermon, Massachusetts, in 1888 by evangelist Dwight L. Moody. Two hundred fifty-one students from eighty-seven colleges in the United States and Canada gathered there for several weeks of Bible study. Out of the conference came the "Mount Hermon Hundred," one hundred students filled with evangelical zeal who pledged their lives to foreign mission service, Mott being number twenty-three to sign the pledge.[29]

Later that year, Mott, along with three other men and a woman, Nettie Dunn, gathered for prayer meetings to discern God's plan for their lives. Out of these sessions, the Student Volunteer Movement was formed on December 6, 1888. John Mott served as chairman of the SVM committee from 1888 until 1915. "The distinctive purpose of the Volunteer Movement," as stated in his report to the Seventh International Convention held in Kansas City in 1913, one year after Harkness's graduation from Cornell, was "to secure student volunteers who will actually go forth from the United States and Canada and spend their lives in non-Christian lands in the work of establishing Christ's Kingdom."[30]

The Student Volunteers sought to supply mission boards of established church denominations in the United States and Canada with a sufficient supply of volunteers to meet the demands of foreign mission work in the twentieth century, in which the world was to be evangelized for Christ. In the first year of its existence more than 2,000 students were recruited and signed the SVM pledge to give their lives to foreign mission work. Over the next fifty-five years, more than 18,000 young people actually went overseas to enter foreign mission work.[31]

Countless numbers of students who signed the pledge, "It is my purpose, if God permits, to become a foreign missionary," did not go into the world mission field. The SVM saw itself directed to these students, too, "whom God does not call to become missionaries to make their lives count most as clergymen and laymen in developing in North America a strong home base for worldwide missions and in backing up that enterprise in all ways within our power."[32]

Georgia Harkness was one of the persons who signed up with the sincere intent, or at least the serious consideration, of becoming a foreign missionary but whose vocational course changed due to circumstances and decisions over the years. As she put it, "When I was at the right age to carry out this purpose I felt that my parents, particularly my mother, needed me, and after they had left me I was too old, and settled in other work. But I do not believe that this purpose and pledge were futile."[33]

Throughout her entire life, Harkness credited that "no purpose has done more to deepen my Christian experience." She was an ideal candidate to fit the "ultraconservative policy for recruiting" persons to sign the pledge. Mott wanted persons who demonstrated the strongest connection with a local church and who were members of the SVM and the YMCA or YWCA on campuses. Further, each quadrennial report also emphasized the need for more women recruits, because "one half of the unevangelized world, and that by far the most neglected half, are women." However, the percentage of persons recruited over the history of the SVM never reached an equal balance of men and women but remained relatively steady, about two-thirds men and one-third women. Finally, Mott sought volunteers who had strong connections with mainline Protestant denominations. Consistently the most recruits came from Presbyterian, Methodist, Baptist, and Congregational churches.[34]

Harkness had the needed credentials: She was an active member of the YWCA, a woman, and a Methodist! Two important pieces of evidence reveal the important place of the SVM and the YWCA in her life.

The first is her description in the 1912 Cornell yearbook. Referring to these two groups as her primary campus activities, the yearbook reads: "An insatiable appetite for a good time is combined with a thorough appetite of the deepest things in life. Her quiet unassuming ways, ready sympathy, and unselfish spirit have endeared her to all who know her best." The yearbook description presents another side of the young woman who had seen herself in college as "shy, green and countrified," and out-of-place in "a big, sophisticated, urban university"; a person who "accepted my inferior social status as being in the natural course of events"; one who, by the time she graduated, felt she was "perhaps as far advanced, in social finesse and the ways of the world, as most people are when they enter."[35]

Granting that a yearbook statement puts a person in the best light, there can be no doubt that Georgia Harkness was blossoming—becoming her own person—during her college years. Further, students and colleagues who knew her most closely in later years, in the private as well as the public sphere of life, consistently point to her good sense of humor and desire to have fun, along with her empathetic and sympathetic nature and her unselfish giving of herself and her goods, as qualities of Harkness that meant the most to them.

Second, one of the most powerful events that ever occurred to her took place at a social event of the SVM. She called the experience a "miracle of deliverance," and it merits description in her own words.

It was at a Student Volunteer picnic, in early May of my sophomore year, that the one, really dramatic, incident of my life occurred. It is quite a story, with not a few elements of comedy, but I must limit myself to its outlines. After singing as students will around a camp-fire, I fell off a 25-foot cliff into Fall Creek Gorge, at 9:00 P.M. of a pitch-dark night. Although fortunately I struck 12 feet of water instead of the rocks all around, I did not know how to swim, and the perpendicular wall of the cliff would not have helped me much if I could have reached it, as I struggled desperately but futilely to do. During this period of facing imminent death I prayed with an intensity that no other emergency has ever evoked in me. I had a clear, visual image of our sitting-room at home with a coffin in it, just as Hattie had lain so many years before. And just as I thought I could struggle no more, some familiar words shaped themselves in my consciousness, "Father, into Thy hands I commend my spirit." At that moment I felt physical support beneath me, for I had simultaneously been carried by the current into shallow water and a rescuer had reached me.

Various factors had to be as they were, or I should not now be here. But the most crucial, I believe, was the fact that during the time I was in the water—certainly not less than five minutes and perhaps nearer ten—I inhaled no water. For this I claim no presence of mind. And I had no prior knowledge of what to do. By a God-given impulse I held my breath while I was under water, catching a gasp each time as I came up. Thus God answered my prayer and a miracle of deliverance was wrought, but within the order of God's world.[36]

93

Georgia understood her fall from the cliff through her faith perspective that was emerging during her student days at Cornell. By birth and nurture, she was evangelical, and the SVM reinforced that stance. As an evangelical, she interpreted the answer to her prayer for life as a miracle of deliverance; indeed, God's offering of new birth. But she had responded to a "God-given impulse" by holding her breath and gasping at the right times. As Georgia internalized the experience, the miracle occurred within the orderliness of God's world, a liberal tenet at the heart of Creighton's philosophical idealism.

In later years, Georgia affirmed this event as one of the profoundly religious experiences of her life. At the time it occurred, however, she must have believed that God was calling her to affirm a special purpose for her life. To be a high school teacher or a foreign missionary were worthy callings from God. But Harkness would have to continue searching and make another choice for her life.

III. "I Had My Own Life to Live"

CHAPTER FIVE

"A New Profession for Women . . . This Was My Calling"
1912–1920

*I*n the summer of 1912, after her graduation from Cornell, Georgia took a temporary job "attempting to sell" *The Century Book of Facts*. It was an unlikely job for her. Feeling shy and awkward, she was uncomfortable in relating to people who were not close acquaintances. But selling encyclopedic books door-to-door was probably the only summer job Georgia could get.

In reflecting back from later years, Harkness remembered herself upon graduation from college "perhaps as far advanced, in social finesse and the ways of the world, as most people are when they enter." That summer she did not excel as a book agent of encyclopedias and earned little more than covered her expenses. However, something more important happened: "Another miracle occurred—my tongue was unloosed! I got over much of my shyness, and from that time to the present I have had relatively little trouble to converse when I needed to. By such strange ways does God lead His servants."[1]

"My tongue was unloosed!" An expressive metaphor for her emerging confidence in talking with people. But Harkness's words symbolize, even more strikingly, her evolving ability to speak in her own voice and determine the direction of her life. She took the giant step during the eight years from 1912 until 1920 to form, articulate, and act upon her own professional vision. As a young adult in her twenties, Georgia Harkness embarked upon her lifetime vocational journey of "making theology understandable to people."[2]

First, however, she had to come to terms with both the vocational goal she had inherited from her father and older sister, and the alternative aim she conceived while in college. Between 1912 and 1918, Georgia left home to take two teaching positions in small towns 150 miles south of Harkness, New York. The first two years were spent in Schuylerville, directly east of Saratoga Springs and slightly northeast of Schenectady and the capital city of Albany. For another two years she taught in Scotia, west and across the river from Schenectady and about eighteen miles northwest of Albany.

"My first teaching position was a stiff assignment of seven periods a day in teaching Latin, French and German, in none of which I had majored in college," Georgia wrote. Though her degree from Cornell carried a more general "arts" major, she had done well in languages. Working hard and also having a natural aptitude for linguistics, she took two years of German, earning a grade average of 95 percent, a year each of Greek and Latin, with grades of 96 and 90 percent, and a semester of French, in which she received 88 percent.[3]

Keeping discipline and dealing with troublesome students proved the hardest part of her assignment at Schuylerville. The study hall duty "floored me, for I had often to teach and keep order at the same time, and much of the time the room was disorderly. I was immature; I incurred the enmity of some students I penalized for cheating; and they were too much for me. At the end of the two years I was asked to resign."

Her forced resignation must have caused Georgia to feel that she had failed not only herself but her father and sister as well. However, the loss of her first job did not lead her to give up high school teaching. With difficulty, she secured her second position in the Scotia High School, not twenty miles away from Schuylerville. She taught the same subjects—German, French, and Latin—and, with the first sobering experience to build upon, "had more sense and no trouble with discipline." Her salary for the first year at Scotia was $700.00, not as large as received by most teachers in western New York schools and by some in the eastern part of the state. After the first year she was promised a raise if she stayed another year. And she did. While teaching at Schuylerville and Scotia, Georgia incorporated her educational interest into a new vocational choice.

> In both situations I threw myself, probably too ambitiously, into the work of the local Methodist Church. Sunday was always a full day, with attending morning and usually evening service, teaching in Sunday School, running the children's Junior League and participating in the young people's Epworth League. Though I enjoyed my second teaching experience well enough, my heart lay elsewhere. When I read an article in *The Christian Advocate* about a new profession for women in religious education which was opening up, I decided forthwith that *if I could not be a missionary, this was my calling.* (italics added)

Georgia was moving vocationally from high school teaching to religious education as she participated actively in countless church activities. As a volunteer, she was doing the work that religious education directors would soon be paid to do in churches that had large enough memberships and financial resources to hire them. And that was where her heart lay.

For a while Georgia planned "to attend the Hartford School, as I knew of no other. When a catalogue of Boston School of Theology came to me, it took me less than an hour to decide that this was where I wanted to go. It had never taken me long to make the crucial decisions of my life when I got the facts." Her decision to enter the newly inaugurated program of Boston University's School of Religious Education and Social Service came during her first year of teaching at Scotia. But she taught for another year in order to save enough money to continue her education.

Georgia now articulated and acted upon a resolve that had been a long time in formation. She began to make this shift unconsciously during her first year at Schuylerville, immediately after graduating from Cornell. During that year, she wrote her first published piece, a story printed in the September 5, 1914, *Junior Herald,* the weekly Sunday school pamphlet for junior high students in the Methodist Episcopal Church.[4] Years later, Harkness might have been glad to forget that she had ever written such a highly moralistic story. But writing for the junior high church paper symbolized the evolution of her vocational direction.

"A Change for the Worse—Then for the Better," is the story of two junior high girls who had to study in late August to take make-up exams for their spring work. Florence had failed her tests, not because she wasn't smart enough, but because she hadn't studied for them and had a sour attitude. Ethel was taking the exams because she had been out of school with scarlet fever for a month in the spring. Cramming for the exams, Florence passed them, but also cheated on one question by copying Ethel's paper. However, Florence's latent good qualities began to emerge when she admitted her guilt to the teacher, who gave Florence another chance to take the test. In turn, Florence became infected, not by the scarlet fever, but by Ethel's disciplined study habits and cheerful, supportive attitude. The following spring Florence passed her tests with higher marks even than Ethel, who was glad that her friend's "change for the worse" had finally issued "in a change for the better." Against all odds and with seemingly little struggle, both girls incorporated the highest ideals of honesty, responsibility, and good will into their sisterly relationship.

Georgia's first published piece reflects shades of her Sunday school days growing up in the church on Hallock Hill in Harkness, New York. In this first of her lifetime ventures to translate theology into ordinary terms, she selected the medium in which she had been nurtured.

To choose the "new profession for women in religious education," and to interpret it as a calling from God rather than as a personal career choice, also followed naturally. The church was a second home to her, from her childhood days through her college years at Cornell. "I loved the church since before I can remember," Harkness wrote of the paradoxical quality of her "definitive conversion" and her decision to become a member of the Harkness Methodist Episcopal Church. Her conversion was not a dislocating move from unfaith to faith. Rather, it was a steady movement of her will, intellect, and emotions to make the decisions of her life based on her faith in God.

Christian evangelism and nurture were one and the same to Georgia. Their inseparable connection provides a basis of analyzing two seemingly contradictory statements regarding her early vocational visions of whether to be a high school teacher or a foreign missionary. Introducing her college years in her statement to the Pacific Coast Theological Group, she wrote: "As far back as I can remember, I expected when I grew up to be a teacher. No other vocational possibility ever crossed my mind." Then, two pages later, she stated: "I became a Student Volunteer during the Spring of my freshman year. It was not a sudden decision, for back in high school I had thought about being a missionary *though I told nobody.*"[5]

In the light of her upbringing, these words are not as inconsistent as they first sound. She grew up in an evangelical atmosphere within her church, where emphasis was put on "making a decision for Christ." Her family attended worship services and Sunday school as faithfully and regularly as they ate their meals, but the transmission of faith within her home does not appear to have been heavy handed. She did not remember their having prayers and periods of Bible reading as a family, for instance. The Christian faith probably was represented as living a wholesome life and doing good, honest work. This experience of religious nurture equated evangelism, in terms of Christian vocation, as responding to God with the whole of her life and in the ordinary round of her daily activity.

The key strands of Georgia's early life interweave in the fabric of her vocational choice. Being intellectually bright and greatly enjoying school, Georgia must have received strong reinforcement from her parents and her teachers to put her life to the service of others by being a teacher. At the same time, with the world mission field expanding at the turn of the century, stories of missionaries sailing to the "dark and heathen continents" must have filled the pages of her David C. Cook Sunday school literature. To conceive of the romantic vision of committing her own life in such a selfless way would have been natural for a serious, religiously sensitive child. While she internalized that vision, she had not yet found her own voice to share this dream with other people. Who could imagine that a shy, awkward girl from a tiny hamlet in the far-northeastern corner of New York state would journey thousands of miles across the sea to the benighted masses to "give her life to Christ"?

Could Georgia herself really imagine it? In stating "if I could not be a missionary" the new profession of religious education "was my calling," she may have decided that foreign missionary service was not the right calling for her, that she was not well fitted for it, and that her aptitude for intellectual pursuits required a career that would relate her more directly to learning and teaching. The idea of a foreign missionary's life may have frightened her, seeing it as more of a break with her upstate New York background than she was capable of making.

Like many other college students who signed the SVM pledge, Georgia Harkness stepped back from her pledge to become a foreign missionary. She may have realized that she had been caught up in a wave of youthful enthusiasm, generated by the fervor of many thousands of students responding to the Social Gospel and the thrill of Christian imperialism. But the pledge helped to confirm her resolve to find a vocation that expressed her Christian commitment.

———

Boston University School of Religious Education and Social Service led Georgia Harkness into worlds more far flung from upstate New York than she could have imagined. It exposed her to the burgeoning cries for home mission work in the new worlds of the inner cities in the United States. The school was opened in 1917, and Georgia entered the second year in September 1918, just two months before the signing of the armistice treaty that ended World War I.

Social conditions in the United States after World War I set the context for the vision of the School of Religious Education. During the next two years, while she was a Master's degree student, the country was stunned by the influx of over ten million immigrants into its urban centers. The term "new immigrants" was used to describe these persons who were arriving from southern and eastern Europe. Prior to 1882, almost 90 percent of the immigrants were from northern and western Europe. Of the same basic stock as the earliest colonists in the United States, the earlier immigrants were easily assimilated.

The new immigrants hailed primarily from Austria-Hungary, the Russian Empire, Italy, and the smaller countries of Romania, Turkey, and Greece. In the decade of the 1880s, for instance, 3.5 percent of the immigrants had come from the Russian Empire and 5.1 percent from Italy. By 1910–1919, 17.4 percent were arriving from Russia and 19.4 percent from Italy.[6]

With their alien speech and culture, these recent arrivals constituted a threat to the older immigrants' understanding of the "inner life" of the United States. National, state, and local governments; public schools; social service centers; and churches developed new agencies in response to two deeply perceived social questions: how to counter the threat to democratic values and how to acclimate the new citizens to American life.

The School of Religious Education and Social Service, an arm of Boston University's School of Theology, was a lay training institution designed to meet the increasing needs of New England rural and city churches for the ministry of laypersons as well as clergy. However, its particular emphasis was placed on the acutely felt urban problems. The school was born out of the vision of its founder and first dean, Walter Scott Athearn, and shared by its other faculty members, including George W. Tupper and Charles E. Carroll. These three men, with Tupper as her primary adviser, made up Georgia Harkness's Master's thesis committee.

Their harmonious perspectives defined the purpose of religious education and social service advanced by the school and influenced both Harkness's thinking and her Master's thesis.

Christianity was born of the social vision of Jesus Christ, who spent a great part of his ministry "in caring for the physical as well as the spiritual needs of mankind," wrote Charles Carroll. Carroll's program included a social ideal of what it meant to be a disciple in Christ's name: "Whosoever will be great among you, let him be your minister. Even as the Son of man came not to be ministered unto, but to minister."[7]

Jesus' understanding of ministry was interpreted as social service. The idealistic purpose of the Boston University School of Theology was an extension of the Social Gospel at the turn of the century:

> to bring religion from the stars to the streets,
> to interpret it in terms of the work-a-day world.
> That social end is a regenerated society,
>
> regenerated bodies and regenerated souls: the achievement of the Kingdom of God in this world, and the better preparation for the realization of the Kingdom of Heaven in the next. As the gardener must first clear and break the soil in which he sows the seed, so the worker for the Kingdom of God must remove the social and economic conditions which are unfavorable for Christian growth.[8]

The chief purpose of the church has been and always will be to save souls, the evangelistic task of "bringing individual souls into a conscious, personal relationship with God."[9] But the church must recognize the indissoluble relationship between social evil and the spiritual side of life. "It must be awakened to the essential wrong involved in a social condition which dooms the millions to hopeless poverty, wretchedness and sin," in Carroll's words. "Its business is to convict men of sin—but sin, not merely in the individual lives of men but in their associated life as well. The church must look back of every individual for the physical, political, industrial, economic, and social conditions which have very largely made him what he is."[10]

At various times in history, the church has been preoccupied with other major passions, including theology, missions, and evangelism. Also in the past, revivalism was the method of evangelizing. But the time had arrived in the early twentieth century for this personal and social evangelical task to be seated in religious education, contended Athearn. In this age, Christian nurture was becoming equated with religious education and, in turn, evangelism.

However, the Boston School professors stated strongly that Christian education was not meant to be a substitute for the "direct and immediate saving and transforming power of grace in the heart." Rather, it offers the best means of "leading the individual into a full realization of this divine power." Parents and Sunday school teachers, as religious educators, start children on their Christian way. In Athearn's words, the religious educator's nurturing task is to give "the child the knowledge, the habits and the feelings which enable him to live a well-rounded abundant and victorious religious life."[11]

Christian education combines evangelical with ethical and moral work in its nurturing function. It seeks to introduce self-control into experience in terms of Jesus Christ, "to present Jesus Christ to the rising generation that every act of every day of every person will be performed in harmony with His holy will." The church's purpose is closely attuned to the public school's aim of citizenship, particularly in such a time as this: to implant in its citizenship the power to control all activities "in harmony with the great ideals which guarantee the happiness and welfare of people."[12]

The need for such training in morality and virtue was particularly acute in the United States in the 1920s, according to Walter Athearn, because of the spiritual illiteracy of American youth, particularly the children of newly arrived immigrants. His calculations were staggering. Probably four-fifths of the young men of this country were growing up with "little or no vital connection with any of the churches" and behind that detachment lay a deep misunderstanding of the faith and the ideals by which Christian persons live. This condition accounted for "the weakest spot in the Protestant church . . . the army of twenty-seven million children and youth in our own land who are growing up in spiritual illiteracy and sixteen million other American Protestant children whose religious instruction is limited to a brief half hour once a week, often sandwiched in between a delayed preaching service and the American Sunday dinner. Let it be burned into the minds of our church leaders that *a church which can not save its own children can never save the world.*"[13]

American youth experienced a vacuum of ethical ideals. Tests revealed their astonishing lack of knowledge of biblical history and literature, and their inability to see a relationship between biblical knowledge and moral sanctions regarding honesty, integrity, and responsibility. However, while scores demonstrated that a large percentage of the rising generation would steal, lie, and cheat with little provocation, they also showed that "virtue can be taught so that it controls conduct." Democratic institutions of the United States—both sacred and secular—of home, church, and state, rested on two closely interrelated principles: first, that the perpetuation of democratic institutions depended on the intellectual and moral integrity of the people and, second, that every normal person was potentially capable of intelligent and ethical self-control.[14]

═══

In writing *An Adventure in Religious Education* in 1930, Walter Athearn looked back over the first decade of the Boston University School of Theology, summarizing the three basic problems it had addressed in the professional training of Christian educators and social workers. The school sought (1) to interpret the curricula and objectives of religious education in terms of personalistic idealism; (2) to organize its training of religious education to harmonize with the democratic ideals that are accepted for the general life of the community, the state, and the nation; and (3) to gain for religious education the scholastic and research advantages offered to other fields of learning and service by the modern university and the great professional and technical schools.[15]

Harkness's Master's thesis on *The Church and the Immigrant*, published by the Doran Company in 1920, demonstrated her grasp of the third component, competence in academic research. It also validated that she had internalized the first two purposes, a belief in personalistic idealism as the basis for development of democratic ideals, through the teaching and writing of Athearn and Carroll.

Georgia's primary intellectual indebtedness, however, went to George W. Tupper, her adviser. Tupper joined the faculty of the new Boston School after serving since 1908 as Immigrant Secretary of the YMCA in Massachusetts and Rhode Island, two states that had more foreign-born residents in percentage of population than any other state in the union. In his valuable first-hand experience with immigrants, he had brought together religious education with social service in the most practical way. *Foreign-Born Neighbors* was Tupper's account of day-to-day work of YMCA programs to aid in assimilating immigrants in these two states. His influence on Georgia Harkness, with her rural and small-town roots, laid the foundation for her mature scholarship and contribution as an applied theologian.

Tupper focused on the great flood of over ten million immigrants from southern, central, and eastern Europe into the United States in the early years of the twentieth century. He sought to counter the storm of unrest and disturbance that their presence, as almost entirely unskilled laborers, had created in the industrial world.[16]

The Protestant churches needed to put aside their theological quibbles and join together in the Federal Council of Churches to lead the United States "to a public confessional," Tupper wrote following World War I. Since the earliest colonial days, the Protestant churches had exercised major influence in shaping the character of American life. Recently, however, the churches had made little effort to reach out to new immigrants, and it was now "high time that they roused themselves from this indifference." The attitude of Americans in general, and of church persons particularly, had to be changed from indifference and hostility to intelligent sympathy. However, "before Protestant Churches are equipped for effective work with the unchurched New Americans they must be converted" to a commitment to work in solidarity for the spiritual welfare of the New Americans.[17]

George Tupper established the cause for conversion of the Protestant churches and their members to enable them to relate to the new immigrants. Georgia Harkness sought in her Master's thesis to address that need in the practical way that would characterize her work over the next five decades.

After mentoring Georgia in writing her thesis, George Tupper wrote the introduction to *The Church and the Immigrant* in its published form. He described the book as directed primarily to young people who were inspired by the Social Gospel to help their foreign-born neighbors in industrial centers but who "realized their helplessness as they invaded this great unknown realm where Old World backgrounds, race psychology and myriad languages loomed large." To these new recruits in the army of workers for Christian democracy, the book asks two important questions: "In what field shall I work? What shall I do?" Both of these questions are "briefly but definitely answered by Miss Georgia E. Harkness in her admirable little book."[18]

These were the same questions Georgia was asking herself as she sought guidance on her own vocational course. During the second year of her Master's program, the movement began to clarify as she took her first philosophy course under Professor Edgar S. Brightman and determined the direction that religious education would take in her professional career. But she had not yet articulated her vocational decision. Writing her Master's thesis was an important step on that journey.

The Church and the Immigrant bore the strong imprint of the Boston University School of Religious Education and Social Service. It synthesized the philosophical idealism and Christian evangelicalism that Athearn and Carroll applied to religious education and social work, the sociological method of Carroll, and the direct application to the immigrant scene by Tupper. In an introductory and methodical way, Harkness laid out the condition of the new immigrants coming to America and the failure of society to welcome them, treat them as brothers and sisters, and prepare them for citizenship. She then turned to her primary purpose: the task of the churches to address the new immigrants' spiritual and social needs. Harkness presented the best of the Social Gospel and its vision for later liberation theology, advocating not only "that there is no necessary conflict between the spiritual message and the social gospel of Christianity," but that the two are inextricably bound together.[19]

In addressing the question of what the church should do, Harkness stated in general outline form a host of highly practical suggestions, most of them drawn primarily from her observation in the Boston School laboratory courses of the wide network of social service work carried on in the city. Her goal was assimilation of the new immigrants into American culture, but always understanding *assimilation* to mean, as did Tupper, a blend of the cherished culture that the immigrants bring from the Old World with that of the New World. Further, the church should address the hard issues of social justice, holding the employer accountable for exploitation of new workers and making the employer responsible for improving working conditions, from sanitation of plants to more equitable wage scales.

Also, the church should serve the immigrants' immediate material needs, sending case workers to help them find jobs and open up less congested housing arrangements. The immigrants' contributions of racial heritage and ideals should be welcomed. Case workers must live out of the principle of genuine brotherhood and sisterhood: they have much to learn from those who would be citizens, as well as to teach them. "Is the American really his neighbor?" Harkness asked. "Too often a barrier of prejudice or superiority raised by the native-born stands in the way of any real Americanization of the immigrant. This barrier is the task of the church to remove. . . . We must not impose our efforts upon the foreign-born, but must give them a share in both the shaping and the execution of plans."[20]

In *The Church and the Immigrant*, Harkness addressed only the relationship of the church to the new immigrants from central, southern, and eastern Europe—a formidable enough task for a young woman from upstate New York, taking her first plunge into the urban world. However, she laid the foundations for ways she would address issues of race regarding African Americans and Asian Americans in years to come.

> The program of the church for racial progress must aim to minister to every side of the immigrant's nature. Giving material aid, relieving bodily ills, supplying a right environment—all are activities worth doing in themselves. But a deeper purpose must underlie our work. Social service cannot be fully successful unless through it we develop the higher spiritual values. Our ultimate goal must be the more abundant life which Christ came to bring to man. We must minister to the souls of men. We must seek to make them, not simply members of one church nor citizens of America, but members of the Church Universal and citizens of the Kingdom of God.
>
> . . . The real foundation of all our efforts must be the spirit of Christian brotherhood. When the Christian people of America fully catch the spirit of the Christ and follow His behest as He says, "Love thy neighbor as thyself," then the immigrant *problem* will cease to exist, for the stranger within our gates will have become our brother.[21]

Both the realism and the idealism of Harkness's statement and her belief in the essential harmony of interests of the "citizens of the Kingdom of God on earth" are distinctive marks of her Christian faith. By writing in plain and simple language, she encouraged her intended readers of *The Church and the Immigrant*, primarily middle-income members of established churches, to venture forth, as she was doing, into new realms—in this case the world of their "foreign-born neighbors."

Georgia had the rare experience of having her thesis published after she received her Master of Arts and Master of

Religious Education degrees. In later years, after she completed the writing of a book, she excitedly told people that she had had her baby, and she shared her children with countless hosts of readers. In content, style, and purpose, most of Georgia's later writings were directed primarily to laypersons, whom she described as "the ultimate consumer for whom churches exist."[22] Because she did not water down the message and summons of the faith, and because she wrote in ordinary language, she reached the congregations as did no other theologian of her age. Undoubtedly, Harkness was the most widely read theologian of the mid-twentieth century.

However, there is great irony regarding the publication of her first book, *The Church and the Immigrant.* In Georgia's words, this baby was stillborn. It did not sell 1,000 copies. The book made little impact on the church in addressing its responsibility and relationship to new arrivals.

At the same time, *The Church and the Immigrant* is vital to understanding Georgia Harkness. The content, style, and purpose of her Master's thesis captured the essential Harkness, which would characterize her written prose and her spoken interpretation of the Christian faith during her middle and later years until her death. Her thesis launched her on a unique journey as a religious educator and embodied much of what would be her distinctive contribution as an applied theologian in her mature years.

CHAPTER SIX

"The Spell of Dr. Edgar S. Brightman's Kindling Mind"
1919–1923

On September 10, 1921, Georgia sent a complimentary copy of her "book on Americanization" to Dr. Edgar S. Brightman, by then her dissertation adviser in the Graduate School of Boston University. "I do not think you will find it much of an addition to your library, for I am very conscious of its defects," she wrote him regarding *The Church and the Immigrant*, "but it represents a great deal of labor expended largely at times when I should have preferred to be doing philosophy."[1]

Georgia's disclaimer of the value of her published Master's thesis points to her intellectual journey during her three years of residency at Boston University from 1918 until 1921. "Those three years in Boston were great years," she reminisced regarding her Master's and Ph.D. programs. Her contentment stemmed primarily from the clarification of her vocational direction during her second year. "I decided definitely, that, if possible, I wanted to devote my life to teaching religion to college students."[2] Georgia began to envision herself in the roles of Brightman and Albert Knudson, in the Graduate School, and other previous professors, including Tupper, Athearn, Carroll, and Creighton.

During her second year toward earning her Master's degrees in Arts and Religious Education in 1919, Georgia began to take philosophy classes under Brightman, the newly appointed Borden Parker Bowne Professor of Philosophy in the Boston University Graduate School. Like a host of his brightest and best students over the years to come, Harkness soon fell under the spell of this brilliant professor's "kindling mind." The initial class she took with him, an introduction to the philosophy of religion, was "beyond question the most stirring and illuminating course [she] ever took," Georgia wrote. It opened a new world for her and was steep sledding, for she received only a "Good +" in the class, the lowest grade she ever received from Brightman.[3]

Other experiences corroborated her sense that these were great years. The academic atmosphere was stimulating and challenging. She had the opportunity to share ideas and professional questions with fellow students who had the same interests, making the social climate in the Boston University Graduate School more comfortable for her than when she was an undergraduate at Cornell. Georgia felt greater acceptance by her male peers in the Divinity School and the Graduate School than by most of the young men in her class at Cornell.

Years later she recalled some of her fellow students at Boston University: Clarence Craig, Stanley High, T. T. Brumbaugh, Earl Marlatt, Dewey Short, and F. Marion Smith. Out of their callings to ministry, these men moved in a host of different ways. Craig became Dean of Drew Theological School, and Marlatt was Dean of Boston University School of Theology. Brumbaugh was a long-time missionary to Japan and was instrumental in the founding of International Christian University, where Georgia took a sabbatical in the mid-1950s. Smith was her pastor in Berkeley earlier in that decade.

High and Short moved into politics. A social activist, High began on the left, authoring *Revolt in Youth* and working with Franklin D. Roosevelt. Then he veered radically to the right, participating in the McCarthy era persecution during the 1950s. During the same years, Short was a United States Congressman and chaired the House Armed Services Committee, while Georgia continued her radical pacifist witness. She remembered these fellow students while on campus as all "boys of promise," using language still acceptable in the 1950s, like so many others in the class who simply had not gained such distinction.[4]

Harkness may have considered getting a Bachelor of Divinity, as had most of these men. Her words to her colleagues in the Pacific Coast Theological Group years later were: "I did not attempt to take a B.D.," perhaps because full conference membership in the Methodist Episcopal Church was denied to women and she did not desire to be a pioneer with partial membership privileges. Or she may have underestimated her ability to accomplish such a course. Another possibility is that she realized that both her talents and her interests better suited her for another type of ministry.[5]

Georgia had begun her Master's program in 1918 because she believed religious education was both her calling and career. As a "theologian of the people," she always would be a religious educator. In shifting the definitive direction of her professional commitment from the institutional church to college and seminary teaching, another new profession for women, she was altering but not changing her definitive vocational choice.

Edgar Brightman, a scholar and teacher of academic excellence and a committed and active churchman, became her most significant mentor and model. Of course, all of Georgia's mentors were male, for there were virtually no women teaching in higher education to whom a young woman could look for direction and support.

———

Lillie Harkness was not a mentor or model of how her daughter wanted to live her adult life. But, paradoxically, Georgia's mother spoke to her the word of liberation from the traditional social constraints placed on a woman.

Comments that Georgia made in her diary when she was twelve years old leave no doubt that her mother's domestic role was not appealing to her. On the other hand, she looked up to her father, whom she deeply valued for his public leadership and whose way of life she secretly envisioned for her own. Georgia probably assumed that her mother, in relating to her husband and family, should adapt her life to his and be "centered in him and the children."[6]

Husbands' and wives' socially prescribed roles were so taken for granted that Georgia, as a child, may not have questioned whether her mother should have an identity or voice of her own. She never remembered hearing scolding and sharp words exchanged between her parents. But, also, she did not recognize until later that such peace may have been achieved by her mother's self-imposed silence. It struck her only after coming to young adulthood that her father had not praised her mother as much as he should have and that "he took her fidelity for granted."

Georgia recorded three events during her years at Boston University that demonstrate how she came to know and value her mother in a new way. Only after coming to young adulthood did she realize, regarding her mother, "how deeply her devotion to her family ran" and how much she had sacrificed on their behalf. These events also indicate that her mother sought for Georgia a different way of life than her own.

One circumstance grew out of Georgia's pressing financial condition as a student. During her second year, she gained her first experience teaching students at the university level, giving an introductory course in Bible to incoming religious education majors at Boston University. "I loved it; apparently they did too; and I hoped to continue." However, despite the positive student evaluations, her invitation was not renewed. "I was told that there was no money; but the money was straightway given to someone else. So, whatever the reason, I was left with no job, and no prospects of one."

Left unemployed, she "expected to borrow the money for this third year, but my mother insisted on turning over to me a small inheritance from her parents." This gift enabled Georgia to focus more exclusively on her course work during her third year at Boston University. And Lillie gained the satisfaction and pride of investing herself in her daughter's vocational journey during that crucial period.

A second event occurred during the Christmas vacation of her first year at Boston University. "I came down with the flu and was ill for six weeks, for half that time very critically. My mother nursed me back to health with night and day attention, though she was never well herself after that."

A final crisis, the most telling of the three for Georgia's identity, grew out of the strains of inter-generational living in the Harkness farmhouse. Through the years, the home was filled beyond capacity many times with members of the extended family, taking a heavy toll on her mother. "Much of her life was made un-happy by having to live, first with her mother-in-law and then with her daughter-in-law, both of whom had sharp tongues." As the youngest child and only surviving daughter, Georgia "wrestled mutually with this problem in the latter instance for over twenty years, often vainly attempting to interpret the viewpoint of each to the other and with my heart torn with sympathy for both."

After Georgia made her vocational decision to pursue a Ph.D. in preparation to teach religion to college students, tension came to a head within the extended family living in the Harkness farmhouse. The problem seemed insoluble, so Georgia offered to stay at home and run the farm to enable her brother Charlie and his wife, Minnie, to go elsewhere. Two considerations prevented such a radical move: "(1) the agreement on the part of everybody that I was incompetent, and (2) the insistence by Mother that *I had my own life to live*, and must not be deflected by it on her account" (italics added).

Undoubtedly Warren strongly concurred with Lillie's unequivocal pronouncement. The necessity for him to sacrifice his vocational dream of teaching and return home to run the farm when he was twenty-three, due to his father's untimely death, paralleled Georgia's dilemma. Further, since Georgia was a young child, her father had done everything possible to provide the education and wider horizons for her that he so desired for himself.

However, her mother's support, even mandate, that "I had my own life to live," made the difference for Georgia in this family crisis, on which she never elaborated further. As a wife and mother, Lillie Merrill Harkness had not led a life of her own. She had "adapted her life to his," and at this critical moment pronounced that her daughter must take her life into her own hands and become her own person.

Georgia Harkness articulated in her own voice "I had my own life to live" when she decided she could become a professor in higher education and asked Edgar Brightman to be her Ph.D. adviser. Brightman may have been testing her when he responded that she "had the preparation, probably the brains, but that [she] lacked the stick-to-it-iveness." And Georgia answered him with a resilience that characterized her entire life: "If that was all, I would see to that."[7]

Edgar Brightman was only seven years older than Harkness when he became Borden Parker Bowne Professor of Philosophy at Boston University in 1919, one year after she began her Master of Religious Education program. He was a fitting choice to receive the chair. Brightman had taken his doctoral preliminary examinations under Bowne in 1910, the same year in which his mentor died. Two years later, he finished his Ph.D. at Boston University, and Georgia completed her BA at Cornell. Bowne had distinguished himself as the founder of Boston Personalism, deemed "the first complete and comprehensive system of philosophy developed in America which has had lasting influence."[8] Brightman followed in his mentor's footsteps as a second-generation exponent of Personalism, and Harkness was among its third-generation representatives.

While studying in Germany before completing his Ph.D., Edgar Brightman married Charlotte Hulsen. After finishing his doctorate, he taught at Nebraska Wesleyan College and Wesleyan University in Connecticut. Charlotte's life was tragically cut short in 1915. The next year, Edgar married a second time to Irma Fall. He fathered three children, a son born to Charlotte, and another son and daughter born to Irma.

During World War I, he was a captain and an instructor in the R.O.T.C. at Wesleyan University, where he taught war issues and military psychology, and he censored German newspapers for the Department of Justice. Brightman later became a pacifist and looked back with regret on his war participation. Throughout his life, he was as committed a churchman as he was a philosopher, being an ordained member of the New England Conference of the Methodist Episcopal and Methodist Churches. Brightman was particularly active in conference social concerns and his local church in Newton Centre, Massachusetts.

Writing in 1986, Walter Muelder, Emeritus Dean and Professor of Social Ethics at Boston University School of Theology, described the profound influence Brightman, as a teacher, had upon him and other outstanding students: "From the first seminary semester, I started taking as many of Brightman's courses as possible. . . . He kept his eye on me, on Nels Ferré and Peter Bertocci—occasionally in the same foundation courses. I owe more to this amazing teacher than to anyone else in higher academe."

Though Muelder is twenty years younger than Harkness, he took courses from Brightman in the late 1920s and is considered among the third-generation Personalists, along with Harkness, Bertocci, Harold DeWolf, Paul Schilling, John Lavely, and others. Martin Luther King, Jr., who expressed deep intellectual indebtedness to his Personalist heritage at Boston University, was a fourth-generation bearer of the tradition.

Reminiscing in an interview in 1990, Muelder precisely described the nature of the relationship Brightman had with Harkness and other top students.

> He was so powerfully brilliant that some people never came to know him personally. . . . However, you persisted with your questions. Edgar loved a challenge. So the good students got to Edgar and Edgar got to them.
>
> And he invited us to take walks with him after class. I would even take the street car out to Newton Centre once a week and walk back to the University with him when Edgar walked into town. We would have a philosophical discussion.
>
> Edgar liked the challenges. He liked the interaction with the students very much. But he was thinking in terms of subject matter. You had to learn to phrase the question in terms of the subject matter, not the question of where I am spiritually.

He was a very spiritual person, though . . . Edgar gave me intellectual consent to pursue my spiritual needs—that it was all right for a critical mind to venture out in faith. And that was what Personalism was really all about. That is, the whole person is to be realized, not just the academic side.[9]

The subject matter, along with his engagement with the material and the students, caused Georgia Harkness to "fall under the spell of Dr. Edgar Brightman's kindling mind" during her second year at Boston University. From James Creighton at Cornell, she gained a foundation in philosophical idealism upon which to build. And from Walter Athearn, George Tupper, and Charles Carroll in the Boston University School of Religious Education and Social Service, Harkness received academic training in Personalist philosophy and evangelical theology and in their relationship to Christian education. All these professors stressed the practical implications of their thought to social service and social justice. However, Brightman officially introduced her to Boston Personalism and put together philosophy and religion for Georgia for the first time.

Brightman's mentor, Borden Parker Bowne, a name almost synonymous with Boston University, began his instruction there in 1876 and remained on the faculty until he died in 1910, teaching in the College of Liberal Arts, the School of Theology, and the Graduate School, of which he was the first dean. During Harkness's study at Boston University, Brightman and Albert Knudson, dean of the School of Theology for twelve years, were among the primary exponents of Boston Personalism. The philosophical school itself declined by the late 1930s. However, a large number of the primary leaders of Protestantism, and particularly those within the Methodist Church through the third quarter of the twentieth century, owed their major intellectual debt to Boston Personalism.

The essence of its philosophical position lay in the interpretation of personality. The person is the ultimate reality and personality the fundamental explanatory principle and value of all of life, both human and divine. Personality "cannot be explained by anything else, but everything else can be explained by it," in William Ernest Hocking's words.[10]

Brightman identified a person as "a highly developed self . . . able to develop self-consciousness, reasoning powers and experience of ideal values."[11] He and other Personalists did not identify reality with the human personality. Rather, they believed that "human persons (not isolated but in community) are the clues to reality with the Divine Person. . . . Humans are not identical to God, nor absorbed into God; instead, they share God's purposes even as they are distinct selves."[12]

Edgar Brightman published two books in 1925, *An Introduction to Philosophy* and *Religious Values,* which contain the essence of Personalism as he developed it in his early years of teaching at Boston University. They particularly reveal the thrust of the first philosophy of religion course that Georgia Harkness took, the class that stirred and illuminated her so much and built upon her previous academic work.

"The philosophical ideal . . . is to take everything into account," stated Brightman, to interpret the whole of life and its values. Its purpose is to be the unifying and idealizing force in education, particularly needed in an age of specialization, in which society tends to ignore or explain away higher values.[13]

Philosophy is not practical in that it "will buy no bread for the starving, will build no house for the shelterless. It feeds and shelters only the mind." However, the philosopher's contribution is more practical than anything money can buy, Brightman continued. "Whatever leads to true value is practical. Philosophy does not furnish the things that make human existence possible; but it casts a new light on the things that make human existence valuable . . . nothing is practical if human existence is worthless."[14]

To be practical, in the philosophical sense, necessitates ideals that provide a more convincing interpretation of the ends, meaning, and values of life than the desires, instincts, and habits that motivate a superficial existence. The practical value of Personalism, as a philosophical school, was that it "finds in the relation of human and divine wills an inexhaustible meaning and purpose in life." Brightman believed that God is a being of perfect goodness and purpose, and that humans live out of an ideal obligation in life to attain the highest values. Though suffering and tragedy are facts of life, the Personalist faced tragedy and saw that there is more to life than that. Deeper meaning can transform tragedy. Because the universe is a friendly place, that hope of trans-formation is possible.[15]

Religion is a person's total attitude toward what the self considers to be superhuman and worthy of worship or devo-tion. In harmony with Personalist philosophy, "all religious experience aims to perform one fundamental function, name-ly, to express man's attitude toward what he regards as the chief value of values in life."[16]

Religion is practical in the same sense as philosophy. It leads people to deeper meaning and purpose in life. Its human value lies in the fact that if "religion is a real part of life, it is supreme; and only the purpose to serve God is in the long run inclusive enough adequately to sustain the server or to benefit the served." Again like philosophy, religion should be inclu-sive of all of life. It transforms our wants and needs from preoc-cupation with mundane goals and "gives an actual unity to life that no other type of human experience can approximate . . . it sets all our thoughts, feelings, and volitions in their relation to God, not merely as an ideal goal of life, but as a real and eternal Power, a Presence ever present."[17]

In all, Georgia took eight semester courses from Brightman, undoubtedly his entire class load, during her second and third years in the graduate school—two semesters of philosophy of religion, practical ethics, epistemology, metaphysics, and a two-semester advanced seminar in philosophy. She did well in all of her work, receiving an "Excellent" in all classes except a "Good +" in the first semester philosophy of religion course.[18]

When Harkness summed up the effect of her residence work at Boston University upon her religious perspective, she stated: "These three years, partially in religious educa-tion, but mainly in theology, philosophy and Bible, greatly deepened and clarified my religious thinking, but wrought no drastic change in it. I had already become familiar with the historical approach to the Bible and the general assumptions of liberal thought." Beyond her academic influences, she gave credit to the Cornell Christian Association, and the voluntary study courses that it gave in Bible, and to a high school minister and life-long friend, the Reverend Emmett Gould.[19]

═══

After three years of residency at Boston University on her Masters' and doctoral programs, Georgia passed her Ph.D. qualifying exams in June 1921, and turned to the immediate realities of gaining employment and beginning her dissertation. That summer a lively and significant correspondence was initiated between the student, Georgia Harkness, and her mentor, Edgar Brightman. During the next twenty-five years, they exchanged more than two hundred letters.

The entire collection of Brightman's personal and professional papers, in the Boston University Archives, contains voluminous correspondence that he maintained with a host of colleagues, students, and friends until his death in 1953. The Harkness–Brightman letters provide information regarding the private side of Georgia's life that is available from no other source. Her public journey over these years has been traced through her writing and speeches. Impressions of her have been gained from relatives, friends, colleagues, and students who knew her in a variety of settings. But no other source provides knowledge of many events that transpired in her life, her struggles to gain teaching positions and professional status, and her feelings surrounding a host of triumphs and trials.

Further, the letters provide the insight of why Georgia, like a long line of other students, "fell under the spell of Dr. Edgar Brightman's kindling mind." They document a notable friendship and professional relationship of mutual trust and esteem that evolved over the years from that of student-teacher to collegial peers, their salutations at long last changing from "Dear Dr. Brightman" and "Dear Miss Harkness" to "Dear Edgar" and "Dear Georgia."

Harkness was forty-nine and Brightman fifty-six when they adopted this more personal greeting!

Almost forty of these letters were exchanged during the two-year period from 1921 until 1923, when Georgia was teaching at Willsboro High School and Elmira College and writing her dissertation. The letters engage three themes: her efforts to gain a teaching position, her mother's health, and how to write a dissertation.

After completing her doctoral preliminary exams, Georgia hoped to begin teaching religion to college students, but the restrictions that she set temporarily created difficulties. Lillie Harkness was suffering from a progressing condition of diabetes, and Georgia felt responsible to be located close to her home and mother. With her brother and sister-in-law living in the Harkness home, it was agreed that she should not return to Harkness to live. But she wanted to be near to help her father when needed.

Georgia hoped to gain a college teaching position in upstate New York, though the possibilities were few. The prospect brightened when Edgar Brightman received a request from Nina Barrows, Syracuse Manager of the Fisk Teachers' Agencies, asking him, on behalf of President Keyes of Skidmore School of Arts in Saratoga Springs, if he could recommend "a good man" to teach sociology, ethics, and biblical literature. She described the school as "a college for girls," which was small, growing rapidly, and had a splendid endowment.[20]

Brightman had a candidate to recommend, not "a good man" but Georgia Harkness! Nina Barrows notified President Keyes, who was resting at home in Delaware under doctor's orders.[21] There is no indication that Barrows ever received a response from the president; at least there was never a positive word. Finally she wrote Brightman that, having heard nothing, she would "hate to have her lose good positions while waiting for something that is so uncertain as the position at Skidmore seems to be at present."[22] There is no indication that anything more was ever mentioned regarding the Skidmore post. Covert sexism may have caused Harkness to lose it, an omen of things to come in the 1930s.

Two other good positions were offered for the fall of 1921, one as Dean of Women at Mt. Union College in Alliance, Ohio, and the other as YWCA Secretary at the University of Michigan in Ann Arbor. Georgia turned down both of them, feeling particular disappointment that the distance from Mt. Union to Harkness, New York, seemed too great. She was gratified, however, that Mt. Union left open a standing invitation for her to join the faculty in the future.[23]

With no prospect for college teaching developing in upstate New York, Georgia welcomed the opportunity that fall to teach English, history, and civics at the high school in Willsboro, only twenty miles from her home. The year's teaching went well; she felt encouraged by the progress of the students and was able to negotiate a teaching load of five classes, in contrast to the previous teacher who had taught eight courses. This schedule gave her time at least to begin her dissertation, though not to make the progress she had hoped to make.[24]

Georgia was overjoyed when the invitation came in the spring of 1922 to join the faculty of Elmira College, founded in 1853 and claiming the distinction of being the first women's college in the United States. She planned to ask for an annual salary of $1,800, indicating that she would not have estimated her services to be worth more than that. However, Brightman encouraged her to ask for $2,000, and Elmira's president, Frederick Lent, granted her request. With her mother's health sufficiently improved, she readily accepted the position. Harkness began a tenure at Elmira in the fall of 1922 that continued for fifteen years, her longest stay in any academic institution of her career.[25]

However, before Georgia could devote herself to being a professor, she had a dissertation to write, a task that occupied her as much as teaching during her year at Willsboro High School and her first year at Elmira. The letters she exchanged with Brightman capture, as probably no piece of literature ever has done, the classic encounter between the Ph.D. candidate, holding grandiose expectations and visions, and her adviser, casting the wisdom of realism.

Georgia asked Brightman for suggestions of a dissertation topic, and she chose to write on the significance of ethical theory for philosophy of religion, one of the subjects he suggested. She wanted to do a sweeping study, comparing representatives of each main type of ethical theory from the standpoint of their relationship to philosophy of religion. Brightman told her that she must hone in. "The subject of a dissertation should be so clearly defined that it can be exhaustively covered," he wrote, "and the more specific it is, the more practicable it is to come to some specific original conclusions."[26]

Harkness protested that Brightman's suggestion, a study of the relationships of ethical theory to philosophy of religion in the thought of T. H. Green, the English proponent of philosophical idealism, was too narrowly conceived. Brightman countered that "Green is a perfectionist; that means that his ethical thought has affinities both with formalism and with hedonism. . . . He is so very rich and synthetic in his thought that I believe you will find all the room you need to turn around in dealing with him."[27]

And when Georgia asked Brightman whether he thought she could finish her dissertation and get her degree in one year, he responded that it was possible, "But I should say very inadvisable." He reminded her, first, of the "unwisdom of haste as a principle," and then of the burdens her mother's condition might bring. But his primary point was that Harkness would not be able to do high quality work in such a short period of time. "I fear that it would be very likely that something would happen to disappoint you."[28]

Georgia took two years to complete her dissertation and graduated in June 1923. The official final draft, which she mailed to the Dean of the Graduate School on February 10, 1923, weighed six pounds and was 399 pages long. Her "stick-to-it-iveness" in writing the dissertation was an example of the productiveness that would characterize her entire academic career. On the same day that Georgia mailed the completed manuscript, she wrote Brightman that only seventy pages remained in the form that he had originally read and 200 pages had been written since she submitted the outline in October. She had been spending about three days each week on her thesis, "and I hope now to have time to teach my classes properly."[29]

She wrote her dissertation on the topic that Brightman had suggested and that they had negotiated: "The Relations Between Philosophy of Religion and Ethics in the Thought of T. H. Green." Ironically, the official manuscript of the dissertation is missing from the library of Boston University.

Harkness published two articles on "T. H. Green as a Philosopher of Religion," both in *The Personalist,* a philosophical journal of Boston University. She capsuled the essence of the philosopher's thought and his significance to her in these articles. Green lived and taught philosophy of religion and ethics at Oxford University in England in the late nineteenth century. He countered the claims of naturalism that were gaining a dominant voice in philosophy by destroying the grounding for faith in God built upon the tenets of philosophical idealism. Through his teaching and writing, Green "established ethics and religion on an idealistic foundation which could command the respect of thinking people."[30]

Green conceived of God in the same way that the Boston Personalists did, through the concept of self-consciousness. God is a "completed self-consciousness, a being of perfect understanding and perfect love, whose life is an eternal act of self-realization through self-sacrifice," seeking "through love to establish a unity of spirit with the object which it loves." God's eternal self-consciousness reproduces itself in human beings and becomes the foundation for their intellectual and moral lives. That harmony between love and understanding can be partial, at best, in human beings.[31]

The keynote of Green's religious faith carried a strong mystical quality. It was "found in the text, 'The word is nigh thee.' The God whom we worship is not far off, but is the immanent God who lives in our moral life, whom we serve in serving our brethren, and in communion with whom we triumph over sin and suffering and have assurance of eternal life."[32]

The desire of persons to live better moral lives is "evidence of an absolute best; and this best or 'possible' self is

God." Communion is realized between God and human beings as persons seek to live more purposeful moral lives. Religion and morality became fused for Green: "Just as goodness increases with the effort of man to identify his life with the 'completer self' which is the life of God; so sin consists in the willful limitation of one's interests and activities to his present fragmented self." Green defined religion as "a God-seeking morality," and moral activity as "the reproduction of God."[33]

Green was a Unitarian, in contrast to Harkness and her strong Methodist evangelical faith. This key difference led her to disagree with his belief that the essence of Christianity did not lie in the historical Jesus and his miraculous birth, death, and resurrection. On the other hand, key aspects of her maturing faith were activated and confirmed by Green's religious convictions, particularly that Christ within a person is a sign of continual resurrection and that the religious life must be a moral one. She also held great affinity for his belief that a religion of the inner spirit needs to replace that of outworn creeds, that prayer is incipient action, that communion with the indwelling God is the way to truest service of humankind, and that outward forms of religion must be preserved to protect its inner vitality.

═════

When Georgia began her dissertation research in 1921, she realized that the thought of T. H. Green probably would not attract wide reader interest. And it did not, attested by the fact that her dissertation was not published and that only two short articles were gleaned from it. Looking back in the 1950s, she wrote that as far as she knew, it "has served no useful purpose to anybody but myself."[34]

However, Georgia's dissertation served the energizing purpose in her own life that such a major project needs to provide for its writer. "The Relations Between Philosophy of Religion and Ethics in the Thought of T. H. Green" launched Georgia on her academic career in the teaching of philosophy. It brought together the work she had done on philosophical idealism and personalism in her undergraduate and graduate academic training and defined the thought out of which she taught philosophy and sought to live throughout the 1920s and 1930s.

By the end of the 1930s, Georgia's mind would have changed considerably. Christian faith and theology would define her personal and scholarly center, with the reasonableness of religion and the academic discipline of philosophy taking a secondary place.

The thought of T. H. Green had played its immediate purpose in Georgia's life by 1923. It had provided her with the academic credentials to establish herself on the faculty of a major institution of higher education. She was now Assistant Professor of Philosophy of Religion and Religious Education at Elmira College in Elmira, New York. By the time she left Elmira in 1937, Georgia would have distinguished herself as a teacher, writer, and church leader, highly sought after in secular and sacred institutions of higher education.

Harkness Family Homestead, Harkness, New York, when Georgia was a young adult and teaching at Elmira College. Left to right: Charlie and Minnie, Georgia's brother and sister-in-law, and Warren and Lillie, Georgia's parents. (Courtesy of Peg Overholt, Georgia's niece, and her husband John Overholt, Kilmarnock, Virginia, Harkness Family Collection)

Harkness Family Homestead, New York (restored). (Courtesy of the Harkness United Methodist Church and Pastor Marion Moore-Colgan)

(BELOW)
Georgia, on far right with a hat on, walking with Gandhi on the plains of India during her trip there in 1939. She was on the faculty of Mt. Holyoke College at this time. (Courtesy of Peg and John Overholt, Harkness Family Collection)

(ABOVE) Georgia, as faculty advisor to the Y.W.C.A., Elmira College, with a group of women students during a summer conference at Silver Bay Camp Grounds, Silver Bay, New York. (Courtesy of Peg and John Overholt, Harkness Family Collection)

Georgia, in center, with Lillian Snodgrass on left and Verna Miller, her thirty-year companion, on right during the 1940s in Evanston, Ill. (Courtesy of Peg and John Overholt, Harkness Family Collection)

Georgia, as a member of the Dun Commission of Christian Scholars on the Moral Implications of Obliteration Bombing and Use of Hydrogen Bombs for Mass Destruction, 1950, meeting at the Princeton Inn, Princeton, New Jersey. Front row: left to r Reinhold Niebuhr, Georgia Harkness, Bishop Angus Dun, John C. Bennett, Chester I. Barnard. Second row: Robert C. Calh Paul Tillich, Edwin Aubrey, Peter K. Emmons, George F. Thomas. (Courtesy of John C. Bennett)

orgia Harkness speaking before a General Conference of The United ethodist Church. (Courtesy of Peg and John Overholt, Harkness mily Collection)

Georgia receiving honorary doctorate from Elmira College in 1962, the year after her retirement from Pacific School of Religion. (Courtesy of Peg and John Overholt, Harkness Family Collection)

orgia, age sixty-eight, returning to Harkness, New York, in 1959, speak at Memorial Service on the site of the "Quaker Union," the gious fellowship from which her great-grandfather, Daniel rkness, was dismissed for marrying her great-grandmother, gail Cochran, a non-Quaker, who was "The Woman in the Red at." (Courtesy of Peg and John Overholt, Harkness Family lection)

Georgia speaking at her ast General Conference of The United Methodist Church in 1972 in Atlanta. She as eighty-one years old while the Conference was meeting and the delegates rose to sing "Happy Birthday" to her on that day. (Courtesy of General Commission on the Status and Role of Women, The United Methodist Church)

Harkness United Methodist Church. (Courtesy of Harkness United Methodist Church and Pastor Marion Moore-Colgan)

Hate-to-Quit-It, for many years, Georgia's summer camp at Willsbore Bay on Lake Champlain, twenty miles from Harkness, New York. She bought it in 1931 and returned every summer for over twenty years. (Courtesy of Harkness United Methodist Church and Pastor Marion Moore-Colgan)

View of Lake Champlain from the front porch of Hate-to-Quit-It. (Courtesy of Harkness United Mehtodist Church and Pastor Marion Moore-Colgan)

IV. "A Woman with a Ph.D. Must . . . Contend Against the Tradition"

CHAPTER SEVEN

"A Pacifist, I Think, Forevermore"
1922–1925

*A*fter Georgia's first month at Elmira College, she received a letter from Edgar Brightman that began with the question: "My dear Miss Harkness, or should I say, 'Professor'?"[1] As if responding to her former mentor's query, she took little time to establish herself as a professional woman with whom to be reckoned. By the end of her second year on the faculty, Harkness was taking the kind of leadership that would characterize her entire professional career. Quickly she became identified as a key member of the faculty and as an advocate of social justice in the college, church, and international movements.

What would have happened had Harkness told Edgar Brightman to address her as "Professor" or "Dr. Harkness"? Over the next seventeen years, he always began his letters to her "Dear Miss Harkness," while she greeted him with "Dear Dr. Brightman." Was he simply blind to the difference of status between the salutations? Or, unconsciously, did he still see them in the professor-student relationship? It was one of those traditions that confronted a woman with a Ph.D.

When Harkness came onto the faculty as Assistant Professor of Philosophy of Religion and Religious Education in the fall of 1922, her immediate interest was to establish herself as a philosopher. No courses in philosophy were required of students, however, and she was the second of two persons teaching in the small field. Her colleague, Professor John Tuttle, was several years her senior, having been on the Elmira faculty since 1913. The courses that each of them taught had small enrollments. Georgia's Philosophy of Religion class, with five members, was typical.[2]

By the beginning of the winter term in her second year, Harkness was questioning whether to stay at Elmira or to search elsewhere for a teaching position. Lack of intellectual stimulation among both faculty and students, along with her feeling that little opportunity would be hers in the Philosophy Department, contributed strongly to her restlessness. When she broached the possibility of leaving to the president, the Reverend Dr. Frederick Lent, "he talked as if he would make almost any concession if I would stay here, though I do not know how much he would actually do if it came to a show-down," she wrote to Brightman. Lent immediately presented Georgia with terms that were very appealing to her: "He says he will relieve me entirely of teaching Education if I want him to, and will use his influence to try to get Philosophy made a required subject."[3]

Finding that she had the president's backing, Harkness became the leader of a faculty fight that resulted in a major curriculum revision. Electioneering most of the influential members of the faculty, she found practically all in agreement that philosophy should be required. Much more was at stake, however. The students were presently required to take fifty hours credit in "Group A," which included English and foreign languages, and twenty five hours in "Group B," which included philosophy, psychology, education, history, sociology, economics, government and law, Bible, and religious education. Students could easily complete their degrees at Elmira without taking any courses in philosophy or in some other areas of the humanities.[4]

"I started the combat in an effort to require all students to take three hours of philosophy. And it ended in a long overdue revision of the entire curriculum modeled after the Smith College system. I decided it was worth fighting for to try to smash the whole system and get a new one. . . . The result is a complete victory for the forces of reform," she wrote to Brightman triumphantly in early May 1924. "Our pernicious former system is now defunct."[5]

The large number of faculty members who taught classes in "Group B" obviously favored the full-scale revision. The change amounted to a victory for the entire faculty and the president over the dean, who had invented the curriculum system two decades ago and had carefully guarded it since. Georgia described the dean, who was also the head of the English department, as having "ruled with an absolute monarchy for twenty-five years."

Harkness did not claim credit for the entire reform, but she was the catalyst and at the center of the movement. She spent a vast amount of time and energy in electioneering the faculty, encouraging its members to hang together, keeping the president favorably disposed and working in committee meetings. "There is not much left of me now," she confessed before school was out in the spring of 1924, "but I feel well repaid, for I think it is the most constructive achievement I ever accomplished. Elmira is on its way, I think, toward becoming a college instead of a boarding school."[6]

With faculty morale higher than in previous years and a curriculum in place for which she had "fought vigorously," Georgia felt that she should stay at Elmira. She did not commit herself beyond the 1925–26 academic year, however, both because of her own restlessness and her recognition that the dean might fire her if he could. But Harkness's position became secure at Elmira. The enrollment in her philosophy of religion and ethics classes rapidly increased, and she emerged as a leader and esteemed member of the faculty.

During the same period that Georgia led the movement for curriculum revision in the college, she also began a drive for equal opportunities for women in the institutions of twentieth-century Methodism. She continued to advocate for the rights of women in the successive denominations of the Methodist Episcopal, Methodist, and United Methodist churches for the next fifty years until her death in 1974. Notably, the first article that bore her name in church journals for clergy and laity was entitled "The Ministry as a Vocation for Women," published in April 1924.

Her article was printed in *The Christian Advocate* of her own Methodist Episcopal Church and was especially addressed to the delegates attending the denomination's 1924 General Conference. With this pronouncement, she began a drive for the ordination of women with the guarantee of full membership within conferences equal to the rights and responsibilities then open to men. The article provided solid arguments against sexism in the church that would apply until ordination was granted in 1956, and long after as ordained women served in local churches and in administrative structures of the denomination.

She was not claiming the sexual superiority of women over men, Harkness wrote, but rather that women have a legitimate sphere outside, as well as inside, the home. "Practically every avenue of leadership today is open to woman save in the Church, and there she must content herself either with rendering volunteer service or working in a subordinate capacity."[7]

Sounding the keynote of the liberal tradition, she continued that it was "a matter of plain common sense that equality of ability ought to bring with it equality of opportunity." Both logic and Christian commitment were defied by the strange dispensation that granted men the opportunity to fill the primary paid positions in the church, while women were valued as volunteers, missionaries, deaconesses, and church secretaries. "But for a woman to preach—impossible."

The need for women clergy was indisputable, Harkness contended, for within the nation's largest Protestant denomination 27 percent of the ministers had less than a full high school education, and a net loss of 613 ministers had been reported in the past four years. Even so, "the Church which would not choose a mediocre man in preference to a superior woman is one among a thousand."

Harkness had the privilege of counseling a good many young women each year who were thinking seriously of religious or social work as a vocation. She told her readers, however: "I do not advise any of them to prepare for the ministry, though I consider it the highest religious calling." Present conditions demonstrated its futility, for after three years of theological education beyond their college training they would find themselves superseded by a less qualified male.

Ordination of women was one area of discrimination, but not the only one, she wrote. The challenge facing institutional Christianity was this: "If the Church is going to keep abreast of the times and meet the spiritual challenge of the new age it must relinquish some of its conservatism; and whatever our theological convictions may be, it might not be a bad idea to introduce some 'modernism' into our conceptions of the function of women in the work of the Church."

The time had come for public opinion to be refashioned, and the clergy and the religious press had to take the lead. They had not done all they could to eradicate this "deep-seated relic of medievalism in the attitude of the Church at large."

Always addressing the mainstream membership of religious institutions, Harkness reminded her readers that a person does not need to be "an ultra-feminist" to recognize the wrong in this situation. She concluded on this prophetic note, which characterized her entire ministry: "We wonder if the advancement of the Kingdom is not more important than the maintenance of an ancient prejudice."

Not surprisingly, the publication of Georgia's article on "The Ministry as a Vocation for Women" in 1924 came at a time when she herself was moving toward ordination. As a student at Boston University, she had taken a Master of Religious Education degree, rather than attempt a Bachelor of Divinity degree for ordination, as she reflected in the 1950s. If she seriously considered the idea when she was at Boston University, she did not articulate it.

However, by the time she came to Elmira, Harkness was receiving invitations to preach in nearby churches. In 1922, she gained a local preacher's license in the Methodist Episcopal Church. She could have been a guest preacher without having the license, but it provided official credentials.

By 1924, Georgia was seeking her deacon's orders, the first of a two-step process leading to ordination. When men gained deacon's and then elder's orders, they could receive full membership in a Methodist Episcopal Conference with a guaranteed church appointment. While women also could be granted these orders for ordination, the benefits of Conference membership and the guarantee of being appointed to pastor a church did not apply to them.

The opportunity to pastor small churches was raised to Georgia in the mid-1920s by superintendents of churches—in the district of central New York surrounding Elmira and in her home vicinity of Harkness—who did not have enough ordained male ministers to fill these posts. She expressed a personal desire to take a church, especially one close to Elmira, where she could both teach and preach regularly. Wisely, however, she declined, knowing that the strain would be too great if she added a part-time church appointment onto her full-time teaching and rapidly expanding extra-curricular responsibilities. But preaching would be a vital medium for the expression of Georgia's voice throughout her life.

———

Georgia thrived on having many irons in the fire at the same time. In February of 1924, with the curriculum revision battle in full swing and her article on the ordination of women underway, she enthusiastically wrote Edgar Brightman about one of her extra-curricular activities: "The most exciting thing that has happened to me lately is the fact that I have been accepted by the Fellowship for a Christian Social Order to go to Europe this summer with the American Seminar."[8]

Otherwise known as "the Sherwood Eddy Party," the seminar was to be composed of seventy-five to one hundred ministers, educators, social workers, and like-minded persons who would spend three weeks in London and one week each in Berlin, Geneva, and Paris, studying economic and social conditions in post–World War I Europe.

Hardly had she received confirmation of her membership in the party than she began to question her decision to make the trip. Academic and church colleagues told her that she would get a propagandistic, one-sided view of Europe, without the liberty to do what she wanted to do. Friends of a more conservative political and religious persuasion branded the seminar an anti-American Socialistic tool spreading misinformation to challenge the total righteousness of the Allied victory and to create sympathy for the German nation. Georgia was not deterred from taking the trip, however, and it profoundly affected her life-time vocational journey.

As Eddy described the seminar, its aim was "not that of the annual invasion of tourists to see the buildings, museums and externals of the old world, to learn where one can get the best mutton chop in London, or the most audacious variety show in Paris."[9] Rather, its participants could "meet the leaders of all political parties and other outstanding men throughout Europe and then return to America to speak and write about their findings."[10]

The American Seminar had a highly focused purpose, just as its detractors argued. "Perhaps this exchange of ideas which the meetings would provide would be one avenue to international understanding and peace,"[11] Eddy wrote. Even more specifically, its leaders sought to promote an idealistic, pacifist vision of a social order "composed of men and women of many nations and races who recognized the unity of the world-wide family and who believed in an approach to life that substituted reconciliation and good will for retaliation and violence."[12]

The annual pilgrimages began in 1921 and continued every year for almost two decades until 1939. They were sponsored by the Fellowship for a Christian Social Order (FCSO), also organized in 1921 and closely affiliated with the Fellowship for Reconciliation. Its leaders were Eddy, International Secretary of the YMCA who became chairman of the FCSO national committee, and Kirby Page, Eddy's secretary in England during the war and a recently ordained Disciples of Christ minister.

Harkness must have felt a close bond with Sherwood Eddy. Though twenty years her senior, he was born into sturdy Protestant stock and had a conversion experience at a student conference led by Dwight L. Moody. "Before he finished I saw myself as I was—no good to my college, to my country, to man, or to God. . . . That night marked a turning point in my life. God became forever real to me." Working both with the SVM and the YMCA, Eddy went to India in 1896, at the persuasion of John L. Mott, and worked with students there for fifteen years. Eventually he became YMCA secretary for Asia.[13]

Invited by the British YMCA to come to England during World War I, Eddy met with their soldiers in the army camps. "My job during the war was to offer religion—a hope, an anchorage, a moral dynamic—to fighting men, living and dying . . . as a reaction to the monstrous evils of World War I, I accepted the ideal of peace and became for a time an absolute idealist and pacifist in the light of what I understood to be Jesus' way of life."[14]

The vision for the American Seminar was born in the summer of 1920 when Eddy, by then International Secretary of the YMCA, and Page returned to England after the war to study the British labor movement. They met prominent leaders of the movement, including Ramsay MacDonald and Arthur Henderson, and Eddy conceived the idea: "Why not bring over annually from the United States a selected group of educators and lecturers for this illuminating and enriching experience?"[15]

The first seminar took place in 1921, and over the next fifteen years nearly a thousand "graduates" took part in the study and investigation. With Eddy and Page, also a committed pacifist, at the helm, the 1924 seminar embarked on June 28 and returned in early September. Three college presidents were among the group members, composed mostly of pastors and college professors, who were "not famous but very companionable." Two of the participants whom Georgia called "our leading lights" were Ernest Fremont Tittle, of Evanston, who later became her beloved pastor for eleven years, and Reinhold Niebuhr, then pastor of Bethel Evangelical Church in Detroit. Describing the party to Edgar Brightman in 1924, she identified Reinhold as the brother of Hulda Niebuhr, who, like Harkness, had studied religious education at Boston University. She also specifically mentioned Judge Florence Allen; Harry F. Ward, leader of the Methodist Federation for Social Service; and Charles Clayton Morrison, editor of *The Christian Century*, who were each with the group for a week or so.[16]

"The trip fully came up to my expectations in every respect," Harkness wrote Brightman on September 21, providing him with a vivid and emotionally charged account of the profoundly moving experience. The seminar participants saw more than an ordinary sight-seeing group would, their stops including Glasgow, Edinburgh, London, Oxford, Canterbury, Stratford, Windsor, Rotterdam, the Hague, Berlin, Lucerne, Interlaken, Geneva, Paris, Milan, Venice, Florence, Naples, Genoa, and Paris. They heard one hundred lectures, each followed by question-and-answer periods, two or three times each day. In London, they heard representatives of the Labor, Liberal, and Conservative parties and got a good view of the workings of each. In Geneva, joint meetings of the American Seminar and the British League of Nations Union were held in the League building.

The group gathered in Berlin on Sunday, August 3, "with thousands of people (estimated at 200,000) banked in for acres in front of the Reichstag . . . to commemorate the tenth anniversary of the beginning of the war." The seminar's experience in Germany had a more formative effect on Georgia than anything else she saw or heard, and bears description in her own words.

> I liked the German people we met very much, and came away with a great deal better understanding of and sympathy for the German view-point than I have ever had before. . . . The economic conditions in Germany are improving, though they are still bad enough. We found that the acceptance of the Dawes report is having a good deal of psychological value,

both in Germany and France. But it is tragic to find so much war bitterness and mutual misunderstanding, with the feeling in both countries that though war has done no good, there is no way out except more wars. My trip to Rheims and the battlefields, with what I saw in Germany of the effects of the hunger blockade and the "war-peace," have made me *a pacifist, I think, forevermore.* I came away with more sympathy, on the whole, for Germany than for France; for while there are still plenty of evidences of militarism in Germany I do not think many Americans realize what Germany has suffered from the hunger blockade, the injustice of the treaty, and the accusation of sole guilt—to say nothing of the Ruhr. (italics added)

Harkness, like Eddy, became an absolute idealist and pacifist as "a reaction to the monstrous evils of World War I." By the 1930s, Eddy moved away from his pacifism in response to Italian and German Fascism and Japanese militarism. He argued that the model of Gandhian pacifism never would have worked against Hitler or Stalin. In later years, he wrote: "I now believe that the absolute ethic of Jesus must be maintained as a frame of reference by which every individual and every society must be judged; but I consider an absolute ethic an 'impossible possibility' and a false perfectionism when set up as a rigid law."[17] Harkness maintained the absolute ethic in the years to follow. Her prophetic contribution continued to lie in pushing the church as an institution, along with laity and ecclesiastical leaders, toward a deeper and stronger commitment to renounce war and the means of war in the name of Christ.

Writing *Grace Abounding* in 1969, Georgia looked back on her American Seminar and succinctly summed up its immediate and long-term highlights for her: "We heard statesmen of many countries speak, making clear the broader causes of the recent war and showing that the blame could not all be laid on Germany. I became acquainted with some outstanding American pacifists and their position made sense. As a result I joined the Fellowship of Reconciliation."[18]

Begun ten years before in Great Britain, the Fellowship of Reconciliation (F.O.R.) was brought to the United States in

1915 by its British founder, Henry T. Hodgkin, secretary of the foreign mission enterprises of the Society of Friends. "Love Our Enemies" was the theme of the organizing conference of the American branch at Garden City, Long Island, in 1915. Jesus' self-sacrificial and pacifistic model of love remained at the center of the F.O.R.'s purpose. By 1917 it offered a bond of communion to ministers who gave up their pulpits because they could not support the entry of the United States into the war.[19]

Scholars warn that precise dating of the F.O.R., in the light of its evolving purpose, is unwise. At some point after 1917, it "was to be the work of the leaders of the FOR not to maintain an historical pacifist witness but to introduce pacifism into, and comport pacifism with, the basic problems of politics." Labor organizing became one of its arenas of social witness, in which F.O.R. members supported remedial legislation, backed attempts of labor to organize, and investigated working conditions to realize a social order in which no person or group would be exploited for the profit or pleasure of others.[20]

Georgia Harkness and other individuals who joined the F.O.R. after World War I, as a result of their participation in the American Seminar, expressed their commitment to the movement's purpose of human unity by speaking and writing on post-war conditions in Europe. The invitations to Georgia to preach and lecture in the central New York area were many. As she wrote in March 1925, "I have preached pacifism and pro-Germanism to the Rotary, Ministerial Association, four women's clubs, and several churches without having yet been thrown out."[21]

Her writings on the subject clearly demonstrate that her position would have been highly offensive to many Christians, both clergy and laity. Beginning in January 1925, several of her articles were published in the interdenominational *Christian Century* and in denominational periodicals, including the Methodist Episcopal *Zion's Herald* and *Christian Advocate* and the Episcopal *Churchman*. Harkness forthrightly stated that the Allies had failed to understand the shared guilt of the war, the atrocities committed by the

Allied as well as the Axis powers, and the point of view of the German people. She summoned clergy and laity to lead the way in the essential reevaluation.

Georgia often began her articles by identifying with her readers' perspective. Disclaiming German ancestry that might have given her a pro-German bias, she acknowledged that during the war she "was as bitter against the Germans and as blind to the real issues at stake as—well, as the average American Christian who believed the war propaganda that was fed to us to keep us fighting." She went to Europe "to try to find out how much of it was true; and . . . I came back with a radically different viewpoint."[22]

No one who had any knowledge of the maelstrom of European politics in 1914 could attribute sole guilt for the war to Germany, she wrote. Study of diplomatic papers since the war demonstrated that Austria, Russia, and France, along with Germany, controlled the outbreak of the war. And even England could not be fully exonerated.

Further, Americans readily branded the Germans as ruthless aggressors, bringing suffering to the rest of the world, forgetting that *"we starved the Germans"* during the war, Harkness told her readers. More than 700,000 people died from the effects of the Allied Hunger Blockade and, among those who survived, the blockade left traces in weakened constitutions, stunted growth, rickets, and tuberculosis. "The undersized bodies of three thousand German children whom I saw being fed by Quaker relief, still haunt me, and make me wonder."[23]

Instead of placing all the blame for the war on Germany, Georgia contended, "we had better blame economic imperialism, secret diplomacy, and the whole war system." She summed up her new, but deeply felt, pacifist resolve in *The Christian Advocate* in February, 1925:

> The more we study the problem, the more evident it becomes that the responsibility for the havoc it has wrought must be laid, not upon any one nation, but upon the whole war system. The sufferings of France may yet bring a blessing to the world if they teach us not to hate our enemies, but to hate war—and to blend all our energies toward banishing it from the earth.[24]

The relationship Georgia Harkness would take throughout her life to issues of social justice was firmly grounded in her positions on pacifism, ordination of women, and curriculum reform during her first years as a professional woman. "A pacifist, I think, forevermore," sums up the unqualified principled positions she characteristically took. Georgia held up to the responsible institutions—in this case college, church, and government—the highest ideals of the moral good. By 1925, she was charting her identity as a social prophet on the radical left.

Harkness was also a centrist, committed to working from within for reform of institutions. Without diluting her own radical positions, she also focused on areas of agreement among diverse viewpoints. Employing an avowed strategic plan, Georgia sought to empathize, even identify, with the perspectives of the wider mainstream of the church in order to lead the institution and its members to a more faithful stance on the issue addressed.

As a centrist, she was also a negotiator. In the years to come, she related directly with others of her persuasion on issues of faculty rights, women's ordination, and pacifism to representative leadership of opposing viewpoints among the administration of Elmira College, delegates of the General Conferences of Methodist church bodies, and members of national and world peace commissions. Characteristically, she sought to reconcile opposing viewpoints and to bring direct action for social change.

Finally, the word, both printed and spoken, was her medium. She did not witness in picket lines or on hunger strikes. Later in life she acknowledged that perhaps she was afraid to make direct public protest. But her gift was the ability to articulate the truth as she judged it. Georgia had found her distinctive public voice.

CHAPTER EIGHT

"A Lack of Feminine Charm"
1925–1929

*H*arkness's self-chosen identity took root during her early thirties, a period now defined as the onset of mid-life. In a confident public voice, she reached out to a national and international audience that would rapidly expand each year. Her strong words of social protest emerged simultaneously as she began to establish herself in her first position as a teacher in higher education.

But what about the inner person of Georgia Harkness, the voice not heard in any of her public worlds? What were the questions, doubts, drives, and conflicts that motivated her, and to whom did she express them?

Georgia's inner voice during her Elmira years emerged in her letters to Edgar Brightman. She saw him very little after her student residency at Boston University, only occasionally having direct contact when she returned to Boston on business or when both attended philosophical conventions. However, over three-fourths of the 200 extant letters that were exchanged between Brightman and Harkness were written during the 1920s and 1930s, while she was completing her Ph.D. and teaching at Elmira. By the end of that decade, when Georgia moved to Mt. Holyoke and then to Garrett Biblical Institute, the correspondence tapered off, and fewer letters were exchanged during the 1940s until his death in 1953.

What was the nature of her relationship with Edgar Brightman? What purpose did he play in her life during that twenty-year period?

The salutations of "Dear Dr. Brightman" and "Dear Miss Harkness" in their letters pointed to a dissonance in relationships between men and women in professional positions that only today is being recognized. However, despite the formality and inequality implicit in their greetings, their relationship changed from one of professor and student to that of colleagues, friends, and confidants. As she evolved into a professional scholar in her own right, they became teachers and mentors to each other.

Harkness and Brightman intellectually stimulated and challenged each other and each was concerned for the other's welfare. Their correspondence demonstrates a high degree of mutual trust and confidence. Georgia deeply needed a relationship with such a person, someone with whom she could bare her soul and exchange advice, a person who valued and trusted her as much as she did him.

Brightman maintained special correspondences with many professional colleagues and friends over the years, though most of these friends were other men. His relationship with Georgia Harkness was exceptional, however, for his sake as well as hers. Catching up on letters on Easter afternoon 1925, he wrote to Georgia, "Discussion with you makes me work harder than discussion with anyone else I know; and your ability to put things in absolutely unambiguous and precise form helps me a great deal in clarifying my own thought."[1] On another occasion he described Georgia as "one of the most thorough minds I have ever known, and one thoroughly capable of a life devoted to philosophical research."[2] Their friendship is described best as "a meeting of the minds."

Brightman was also something of a father figure to Harkness. The respect that Warren Harkness showed to his daughter, the encouragement that he gave her from her earliest years, and the drive he instilled into her also were demonstrated in the way Brightman related to her. Further, she looked up to her own father for his intelligence and the patience he showed toward her. Brightman bore that same patience with Georgia in response to the multitude of academic questions she often directed to him.

Georgia looked up to and idealized both of these men. However, her relationship with Brightman went beyond that of daughter-father or student-teacher. It became one of equality and mutuality because she took him off the pedestal and shared frankly with him her critique of their relationship. Further, Edgar Brightman was a genuinely caring person and teacher, and he needed collegiality with her, just as she cherished it with him.

A person's inner voice, a release of one's frustrations, longings, and private feelings, emerges through a trusting relationship such as Georgia shared with Edgar Brightman. One of the strongest expressions of her private self revealed in these letters is her determination to succeed professionally. She had experienced wounds from the hurt of being "shy, green, and countrified," an outsider and social misfit, at Cornell. Harkness had proved to herself, however, that she stood number one intellectually. She knew that she could use her intellect and her will to excel in professional leadership and to gain the social stature that some women would have sought through personal popularity.

A need to prove and fulfill herself—to herself, to Brightman, to her parents, and to the world—was closely tied to Georgia's determination to succeed professionally. She was proud of her effectiveness as a teacher, and she wanted Brightman to be proud also. When Georgia came onto the faculty of Elmira in 1922, twenty-five students constituted the entire enrollment in all philosophy classes. A startling gain, both in the count of students enrolled in her classes and the number of courses she taught, characterized her academic record through 1929.[3]

She told Brightman in October of 1923, after one year of teaching, that five students were taking her philosophy of religion course and that she was reorganizing her ethics course. By 1927, sociology and ethics drew the highest number of enrollees of all classes on campus, except the required freshman subjects. Letters every year document the exact count of students electing to take her classes. By 1929, ninety-nine young men and women took ethics, clearly the favorite subject of the teacher as well as the students. "Ethics bids fair to devour everything else in the Philosophy department," she wrote in December.

"I seem to be 'hogging' the department," she wrote in May of 1924, "but Dr. Tuttle is so busy that he seems willing to relinquish part of his courses."[4] Warmth and cordiality characterized her relationship with her colleague in philosophy, Dr. John Tuttle. But unavoidable strains were also present, for Georgia was teaching an increasingly larger number of classes in the department—some semesters all of the courses—while her colleague was assuming more administrative responsibilities. At times, it appeared that President Lent wanted her to teach more classes because of her effectiveness and popularity. At other times, he exerted pressure on Dr. Tuttle to pick up courses in order to share a more equitable distribution of teaching assignments.

In May 1925, Harkness wrote Brightman that class lists for the following fall had just come out. She itemized the projected enrollment of the six classes she would be teaching, coming to over 160 students. Dr. Tuttle's one course, History of Ancient Philosophy, had to be canceled because only two students had pre-enrolled. "I admire his kindliness of spirit in not displaying any jealousy over the registration," she wrote. Tuttle must have been deeply hurt. The imbalance inevitably created some awkwardness between the two colleagues, despite the effort of both to handle the situation gracefully. Though Georgia felt sorry for Tuttle, she could not hide from Brightman her own pride and happiness at her obvious popularity. Further, she had an inner need to share these feelings with a confidant.[5]

A personal restlessness also characterized her inner voice. The most direct manifestation of her restlessness was her desire, after being at Elmira for only one and one-half years, to begin to look about for other teaching possibilities. In November 1923, she wrote Brightman that she "did not relish the atmosphere of polite superficialities and intellectual lethargy enough to stay permanently." The intellectual level of the students was not high, she told him later in the same month, and little mental stimulation was gained from other faculty members. Further, the Fundamentalists were strong in Elmira, both in the community and in the college, and Georgia found herself in situations with them of "attack and counter-attack." Also she wanted to be relieved after the first year of teaching religious education. While that assignment was soon removed, strains within the philosophy department could not be avoided.[6]

Conditions improved remarkably and created a happier and more positive working environment for Georgia after her second year at Elmira. The curriculum revision she had such a formative part in bringing about upgraded the academic reputation of the college. Faculty members began to meet regularly for exchange of ideas regarding their scholarly projects, another reform that Georgia helped to initiate. "My children are beginning to show a few signs of life and I can see some slight results of my labors," she wrote regarding her students in early 1924. And President Lent continually evidenced his esteem for Harkness by giving her salary raises, even though the increases were small, and adjusting her teaching responsibilities. Overall, her working relationship with Dr. Tuttle was more positive than negative, and she enjoyed working with Dr. E. W. K. Mould, the valued scholar and teacher of biblical studies.[7]

As a result of improved working conditions, Georgia was open to moving, but not overly anxious to do so, during the 1920s. She was offered a position at Lindenwood College in St. Charles, Missouri, and a one-year post at Goucher College in New York state, both of which she declined. Other opportunities never materialized, such as openings at Wellesley, Mt. Holyoke, and Radcliffe, the last being a blatant case of sexism. She stated directly to Brightman that she would like to teach at a larger institution and one in which the academic level was higher and the religious influence less conservative. In balance, however, her experience at Elmira was a happy one. Returning refreshed in the fall of 1929 after a sabbatical at Yale, she described herself in this way: "I have not felt so well or happy in years. I get a real thrill every day over being back here, and it seems to me we have never had so fine a student body as now. Now and then, I perceive real gleams of intellectual interest."[8]

Georgia always threw herself unstintingly into her work, though she realized that this habit was not always a strength. In November 1925, Harkness wrote to Brightman stating a weakness she believed they shared in common: They both worked too much "resulting in a rather excitable state of nervous tension." On another occasion, after describing a heavy extra-curricular schedule of lecturing and preaching, she added: "But I seem to thrive on it."[9]

Both evaluations were correct and add up to a third word coming through her inner voice: Georgia evidenced a driving need to be busy, literally, never to experience a dull moment! In her early years at Elmira, her letters document an incredibly large number of speaking engagements on highly diverse subjects in the local and nearby areas of central New York: preaching at the Union Service in Troy, addressing the Elmira Daughters of the Revolution, teaching at the Riverside Summer Epworth League Institute and the Round Lake Summer School of Missions, preaching on Jonah to a crowd of Baptist Fundamentalists, talking to the Jews about religious education, and discussing child psychology at a six-week School of Religious Education.[10]

Georgia was cognizant that she was being used at times because of her good nature and her lack of family involvements, that she was being pulled in different directions, and that she needed to exert more control over her schedule. She stated this reality candidly to Brightman: "Dr. Lent sends me around to the places that are too small for him to waste his time on. I like to do it but I think I shall have to call a halt if I am to have time for any writing."[11]

As a new professional woman, Georgia had not yet gained a stronger inner voice to temper her drive to extend herself too far and too thinly. However, she was also a stand-out, an exceptional pioneer professional woman who bridged the practical and the academic religious fields, and she was highly sought for the contributions she could make to a multitude of audiences. By the late 1930s, the conflicting tugs from the outer world and from her inner self would constitute a serious peril to her emotional and physical health, leading her to a deeper understanding of herself and her spiritual needs.

During the 1920s, however, Georgia found sufficient spiritual renewal through her involvement in social justice causes. Her participation in the Summer School in Creative and Humanistic Education and the Summer Conference on Economic, Political, Racial and International Problems in August 1925 provided a balance for her between a widening social involvement and a deeper spirituality. The conferences were sponsored by The Fellowship for a Christian Social Order and were held each summer on the campus of Olivet College in Olivet, Michigan. She thrived on the "ferment of argumentation" over national and international issues "from morning till night, with time off for volley-ball and swimming." The month brought needed renewal, Georgia wrote, increasing her "zeal for a Christian social order," and providing a catalyst for "intellectual and spiritual regeneration."[12]

Finally, Georgia's inner voice emerged during the 1920s in her growing ability to find her own voice and to speak with professional authority in her relationship with Edgar Brightman. As noted, they continued to address each other by "Dr. Brightman" and "Miss Harkness" until the end of the 1930s. But Georgia began to recast the terms of their relationship by 1925, when she ventured to criticize him in a manner that only the most trusting of friends and colleagues could do.

In 1925, Brightman's name was identified with Boston Personalism as closely as Borden Parker Bowne's had been in his day. Georgia proceeded to write Brightman on November 8 about something that had been on her mind for a good while. She was beginning to strongly question aspects of the Personalist school: "Quite often after I get through defending something I get to wondering whether I really believe it myself. I am not sure whether this betokens an awakening of intellectual honesty or a belated case of losing my religion!"[13]

While she disavowed any intention of criticizing his courses specifically, Harkness described the general spirit of the School of Religious Education and the Department of Philosophy as "unwholesomely dogmatic. It is anti-behavioristic, anti-deterministic, anti-Deweyite, anti-Columbian, anti-everything-not-personalistic." While other systems of thought are studied, "care is taken to point out their deficiencies rather than to consider sympathetically their merits, and students are left with the Boston brand of religion firmly planted in their systems and a sort of 'superiority complex' regarding any other view." In her direct critique of the philosophical school on which she had been raised, Georgia was moving to a root problem of "whether, on a somewhat glorified intellectual plane, it is not really a resort to Fundamentalist tactics. . . . I suppose the question really depends upon which is more to be desired, loyalty or open-mindedness. It is the same question," she continued, "that is involved in the relation of Christianity to non-Christian religions—whether it is better to send people out with evangelistic fervor to make converts, or to try to eradicate from Christians their superiority complexes."

Georgia carefully distanced herself in this letter from accusing Brightman himself of this "unwholesomely dogmatic" spirit. However, in a letter written the next week, on November 15, she moved in more directly. "I do not think it would be correct to say that you are either dogmatic or conceited (though I have known such charges to be made!); but I wonder if perhaps you may not have, subconsciously, a somewhat over-developed 'defense mechanism' where your own views or productions are in question." Becoming increasingly specific, she stated: "In the years that I have known you I have never heard you admit yourself to be in error on any point, and only a few times to acknowledge any uncertainty." Granting that she had no reason to suppose that he considered himself infallible, "Consciously, I think you want your students to be intellectually independent. Subconsciously, you like to have them agree with you." She acknowledged, however, that perhaps any author expects and desires words of approval more than criticism.[14]

Edgar Brightman, of course, was not left without words of response. He granted that there was a tendency at Boston

University "to frown upon those whose search for truth leads them to conclusions other than those of the accepted Boston pattern." However, Brightman defended himself by saying that one of his own best students the previous year was sympathetic to almost everything with which he personally disagreed![15]

He then shifted the argument by stating that he and Georgia were alike in both their merits and their defects—and focused on two defects, their obstinacy and stupidity! Their obstinacy, he wrote, "is tremendously increased when we are talking with or about another in whom we recognize that same quality." While a teacher should not yield ground for merely tactical or pedagogical reasons, "you and I have both passed the limits at times" beyond which obstinacy "ceases to be beautiful or useful." Further, Brightman pointed out, "we are in some respects rather stupid. I admit that I have to work like sin to get a student's point, and then often fail; likewise, to get your points . . . as regards my points I could wish that you might treat them a trifle more sympathetically." Continuing full steam, he told Georgia that "rather than attribute my vagueness to a lurking dogmatism and conceit . . . would it not be better to try again to enlighten me rather than to 'shut up clammishly?' "

By shifting the discussion to their "shared defects," Brightman and Harkness each had to face up to some hard realities that neither liked to claim. They concluded their exchange of letters by having "reached amicable agreement." The banter was friendly but pointed, and Georgia had notably changed the balance of their relationship by the initiative she took and the forthrightness with which she pressed her points.

The most telling episode in which Harkness assumed the authority to shift the grounds of her adviser-advisee relationship with Brightman came in 1928 when she applied for a Sterling Fellowship for a year of post-graduate study at Yale University. Brightman, as her Ph.D. mentor, would be her most important commendor, and he graciously responded to her request to write on her behalf. He sent Georgia the original copy of his recommendation, with the intent that she would send it on to the Scholarship Committee of the Yale Graduate School with her completed application.

After reading his highly complimentary evaluation of her, Harkness responded to Brightman immediately, expressing appreciation for his "many gracious words. In fact, my head swelled several sizes while I read it," she told him. More than thanking him for his recommendation, however, Georgia asked Brightman to do two things further regarding the recommendation. First, he should send the statement directly to the Dean of the Graduate School, for the candidate was not supposed to see the recommendation.[16]

Second, Harkness asked Brightman to change a phrase in his letter of recommendation. Certainly such a request would be unacceptable by most codes of ethics—but the particular situation demonstrates the necessity of an exception. After his several complimentary statements, Brightman referred to Georgia's "lack of feminine charm." She undoubtedly interpreted his comment as a reference to her large body and her physical awkwardness, as well as her feeling of discomfort and social inferiority in relationships with men, a condition she had long experienced. "I know what you mean, and am not offended by it," she stated, though she undoubtedly was offended. "If it would be taken at its face value, as you meant it, no great harm would be done. But will it? . . . I suspect that a committee might be prone to read this as suggesting freakishness, or at least a conspicuous masculinity of dress or manner. And if so, the fellowship would probably go elsewhere." Then she asked him directly, "If something less dangerous could be substituted for this half-line, I should appreciate it: if not, let it go."

Harkness continued to pierce to the heart of the matter by confronting Brightman with the blatant sexism of his reference to her "lack of feminine charm."

In this connection, I wonder whether you realize the extent to which *a woman with a Ph.D. must, among other obstacles, contend against the tradition* that female Ph.D.'s are so "intellectual" that they are freakish and sloppy. A degree of queerness that would be overlooked in a man is unforgivable in a woman—when both are contending for the same prize. (italics added)

She might well have taken her position one step further and told Brightman that any reference to "feminine charm," whether positive or negative, was out of order. He would have been horrified to think of anyone raising the issue of a man's "masculine charm" in a letter of recommendation.

Brightman's response could be anticipated, especially in the light of Georgia's discernment of his "defensive mechanism" in the previous exchange of letters. First, he was the gentleman, acknowledging that he wronged her by including the phrase. But he missed the point that he had acted in a highly sexist manner: "It was crude of me to put that charm passage in a letter *that you were to read, and I regret it for that reason*" (italics added). After such a cursory apology, he continued by putting up his defenses. Objectively considered, the matter is not so bad as it sounds, he contended. "A testimonial which contains no frankly unfavorable comment is always under suspicion. On the other hand, women applicants for scholarships are always under suspicion of being candidates for matrimony and using the funds of scholarships as stepping-stones thereto."[17]

Brightman did his best to personally apologize to Georgia. "I hope that the 'strong personality . . . dignity and poise . . . presence and confidence' will serve to obviate any inferences as to freakishness, masculinity, or sloppiness, which of course are far from the truth. . . . I am very sorry about my thoughtlessness." He would not retract his statement, however. "Chiefly, then, because I don't have another blank form and a corrected one would make a bad matter worse, I think I'd better let it stand."

Did it occur to Edgar Brightman that he might have discarded the recommendation form and simply sent a letter to the scholarship committee, certainly an acceptable alternative in today's academic world? This thought probably did not occur to him, for the entire incident pointed to the truth in his self-evaluation: "I have to work like sin to get a student's point," as he had written to Georgia earlier. Brightman had demonstrated an obstinacy, even a stupidity, in failing to recognize or acknowledge the inherent sexism in his act. Harkness had sought to relate frankly but sympathetically to him and to enlighten him regarding his misguided statement. Her response to him also verified his evaluation of Georgia, that "discussion with you makes me work harder than discussion with anyone else I know; and your ability to put things in absolutely unambiguous and precise form helps me a great deal in clarifying my own thought."

In this particular case, however, Brightman was incapable of hearing Georgia's emerging voice. She was moving on to a new inner identity, regardless of whether Brightman could discern it.

Georgia forgave Brightman for his inappropriate statement in his letter of recommendation for her. Their relationship continued to be cordial and trusting. But her forgiveness could never erase the hurt she experienced. After Georgia had been dead for over fifteen years, her niece remembered her Aunt Georgia telling her of the experience she had, when she was thirty-seven years old, of "applying for a job or something and whoever had written this recommendation let her see it. One of his statements was that she was completely without sex appeal."[18]

V: "A Spiritual Pilgrimage: How My Mind Has Changed"

CHAPTER NINE

"I Ran Myself Ragged"
1929–1939

Georgia confronted the tradition that few women with Ph.D.s had reached positions of stature. Contending against this reality created an uncharted obstacle course on her vocational journey. By the end of the 1930s, she was in an inevitable but precarious position as a result of her successful and rapidly escalating career. January 1939 provided the opportunity for her to step back from a busy schedule and trace the strands of her public and private journey since beginning her professional career at Elmira.

The setting was right for personal reflection. Relaxing on board ship, Georgia was returning from India where she had been a delegate to the Madras Conference of the International Missionary Council meeting at Tambaram, Madras, from December 12 until 29, 1938. It was the second international ecumenical event she had attended, the first being the Oxford Conference on Church, Community, and State, convened in England in the summer of 1937. Madras was an exhilarating time for Harkness, "the most significant ecumenical gathering I have attended," she reflected fifteen years later, "with its disclosure of the virile quality of Christianity among the younger churches and its realistic vivid demonstration of the reality of the world Christian community."[1]

The entire trip was thrilling for Georgia. She enjoyed her distinction as one of the few women at the meeting. And she took time before and after the conference to see northern India, including the church mission stations and the Taj Mahal, where she sat silent before the exquisite beauty and "felt a sense of the numinous such as has never been stirred in me by any Christian art." Especially memorable was her visit, as an overnight guest with Muriel Lester, at Gandhi's ashram.[2]

On her return trip to the United States, Harkness was physically exhausted and spiritually uplifted from the entire experience. Now she had several days to meditate and make some sense out of her swirling schedule of the past decade. But there was a purpose guiding her reflection. "These words are being written on shipboard as I return from the Madras Conference, and whatever I say is likely to be colored by it," she wrote in the opening paragraphs of her autobiographical essay, "A Spiritual Pilgrimage: Ninth Article in the Series 'How My Mind Has Changed in This Decade,' " published in the March 15, 1939, edition of *The Christian Century*.[3]

To be asked to share her spiritual journey in this distinguished series confirmed that Georgia Harkness had arrived as a scholar in the theological world. Only persons of prominence in the wide mainstream of the church and the academy were selected as contributors. In 1925, Edgar Brightman had commended Georgia on her early publications of uniformly high quality that were making her rapidly into one of the most prominent contributors to the Methodist press. In the letter, he encouraged her to take a big leap and to "try *The Christian Century*." Indeed she had, and now, fifteen years later, *The Christian Century* was acknowledging her mantle of leadership in the national and international ecumenical church.[4]

In 1937, two singular distinctions came to Harkness. She was tapped by the American Theological Society to be its first woman member, after its male members decided to "admit women in moderation." And *Time* magazine brought her to the attention of the larger secular world by entitling her "famed woman theologian." The invitation to compose her essay in the aftermath of Madras attested to the high stature she had gained during the decade. She had been selected to serve in two key sections at the conference, on "The World Mission of the Church" and on "Faith and the Changing Social Order," and she had been a member of the drafting committees for reports from both sections to the full conference.[5]

"I was in the sections where theological cleavage was the sharpest," she wrote to Edgar Brightman, "and it was one long process of butting one's head against Kraemer theology. However, I came out with my head 'bloody but unbowed' and I am bold enough to think that the reports in both sections are somewhat different than they would have been without my presence."[6] Georgia was speaking her own mind in a strong and widely heard public voice. And her statement to Brightman reflected her own sense of being a leader of the church with whom to be reckoned.

Harkness's article in *The Christian Century*, as those of the previous eight contributors, was to address ways that the past ten years had affected her religious thought. However, she could not isolate how her mind had changed from how she had changed as a person. Georgia had been transformed by external events of the public world. "The collapse of economic and international security, of brotherhood and mutual trust, which the world has witnessed in this decade has affected my thinking, as it must that of anyone with a shred of ethical or religious sensitivity. The rise of continental theology has led me in part to accept it and in greater measure to reject it," she wrote. "Yet more determinative for me than what has happened in the political or theological world have been the events of my private world."[7]

Georgia proceeded to identify a few of the key events in her public life during the 1920s and 1930s as background to how her mind had changed. She had participated broadly in the life of the church through national and international preaching and lecturing, ecumenical leadership, and productive sabbatical leaves, resulting in definitive writing projects. Further, she had immersed herself in the daily life of Elmira College through her teaching and work for the vitali-

ty of the institution during difficult years of the Depression.
Tracing the course of Harkness's professional life during
these years, in the light of her personal commentary, helps
to discern the connection of her rising professional stature to
her spiritual and intellectual pilgrimage.

She had come a long way as a pioneer in the world of academics and the church since she wrote to Brightman in the
1920s, telling him about every speaking engagement for
church and community groups she was invited to fill within
a wide radius of Elmira. Her vision of the church and the
world broadened, moved from a local to an international
plane, after she joined the 1924 and 1926 American Semi-
nars, led a tour to Palestine in 1926, and participated in the
Oxford and Madras Conferences in the 1930s. Membership
in the Fellowship of Reconciliation and its Advisory Council, on which she served until her death, continually reaf-
firmed her resolve to be a pacifist and a socialist.

During these two decades, Georgia also took significant
sabbaticals at Yale, Harvard, and Union Theological Seminaries, where she studied with men who were the philosophical and theological giants of the mid-twentieth century.
These periods to focus on research and writing were refreshing and productive for her. On a semester's leave of absence
from Elmira in the fall of 1926, she worked with William
Earnest Hocking and Alfred North Whitehead at Harvard. "I
owe much to his great mind and soul," she wrote of Hocking.[8]

Georgia received the Sterling Fellowship for a sabbatical
at Yale in 1928–1929. She described the year as "one of
varied experiences: stimulating courses with D. C. Macintosh, Roland Bainton and Bob Calhoun; delightful fellowship with the Yale community, especially with Hal and
Mary Luccock with whom I had become acquainted on the
Mediterranean trip; an abortive love affair, from which I
now profoundly thank God I was delivered."[9] Oral tradition at Yale Divinity School, handed down over many
years, holds that the romance was with Kenneth Scott
Latourette, the distinguished professor of church history
and world missions. Their relationship supposedly broke

off because they could not reconcile commitments to marriage with their Christian callings and careers.

During the winter and spring of Georgia's sabbatical year at Yale, her mother's health took a turn for the worse. Georgia made numerous trips to upstate New York, stopping "everything else in the Spring to go home and nurse her through her last illness." In her later years, Lillie Harkness had diabetes, which resulted in blindness. Before losing her sight, she occupied much time in making and tying quilts. "For a while after going blind, she could still knit, and then she just sat," her granddaughter, Peg Overholt, remembered. Lillie Harkness's death came in May 1929, "a release from suffering for a patient soul," Georgia wrote.[10]

Immersion in work served as a therapeutic release for Georgia. She had developed a research proposal for her sabbatical at Yale on the relationship of the ethics of Calvinism to the growth of capitalism, a topic that had captured her interest in discussions with Reinhold Niebuhr that began while they were both on the American Seminar in 1924. During her sabbatical year, however, most of Georgia's attention was directed to her book on *Conflicts in Religious Thought*. Before her leave was over and in the midst of the strain of her mother's illness in the spring, Georgia completed the manuscript. Her first book since publication of her "stillborn" Master's thesis, *Conflicts* remained in print for over two decades and went through a revised edition in 1949.

Georgia returned to John Calvin after her mother's death and "went back and spent most of the summer amid the hot, dirty stacks of the old Yale Library, poring over the Latin and French of the *Calvini Opera*." Her work came to fruition with the publication in 1931 of *John Calvin: the Man and His Ethics*. However, by the time her sabbatical was over, she was "pretty well 'shot' with anemia, hypothyroid, a sacro-iliac trouble, and nerves more frazzled than usual." The combined effects of her mother's death, writing two books within two years, and returning to full teaching responsibilities had taken a severe emotional and physical toll on Georgia. She described herself as "so drained dry that I don't know whether I shall ever write another. Perhaps I shall, but not until I can take a year off to do it. I have not your rapidity of execution," she wrote to Brightman, "not enough physical vitality to do my college work and write a book at the same time by my plodding methods."[11]

Of course, Harkness did write again, and her methods hardly seem plodding. From 1931 through 1934, she kept her teaching fresh by developing new courses and teaching materials that would be turned into books later in the decade. In 1935, when Georgia was forty-four, she was again due a sabbatical. She decided to spend it at Union Theological Seminary in New York City, where she could work with Reinhold Niebuhr, Paul Tillich, Eugene Lyman, and other members of the faculty.

"I have been here since last Wednesday, and am wholly, and jubilantly happy. In fact, I get more thrills every day than I supposed possible at my middle-aged station in life," she wrote after being there for less than one week. "The spires, the atmosphere of the place, the delightful people one meets every time one turns around, the classes dripping with ideas, the cordial welcome everybody here has given me, with complete freedom to do as I please, everything seems as near an earthly paradise as it could be." She surmised that she would enjoy herself here more than she had at Harvard and Yale, where she felt like a nonentity. "Here a good share of people I meet seem to know who I am, and the faculty have been more than cordial. All of which is an adolescent reason for being happy, but a real one."[12]

Georgia's enthusiasm for Union Theological Seminary did not ebb; rather, it resulted in a burst of creative intellectual energy. She had planned to work on a textbook, a survey of the origins of Christian ethics. Instead, she wrote *The Resources of Religion*, which grew out of another course she had recently introduced at Elmira, "Present Day Problems in Religion." She began *Resources* on the morning of September 28 and finished it at midnight of November 14! The book was well-received and became a selection of the Religious Book Club.[13]

After returning to her teaching position at Elmira in the winter and spring of 1936, she was enabled to go back to Union for an extended sabbatical and leave of absence in the fall of 1936 and winter of 1937. In November, she wrote of the toll that physical and emotional strains had taken on her: "I feel less inspired this fall than last. . . . Too many odd jobs—too many attempts to serve the Lord here and there. I am trying to get resolute."[14]

Harkness gained her resolve very quickly. Again, she intended to finish the ethics text, but could not put herself to it. In an experience similar to the writing of *Resources of Religion,* Georgia immersed herself in her manuscript of *The Recovery of Ideals* and completed it by Christmas. It, too, was selected by the Religious Book Club.[15]

On the crest of enthusiasm, Georgia turned in January 1937 to the manuscript for her lectures at the Hazen Foundation Conference the next spring that would be published under the title *Religious Living.* In a style of work that was becoming a pattern, she described the month in a letter to Edgar Brightman: "I have had a great burst of energy, the Lord inspired me, and my Hazen manuscript on 'How to Find Religion' is done—writing time two weeks and one day. Since during this period I went to Lynchburg to speak, made six addresses over in Harlem, read the proof on 'Harkness's Recovery' and did the appendix for it, I think perhaps I had a 'reason for living' during that period."[16]

In a postscript, she queried of Brightman: "Do you remember that when I asked you in the spring of 1920 whether I should go on to get a Ph.D. you spoke doubtfully on the score that I lacked physical vigor and gave up on things too easily?" Harkness conceded that she was going to loaf for a week or two and then plunge again into her ethics book! In fact, the ethics text remained unfinished in her drawer until 1953, when she finally completed it after joining the faculty of Pacific School of Religion. But the inability to turn to it in 1936–1937 hardly tarnished her work sheet for that period.

Her prodigious output of book-length manuscripts was coupled with an equally amazing production of articles during the 1920s and 1930s that appeared in a host of interdenominational and denominational church publications, among them being *The Christian Century, The Christian Advocate, Zion's Herald, World's Y.W.C.A. Monthly, The Presbyterian Tribune, The Intercollegian, Journal of the National Association of Bible Instructors, World's Call, World Outlook,* and *World Christianity.* Virtually a countless number of essays, they also related to a wide diversity of subjects. A representative listing includes:

"The Ethical Approach to the Study of the Bible"
"What It Means to Believe in God"
"Ethical Values in Economics"
"Prayer and Life"
"Peace Asks a Hearing"
"Impressions of the Oxford Conference"
"Wanted—Prophets!"
"The Church and the Student"
"John Wesley as Hymnologist"
"Are Pacifists Romantics?"
"The Last Stronghold of Male Dominance"
"Protestants Plan World Strategy for Peace"
"Ecumenicity Marches On"
"The Theological Basis of the Missionary Message"
"Young Women Leaders in the New Methodist Church."

While the above list is only a sampling of her articles written during the decade of the thirties, it points to many things about Georgia's spiritual pilgrimage. She had amazingly wide vision of the issues. Systematic theology, spiritual guidance, pacifism, women, ecumenism, hymnology, ethics, religious education, and student life account for some of the broader themes. Amid countless calls for her attention, she could focus on the task at hand and turn, almost without skipping a beat, to the next one. Her name and message were reaching an increasingly wider audience in professional church positions, volunteer church service, secular occupations, and management of the home. Finally, her essays are her best writing—more alive, vital, and confessional than most of her longer, book-length manuscripts.

It is no wonder that Georgia's ascending position as the first woman theologian of distinction in the United States was rapidly being recognized by agencies that bequeathed that official status. In January 1935, she noted: "Some things which have brought me satisfaction are 1) entrance into 'Who's Who' 2) ditto into 'American Women' 3) an invitation to join the 1935 Anthology of Magazine Verse 4) an invitation to join the 'Fellowship of Younger Christian Thinkers' of which Pit Van Dusen seems to be the presiding genius."[17]

She went to New Haven at the end of the month for her first meeting of the Younger Theologians, a group of about twenty-five men—and now Georgia—in academic positions related to religion on the East Coast. At this session, "we spent two days discussing sin and salvation under the stimulus of papers prepared by Bob Calhoun, Gregory Vlastos, Richard Niebuhr and Bill Pauck, with Ed Aubrey as summarizer and correlator." As she participated regularly in the semiannual meetings, some members cast sexist aspersions and only politely tolerated her presence, as one whose work was directed as much to laity and practicing clergy as to fellow academics. They undoubtedly saw her as beneath their scholarly distinction.[18]

Whether or not Georgia was aware of their miserliness, the group provided a much needed breath of intellectual fresh air for her. It meant good fellowship on a "trenchant intellectual plane. . . . I have seldom enjoyed anything as much as this discussion meeting, and I think I can live with more intelligence and vigor now in the hope of having it to participate in twice a year."

Beyond the Fellowship of Younger Theologians, admission into the American Theological Society as its initial woman member in 1937 constituted a parallel but more official "first" for Georgia. She reacted frankly to her election in a letter to Brightman in early April 1937. "It swells me up to think of being the first woman to have achieved this distinction."[19]

Georgia's voice also was sought by the wider ecumenical church. It was heard prominently at the Oxford Conference in the summer of 1937, and events precipitated by her words brought increasing public fame. "My globe-trotting to

Oxford, Colorado, and New Mexico left me much refreshed," she wrote in late September. She thrived on her place in the public spotlight, but it also brought her inner trauma. She described the personal consequences of the Oxford Conference in this way: "I made a four-minute speech on the place of women in the church which caused quite a stir, and being cabled under the Atlantic in an AP dispatch, gave me a good deal of publicity at home. This would not be worth mentioning except that it precipitated so many invitations to speak here and there that *I ran myself ragged* in the attempt to keep up my school work and accept even a few of them."[20]

Her speaking engagements confirm that she represented women's participation in the church to much of the ecclesiastical world. In the 1930s she no longer wrote Brightman of every nearby church group that invited her to speak. But she continued to tell him about some of her addresses that brought her singular distinction.

Georgia wrote to him in October 1938 about her major leadership roles in the past few months. She had a grand time during the summer with the Southern Methodists— two weeks each at Dallas and Lake Junaluska, North Carolina. The intervening three weeks at Pendle Hill in Pennsylvania had not intrigued her so much, "probably partly because I was weighed down during that time with the responsibility of formulating the faith of the North American churches in preparation for the Madras Conference. I don't mean to imply that my feeble shoulders had to bear the whole burden," she emphasized, but she knew that her contribution was crucial. "The committee made quite an extensive study and Pit Van Dusen, George Buttrick and I formulated the results. My job was to shorten and clarify Buttrick's somewhat flowery rhetoric. It would have been much easier to start from the beginning."[21]

She would not attempt to give Brightman a catalogue of her comings and goings, Georgia stated in the same letter. But among other highlights were trips to Denver by plane to address the Disciples of Christ on "Women and the Church," and to West Point to lecture at the Methodist pastors' retreat. The incongruity of the situation, "in refusing to admit women to the Pastors' meetings and then asking one to make two of the speeches," was not an isolated instance for her. "The Methodist pastors received me with proper Methodist cordiality and I had a good time," she wrote. But she also felt the responsibility to address the "powers-that-be" of the conference with the reality of their sexism. The retreat director, Dr. Christian Reinner of the Broadway Temple in New York City, invited Harkness to come again the next year. She responded that she was not at ease in accepting an invitation when women pastors were not allowed to attend. "If participation is on the basis of professional connection with religious work and not on that of sex, I am glad to come. Otherwise, I must decline."[22] No record exists of the outcome of their exchange.

One further invitation extended to Harkness in January 1939 illustrates the glory, burden, and pressure of the mantle of leadership resting on her shoulders by the end of the decade. On January 13, Brightman wrote to her that she would soon be hearing from Katharine Gilbert of Duke University, who had told him at the Philosophical Association that Duke was holding a celebration sometime during the spring. "She was convinced that you were the speaker that they wanted to represent the leadership of women in the church." Then he bore in, supplying a rationale for her acceptance of the invitation from Duke in the light of the unification conference, scheduled for September, which would bring together the Methodist Episcopal Churches of the North and South, which had been sundered for almost a century.

> Your position of leadership among women in America in the field of religious thought is undoubted (of course you have heard of how *Time* christened you "famed woman theologian"), and I am convinced that your acceptance of the invitation will mean a great deal in promoting good feeling between the Church North and the Church South in the unification. As a delegate to the Uniting Conference you will have additional reason for accepting this invitation. . . . I understand

that the Committee is fighting hard to have you also invited to preach in the chapel on Sunday. If this invitation does come, I hope you will see it in the light of no mere routine item, but an extraordinary victory for the cause of woman's place in the church, especially in the South.[23]

Just over two weeks later, after Georgia had returned to the United States from the Madras Conference, she responded to Brightman. His letter had reached her at Cherbourg, France, in the same mail with one from Katharine Gilbert. Yes, she had been invited to participate in the Women's Symposium at Duke University with President Mary Woolley of Mt. Holyoke and Judge Florence Allen as her colleagues. She was also scheduled to preach in the Duke Chapel on the following day, undoubtedly a historic first for women. She would receive an honorarium of $150 for the symposium address, twice as much as she had ever gained from a speech. "This double-header is quite overwhelming and while I have accepted the invitations I have not quite come to," she confided to Brightman.[24]

Georgia's schedule in the 1930s amounted to a pace that only a person of enormous psychic and physical energy could keep. However, it provided some relief from her day-to-day working conditions at Elmira. The immediate strain did not come from teaching responsibilities, even though she often taught a heavy load of five courses during one semester. She was a highly popular and able teacher who drew large numbers of students to her classes. She loved to teach and enjoyed immeasurably her work and friendships with students.

Harkness often spoke of the spontaneous interest and scholarly work of her classes. In one class on the history of modern philosophy, she evaluated almost all the students to be of graduate-school caliber. And in a course on present-day problems in religion, the students broke the record for outside reading. "When one asks for reports on 500 pages and gets 5000, it is evident that interest in religion in the colleges is not dead!"[25]

Louise Proskine, formerly Louise Benning when a student at Elmira, valued the comments Harkness made on her reading reports. "She asked her students to respond to the assigned readings with a brief 'original idea.' On one of my papers, Dr. Harkness wrote, 'This is hardly an original idea'! Even though we were friends, she didn't give favors. She was very honest. Then on another paper, one that I am so proud of, she said 'This is a good observation.' For her to say 'a good observation' was something. . . . She expected a lot."[26]

Now living in retirement near Ithaca, Louise particularly remembers her friendship with Harkness as well as their student-teacher relationship. "I made muffins and coffee and had her over sometimes for Sunday morning breakfast. She was a friendly person, and she seemed glad to come." Louise was a nutrition major at Elmira and became a nurse, but "I took many electives from Dr. Harkness, who had a strength that attracted my attention from the beginning . . . a feeling that here was someone who rang true to all that I had experienced and sensed in my brief eighteen years. Here was someone broad enough to greatly expand my horizons."

Further, Peg Overholt, Georgia's niece, now living in retirement in Maryland, remembers living in her aunt's home in Elmira. "Aunt Georgia" had been able to bring her to college on a "faculty scholarship," by declaring Peg as her heir. "During those depression days almost everyone had scholarships or worked. Hardly any student could pay her own way," she recalled.[27]

Georgia's niece, then Peggy Harkness, and Ruth Edwards, the daughter of a close friend, lived with Georgia during their student days in the early 1930s. Georgia spoke of their companionship as a great blessing to her. After they had been with her one year, she described herself as "feeling maternal and generally amiable in the company of two nieces." Before long, she was referring to them as her two daughters. In looking back from 1990, Peg remembered her aunt as a caring person, but one who related to them more distantly than a mother or sister would. "She was not that affectionate. It seemed more like a teacher-student relationship" to her niece. The difference between their two perceptions probably stems from the reality that Georgia simply was not demonstrative in expressing her feelings.[28]

However, both Georgia and her niece remembered that many friends visited in their home. Peg particularly recalled the families of her aunt's close colleagues, Dr. Tuttle and Dr. Mould. In terms of teaching and colleagiality with other faculty members, Elmira College was a happy environment for Georgia.

Administratively, however, the college was in "an unholy, sickening mess," Georgia wrote in the early 1930s. Enrollment shrank severely during the depression years, dropping by 100 students in 1932 and by 80 more the following year. In 1934, total registration was only 322, with 150 of those living in town rather than residing on campus, a drop from a peak of 590. She did not see the entire loss as being caused by the Depression. Much was due to the struggle between the president and the new dean, a woman who smoked and allowed students to do so, and had little religion. Georgia felt that more conservative-minded alumnae were no longer recommending Elmira to prospective students.[29]

Decreased enrollment resulted in drastic cuts in the faculty, with nine members released in 1932 and fourteen the following year. The faculty received a 5 percent cut in salary in 1932. Harkness and her colleague in Bible, E. W. K. Mould, led a campaign to get the faculty to agree to a 10 percent drop, in order that the first nine might not be fired, but their effort was to no avail.[30]

The president brought together Harkness, by then head of the philosophy department, and other departmental chairs to assure them that they would not lose their positions. While Georgia felt reasonably secure that she would not be dropped, the possibility always loomed in the background, due both to financial stringency and to Georgia's forthrightness in standing up for faculty causes.

As a consequence, Harkness almost constantly was looking for another teaching position. However, the Depression caused drops in student enrollment and faculty employment in all institutions of higher education. Through the 1930s, she wrote often to Brightman of positions that became open, asking him to write letters of recommendation for her. Sometimes, she withdrew her name, as she did after applying to Rollins College, where nine faculty members had been released and she felt it would be "good to stay out of that mess."[31]

However, in many cases Georgia experienced overt sexism in hiring practices. Such was the case at Radcliffe in 1926. After she had graded papers for William Earnest Hocking while on her sabbatical at Harvard, he was highly impressed with her work. With a position opening at the sister college, Radcliffe, Hocking pleaded her cause vigorously and "was very anxious to have me stay." Strong sentiment existed against permitting a woman to do any teaching, and even when women had been appointed as tutors in history and mathematics, higher requirements were imposed on them than on men. Tradition prevailed, and the Radcliffe possibility turned out to be a fiasco. When positions opened at Mt. Holyoke and Smith in the early thirties, "the desire to hire a man" again caused her to be eliminated.[32]

Losing a position at Mt. Holyoke in 1932, because President Mary Woolley thought it better to hire a male, Georgia described herself as "an also ran."[33] This feeling must have increased when she was passed over for several faculty positions during the ensuing years of the 1930s.

Georgia was in line for a faculty post in religious education at Chicago Divinity School in 1937 when a position was offered at Mt. Holyoke. She accepted the Mt. Holyoke position with the title of Associate Professor in the Department of the History and Literature of Religion and a salary of $3,000 annually. The intention was that she would be promoted to full professor, at a $4,000 salary, in three years. When she informed the new president of Elmira, Dr. W. S. A. Pott, that she was leaving, he simply responded with a "thank you." He undoubtedly found Georgia threatening because of her efforts to organize the faculty during the employment crunch, even though she was esteemed within Elmira College and highly recognized outside the college.[34]

Harkness was overjoyed to join the Mt. Holyoke faculty, both because of the higher caliber of the institution and because it enabled her to move from a department of philosophy into one of religion. Her selection was another confirmation that she stood among the leading women pioneers in academia as well as the church. To briefly survey her comings and goings of research, writing, speaking, and traveling, during a period of severe political strain in the daily campus life, leaves one almost breathless. It is little wonder that she ran herself ragged.

CHAPTER TEN

"The Most Impregnable Stronghold of Male Dominance"
1929–1939

*T*he editor of *The Christian Century* wanted the contributors to the series on "How My Mind Has Changed" to discuss the turns their understanding of the Christian faith had taken in recent years. Georgia's response was that she could not separate her thought from her life experience. One reflected the other! This interaction between the way she thought and the way she lived is strikingly demonstrated through the four categories she chose regarding the changes in her faith: theology, worship, social action, and the church.

Foremost, her mind had changed in the 1920s and 1930s in terms of theology; she had become more theological than philosophical in her approach to truth and more Christ-centered in her faith. "These two movements are part of one process," she wrote, "a movement away from an ideal of philosophical objectivity to one of more overt Christian commitment."[1]

For many years, the philosopher and the theologian had existed within her in "friendly rivalry." Her graduate training was in philosophy, though in the personalistic school that was cordial to religion, and she had taught philosophy for fifteen years. "My academic conscience has the conviction that philosophy should be taught philosophically. . . . But while I was teaching philosophy I was writing religion."

The opportunity to transfer to a department of religion was a welcomed means of terminating the rivalry.

Further, she was still a liberal, "unrepentant and unashamed," as she had been ten years earlier. However, her liberalism, with its overly optimistic view of humans' ability to remake the world, had been chastened and corrected. This was due, primarily, to the influence of neoorthodoxy, with its understanding of "the profound fact of sin and the redeeming power of divine grace."

Georgia and liberals more generally in the 1930s made their essential theological change in their understanding of the Bible. They came to see it as more than a collection of moral adages, and Jesus Christ as "more than a great figure living sacrificially and dying for his convictions." Liberalism had been "recalled to the meaning of the cross and the power of the resurrection." Her mind had changed the most, Harkness wrote, in coming to focus on God's incarnation and the presence of the crucifixion and resurrection in Jesus Christ's life and our own lives.

Harkness pointed to her second book, *Conflicts in Religious Thought*, which was written eight years after publication of her Master's thesis, as the fullest statement of her earlier, philosophical self. "At ten o'clock on the evening of February 8, 1929, I put the last words to the writing of *Conflicts in Religious Thought*. At the awareness that at last the long job was done I felt a wild exhilaration such as makes one want to 'paint the town red.' Being thoroughly conditioned to sobriety, I went to bed. The content of this book affords a measuring-point from which I can reckon the changes of the past decade."

The impetus to write *Conflicts* came in 1925, when she began teaching the course on present-day problems of religion. The class was introductory, not meant to give students a thorough knowledge of philosophy of religion or theology but to stir up their thinking and give them some constructive answers to questions "as far as their baby minds can grasp them." She wrote to Brightman, asking him whether she should put these ideas into a book out of her conviction that "what helps my children might help others, and I am a firm believer in the need of 'the popularizing of knowledge.' "[2]

She was struggling with the traditional belief that scholars first should publish their ideas in academic form, and then turn them into more popular pieces. Brightman encouraged her first to write in popular form directed to the masses. A good case can be made for building up to one's scholarly contribution, he stated. Too, Brightman may have realized that Georgia did not have a traditional academic style of writing and that she would always write more naturally to educated laypersons and students than to so-called scholars.[3]

Conflicts in Religious Thought was published in 1929, and it reached its desired audience well. Its original publisher, Henry Holt and Co., reported that after one year thirty-seven colleges had put it on their adoption lists, including Colgate University, with an introductory course of 300 students. The book remained in print for over twenty years and went through a revised edition in 1949. "Miss Harkness has dealt with the various basic religious problems with scholarly accuracy and real insight," wrote Reinhold Niebuhr, "and her book will be helpful to all who wish to clarify their thought on the perplexing problems which face those who deal with ultimate things." William Earnest Hocking judged the book as "admirable in directness . . . clarity . . . unaffected language . . . the work of a real teacher dealing with the problems of students as they actually arise." Such an evaluation would succinctly describe the corpus of Harkness's writings, not only *Conflicts in Religious Thought*.[4]

Specifically, *Conflicts* sought to address the most profound questions of human thinking, but to do it in the language of ordinary people. The book captured the essence of Harkness as the philosopher of religion, not the theologian. It spoke to universal problems of religious faith, rather than to issues of Christology and biblical interpretation that relate to a single religion. "I waited for someone else to write it," Harkness stated in her preface. "None came to hand that met the need of my students; and I decided to write it myself."[5]

Religion, as Georgia defined it in 1929, is a total attitude toward life that posits belief in a more-than-human determiner of destiny, a divine Controlling Cosmic Power. It is a way of life, rather than a set of intellectual beliefs, that leads a person to pursue a course of conduct that he or she believes to be the will of God. There are two functions that "religion at its best has always had . . . to make men better and to make men stronger. Keenness of moral vision, strength to meet the storms and battles of life—these have been the dual gifts of religion."[6]

Conflicts was a study of religious values, as were most of Harkness's writings through the 1930s. Religion serves the double purpose of adding new and deeper meaning to all the values of life and of supplying a value that is uniquely religious. Values such as economic self-mastery, health, vocational adjustment, play, friendship, and the quest for beauty, truth, and goodness are not uniquely religious, but a spiritual understanding can provide greater meaning to them all. Quality of life, not abundance of possessions, for instance, is the value that religion brings regarding the possession of material goods. Similarly, a physician helps to bring physical health, while religious value can help people know how to live, and bring mental health. "Through a sane, steadfast religious faith do we find release from obsessions and fears, and find guidance for an aimless drifting life." Further, to work without a vision makes a person a drudge, but if work can be viewed as a task committed to the person by God, the person is likely to find something worth doing.[7]

However, for all the good that religious faith can add to each of the major values of life, it alone addresses the question: What are we here for anyway? What is the purpose of life? Happiness or enrichment of personality is the chief end of life, according to Harkness. And religion brings happiness, though not the superficial sort of hedonistic gratification. "But if happiness be interpreted as the enjoyment of the richer satisfactions of life, as contentment, serenity of spirit, joyous self-mastery, as power to rise above the 'slings and arrows of outrageous fortune'—then religion is *par excellence* the source of human happiness. The fruits of the Spirit are love, joy, peace. . . . Looking over humanity in the large, experience bears witness to the fact that the most sanely spiritual people are also the happiest people."[8]

Harkness's description of God provides an excellent translation of the personalistic school into nonacademic language to address the experience of students and laity. "As the highest reaches of human personality are found in love and goodness, wisdom and creativity," the most profound expression of the uniquely religious value, "so also the personality of God may manifest these qualities in infinite degree. . . . We must think of God, if at all, in terms of the highest that we know. Life gives us nothing higher than personality."⁹

Finally, though Harkness devoted little space to Jesus Christ, she gave him a unique place in two ways: "To Christians, God is most readily conceived as revealing his true nature in the personality of Jesus." Further, the "Christian revelation is not the only avenue to God, but it is the highest the world has seen." For a person within or outside the Christian faith, the "essence of the doctrine of Jesus' divinity lies in the fact that in his life and teachings we learn what God is like."¹⁰

When Georgia wrote her essay on "How My Mind Has Changed" in 1939, she described herself as "quite a different person than the self of ten years ago." While there was nothing in *Conflicts of Religious Thought* that she would seek to retract, "Were I writing it now there is much that I should wish to add." Georgia did exactly that when she wrote *The Resources of Religion* in 1935, a book that she described as "a companion and supplement" to *Conflicts*. *The Resources of Religion* was written like her other books, in a burst of enthusiasm and energy, begun on the morning of September 28 and finished at midnight November 14.¹¹

The primary difference, as Georgia stated herself, was that *Resources* was more religious than philosophical. "I suspect that no other Philosophy department will accept me into its midst after it gets published! But I have a sort of messiah complex about it, so think I shall go ahead and publish it."¹² The book marked a significant step in her spiritual and professional pilgrimage. She wanted to put behind the friendly rivalry within herself that had been present for the several years she had been teaching philosophy and writing theology. *Resources* helped her to do that. Accurately reflecting how her mind had changed in the 1930s, it made her a highly suitable candidate for the position in the Department of History and Literature of Religions at Mt. Holyoke in 1937.

The Resources of Religion went considerably beyond *Conflicts in Religious Thought* in two ways that Harkness identified: It set forth the basic elements of an avowed Christian philosophy for the individual life, and it provided a Christian strategy for social change to address the neopaganism of the day. Her declared purpose in this book was to focus on Jesus Christ, to write a Christian theology and ethics. Indeed, Georgia devoted considerably more content in *Resources* to Jesus Christ than she did in *Conflicts*. But it is questionable whether her understanding of God's incarnation in Christ had changed by the mid-1930s as much as she thought it had.

Georgia set forth an understanding of the death of Jesus on the cross as "the eternal symbol of a loving, suffering God," providing a foundation to develop this essential emphasis of the Christian faith in the 1940s. At this point, however, she focused on the resurrection as the means to "triumphant living" that Christianity calls salvation.[13] Georgia said that she was bringing together the cross and the resurrection in her theology. Her declaration is unconvincing, however. The primary purpose of religion, and specifically of Christianity, as she understood it in 1935, was to provide an influx of power to enable the individual to meet the high moral demands of life. Her emphasis was still on moral striving.

By Jesus Christ, Georgia continued to mean the man Jesus: "no other man ever lived with so perfect a harmony of precept and deed. . . . Jesus believed himself to have a divine mission to reveal the way of God to men, and he embodied in a life which led him to the cross the self-giving, suffering love of God for men . . . the moral meaning of the incarnation . . . the high mark of ethical idealism" was still central to Harkness's Christian faith.[14] She had not dealt yet with the reality of the cross in Christian theology—or in her own life.

The model of a "Christlike personality" is the primary spiritual gift that Jesus, the human being, bequeaths to those who would follow after him, Georgia wrote. Such a personality does not exude piety or try to convert people. "Christlike personality *may* exist along with peculiarities. Evangelistic zeal which proceeds tactfully from high motives is not necessarily offensive. But neither queerness nor religious obtrusiveness is *per se* a mark of Christlike personality."[15]

In fact, the Christlike personality added up to a beautifully well-rounded way of life and grew out of a solid biblical base for Georgia. However, at this stage of her life, she believed that a person came to such a personality through high moral striving, not through a genuine grappling with a deeper experience of spiritual death and resurrection.

Her own words from *The Resources of Religion* best sum up the nature of her theological ethics in the 1930s.

> When I think of the most Christlike personalities I know, I find them marked by a concern for spiritual values—not religious values alone in the narrower sense, but beauty, knowledge, fun, friendship, all the higher things of life; I find them able to control their tempers and meet the vicissitudes of life with serenity and courage; I find them humble, confident of their abilities but never boastful; I find them sensitive to others' needs and feelings, never willfully giving pain and always eager to heal; I find them gentle but dynamic with a power so evident that it does not need to be talked about.
>
> In short, I find such personalities conforming to the ideal of love set forth by Paul in the thirteenth chapter of First Corinthians. A paraphrase of this may suggest more clearly than the familiar words what it means to be Christlike, and therefore a truly great person. The Christian religion demands greatness, and will be satisfied with nothing less.
>
> A great person is patient and kind;
>
> A great person knows neither envy nor jealousy;
>
> A great person is not forward and self-assertive, not boastful and conceited;
>
> A great person does not behave unbecomingly, nor seek to aggrandize himself, nor blaze out in passionate anger, nor brood over wrongs;

A great person finds no pleasure in injustice done to others,
    but joyfully sides with the truth;
A great person is full of trust, full of hope, full of patient
    endurance;
Love never fails.[16]

Georgia could have summed up her paraphrase by saying that "a great person never falters in living out of the idealism of the Christian life." However, she had not confronted yet the reality that great persons who strive to live out of these ideals, even she herself, do falter and fall. When this happens, the way is open for them to come to a deeper meaning of the cross and resurrection in the life of Jesus Christ and in their own. This would be Georgia's experience within a few short years.

═══

Harkness's mind changed in the 1920s and 1930s more significantly regarding social action than personal theology. The awakening of her mind to the necessity that social justice be at the center of the individual's and the church's witness came from her participation in the American Seminar in the summer of 1924. By 1939, the steadfast march of nations toward another world war led her to a deepened pacifistic witness.

"But perhaps I should explain why I have become a more convinced pacifist in a day when many better Christians than I have felt impelled to surrender their pacifism. The reasons are both pragmatic and theological. War destroys every value for which Christianity stands, and to oppose war by more war is only to deepen the morass into which humanity has fallen," Georgia wrote in her "Spiritual Pilgrimage."[17]

In *The Resources of Religion*, Harkness applied her idealism to the necessity for social justice and envisioned a Christian strategy for a society built along the lines of the Kingdom of God. Ideals alone are strong enough to stand against humans' most powerful physical impulses, she wrote. "Ideals are the stuff that great movements are made of." And respect for personality was the root value upon which the Kingdom of God on earth was to be constructed.[18]

Deeply influenced by Reinhold Niebuhr and his *Moral Man and Immoral Society,* Georgia wrote:

> There is no record in history clearer than the evidence that honest, pure, unselfish, loving personality in large numbers of individual Christians has not abolished war, capitalism or racial prejudice from the earth. As long as society has colossal systems antagonistic to respect for personality, individual character will be like a flower rooted in a muck-heap—it will shed beauty and peace, but it will not obliterate stench and filth.[19]

Harkness, like Niebuhr, overestimated the goodness of individual human beings and underestimated the potential of groups to bring reform and renewal. But, in large part through the influence of neoorthodoxy and particularly Niebuhr, Georgia was coming to a clearer understanding of the nature and relationship of tragedy and triumph on the social and global levels. "I believe that life is inevitably a sphere of conflict and that our choices are not often to be made between good and evil, but between alternative evils," she told her *Christian Century* readers. "In all life's dark areas the triumph which shines through tragedy comes not with the sword which our Lord rejected but with the cross toward which he walked. I believe that only in the union of justice with suffering love is any human force redemptive and permanently curative, for only in such union is force more than human."[20]

Harkness believed that an "aggressive pacifism" was essential, and she challenged the church in unequivocal language to make that witness. Such an article as "Wanted—Prophets!"—published in 1937—demonstrates how far Georgia had come in her own prophetic witness and the witness to which she was calling ecclesiological bodies, nationally and locally.

If the church is to have a prophetic function, Christian leaders must be willing to challenge comfortable, traditional modes of thought, and do it in terms not glossed over with vague generalities. Such challenge is imperative in the areas of economics, of militaristic nationalism and of race, and because in these areas we are now least Christian, it is in these most dangerous to be prophetic. It is safe to talk of social justice in general, but not to be a socialist; to read Isaiah's vision of a warless world and preach an eloquent sermon from it, but not to be a pacifist; to quote, "God hath made of one blood all nations of the earth," but not to invite a Negro to one's home or to one's pulpit. So one chooses the safer course, and tells himself he must not undermine his influence by rashness. Caution is the mother of pseudo-prophetism.

Prophetic courage, to be sure, should not be made an excuse for blundering obstinacy. Lyman Abbott had a wise adage, "Let courage teach you when to speak, and tact teach you how." But neither must expediency be made an excuse for retreat. There is need of a resurgence of the spirit of William Lloyd Garrison who said: "I am in earnest. I will not equivocate. I will not excuse. I will not retreat a single inch—I will be heard."

If the church has not produced many prophets in our day, it is largely because congregations have not wanted them. Pulpit and pew must share the blame. "Passing the buck" is a practice at least as old as the story of the garden of Eden, and one which is antithetical to prophetism. What eventuates from it is lack of vision on both sides of the chancel rail. And where there is no vision, the people perish.[21]

Georgia *became* a prophet of social justice during the 1920s and 1930s, a new dimension of Christian experience for her. James Creighton had taught philosophy at Cornell by applying his idealism to practical life issues. This approach gave Georgia a foundation upon which to build a social ethic during her Master's and Ph.D. programs. However, it was not until she began teaching and traveling internationally that she gained firsthand exposure to the evils of sexism and militarism. These experiences enabled her to make the close and necessary connection between theology and ethics. So, while teaching philosophy at Elmira College for fifteen years, Harkness was becoming an applied theologian.

Harkness's personal experience and its application to social justice issues led her mind to change, thirdly, in her understanding of the church. Georgia had never strayed from the church since she was a week old and her parents first carried her to services, she told her *Christian Century* readers. "Yet within the past two years the church has taken on new meaning."[22]

She traced the change through her response to the hymn whose rhythm had stirred her since childhood, "Onward, Christian Soldiers." Becoming an adult, she was repelled by its militaristic language and "bombastic assertion of what seemed flat falsehood":

> We are not divided,
> All one body we,
> One in hope and doctrine,
> One in charity.

Nothing was more obvious than that the church was not "all one body." However, at the Oxford and Madras International Ecumenical Conferences during the last two years she had come to experience the "world transforming truth" of these words. "There were enough divisions in hope and doctrine, if not in charity," at both conferences "to tear any group in the world asunder." Yet the delegates worked together out of an underlying unity. "This vision of the church came to me at Oxford. But it remained for Madras to show me what the church has actually accomplished in the world community."

The first major ecumenical event that Harkness, or almost any other woman, ever attended was held at Oxford July 12–27, 1937. Here the delegates voted to unite the two ecumenical movements that had existed side by side during the early twentieth century, setting the stage for the constitution of the World Council of Churches in 1948. Oxford represented the wing of Life and Work, and was successor of the Universal Christian Conference on Life and Work, held at Stockholm, Sweden, in 1925. Its sister conference on Faith and Order met at Edinburgh the following month, being preceded by two conferences of the Faith and Order Movement at Geneva in 1920 and Lausanne in 1927.[23]

Harkness did not attend the Edinburgh meeting, where even fewer women were delegates than at Oxford. In attendance at Oxford were 425 delegates from 40 countries and from all branches of Christianity except Roman Catholicism. Though Georgia referred to herself as a consultant, she was listed as one of 300 delegates representing their official denominations. Of the total number of delegates to Oxford, 23 were women, in comparison to 6 women and 353 men at Edinburgh.[24]

The theme of the Oxford Conference was the relationship of the church to the state and the community, particularly to "the life and death struggle between Christian faith and the secular and pagan tendencies of our time." By then Associate Professor of Religion at Mt. Holyoke, Harkness participated in Section Four of the working groups on "Church, Community, and State in Relation to Education."[25]

In presenting its report to the general body, Harkness's section came out strongly in favor of freedom of thought and the equality of all persons to a secular and sacred education. It also condemned the curtailment of these rights as one manifestation of the international crisis.[26]

Addressing the march of totalitarian regimes, the report called to task totalitarian governments that were gaining strength in the 1930s, without naming them specifically. It responded to racial injustices within these states by declaring that the church "cannot be blind to the fact that all races are not equally advanced" and must teach the equal worth of all people before God. It condemned the fact that education was being used by some national powers as a means of separating people along class and race lines. The church and Christian education must hold governments responsible for persons, not persons for governments. A person who receives a Christian education should be "both a grateful recipient and a critic of the cultural heritage. He is a patriot, but a discerning patriot," the report read.

Georgia saw the Madras Conference, which met December 12–29, 1938, continuing in the spirit manifested at Oxford. The vision of unity transcending this world was demonstrated at Oxford as the ecumenical church took stands on the most basic human rights and social issues of the day. "But it remained for Madras to show me what the church has actually accomplished in the world community."[27]

To Harkness, the most distinctive feature of the conference was the parity of representation from the younger and older churches of the world. Too, the strength of the diversity of cultures present was balanced by the common ties of friendship that were developed. Women also had a larger part in leadership than in any previous ecumenical gathering: one-seventh of the total delegates were women and fifteen of the forty-five representatives from the United States and Canada were women.[28]

Madras demonstrated the living fellowship of the Church Universal by witnessing to the exceedingly able leadership of young churches in the mission field. Representatives from the established churches of the West became aware of a freshness, vitality, and life-transforming power in Eastern Christianity that could inject a note of hope into a baffled world. The younger churches have much to teach us, Harkness wrote. They do not feel the despair that grips the Western world. "Their faith is more elemental, more Christ-centered, and consequentially more victorious."

Georgia experienced "the great democracy of God" in action. "I have never seen elsewhere so complete a transcendence of distinctions of race, color, age, sex, denomination, and (most difficult of all) ecclesiastical prerogative."[29] Theologically, Madras gave her a deeper understanding of the church as the Body of Christ: a highly diverse gathering working together because it was unified by one faith.

But she also saw ways that such pronouncements regarding Oxford and Madras were still glaring generalities. The status of students and women was her particular concern. Though no women made major addresses at the plenary sessions of the Oxford Conference, Georgia made a short statement that she entitled "Remarks Regarding Students and Women." Her comments ran no more than four or five minutes, but they were sharply critical of the marginalized status of both groups.

The church had failed to state its message in terms that applied to young people and to the problems of the world in which they lived. The challenge of the gospel had not been addressed to the whole of their lives, and religion remained "something which happens on Sunday." While the church had done much *for* young people, it had done less *with* them, often failing to give youth a responsible place in their own life and leadership.[30]

At the same time, colleges were becoming increasingly secularized and young adults were expressing their idealism in movements and institutions outside the church. The unfortunate fact was that "they are losing the fullness of the Christian Gospel, while the Church is losing its best lay leadership. I consider this to be the most serious menace confronting the Church, for without an able and intelligent leadership it cannot survive."

The same circumstances applied to women and the church. While women always had done much of the educational work in the local church, in many instances their energy and intelligence were drained away from the church and channeled into various secular programs. Harkness focused on a major reason for this tragedy: "In such secular enterprises and in professional life in general outside the Church, women find an opportunity for *creative leadership, for expression of their talents on their own initiative,* and in turn, a *recognition* which they do not ordinarily find in the church." Here she was not speaking to the issue of ordination, she added, but to the broader concern of wider lay leadership.

In concluding, Harkness affirmed the conference report *"that the Church is a supra-national, supra-racial, supra-class fellowship."* But she hastened to remind the delegates "that the Church is also a *supra-sex* fellowship."

Harkness's words received wide press coverage, undoubtedly because she was recognized by then as both a noted author and lecturer who spoke with authority. Further, she minced no words on a subject becoming important to an increasingly larger number of people. These were the "remarks" that were cabled under the Atlantic and circulated widely by the religious press in 1938, causing her to run herself ragged keeping up with increased speaking engagements and regular school work.

Georgia's strong challenge to the church to address sexism within its own house symbolized the way in which her mind had changed. She was thrilled by the potential oneness amid diversity of the body of Christ that she experienced at Oxford and Madras. She was not bleary-eyed by it, however. Rather, she was developing a sensitive and courageous prophetic consciousness.

Only the month before she went to England, *The Christian Century* published an article by Harkness that spelled out in greater detail her arguments at Oxford, attacking the paternalism of the church and the reasons for diversion of women's activity into secular professions. In unequivocal language, she stated her basic point: "It is a paradoxical fact that the Christian gospel has done more than any other agency for the emancipation of women, yet the church itself is *the most impregnable stronghold of male dominance*. It is this fact more than any other which makes women of intelligence and ability restive, and skeptical of the church as the most effective channel for their effort."[31]

Upon returning from Oxford, Harkness spoke before increasingly wider audiences of the church, warning them that secular agencies were offering women an opportunity for leadership and creative expression of their talents on a level not being duplicated in the church. A speech delivered to the annual Leadership School at the Methodist Assembly in Lake Junaluska, North Carolina, was entitled "The Last Stronghold of Male Dominance." She pressed her point that until the men of the church recognized the loss the church was suffering, "to deplore the defection of women will largely be wasted breath."[32]

The editor of the Methodist *Christian Advocate* printed excerpts of Georgia's address and was powerfully moved by her words, commenting that Harkness was so completely right that many critics would be impatient with her. But those who were not worried by the losses of which she spoke would be "short-sighted and superficial critics." Then the editor followed with this critique:

> Strangely enough, women in the church and the colored people in industry have this in common: each is much in demand for the humbler tasks; each is praised for faithfulness in lowly duty; and each is directly or indirectly discouraged from seeking to rise above a fairly definite level. Above that line in industry this is a [white] man's country; in organized religion, despite woman's preponderance in the membership, the church is a man's church.

Harkness focused on the response needed from women when she spoke at the National Meeting of the Presbyterian Women's Missionary Societies, at Buck Hill Falls, Pennsylvania, and at the International Convention of Disciples of Christ, at Denver, within the next few months. Women must rethink their approach to mission work, she told these organizations. A need existed for closer connection between service to other races abroad and elemental racial justice at home. "Women—and others—have often shown more enthusiasm for Christianizing the Negroes of Africa than for being Christian toward the Negroes of their own communities. Similarly, missionary education ought to be linked with peace education. What shall it profit if we evangelize Japan, yet cannot maintain our good will under strain?"[33]

Georgia continued by telling her listeners about women who had come to her, directly sharing their experience of sexual discrimination in the church. A forty-two-year-old woman had been asked to resign from her position as director of religious education so that a man could replace her as assistant pastor. Should she seek another church position, running the risk of being asked to leave again in a few years, or try public school teaching? Another director of religious education had gained success in her position at the price of constantly seeing an ordained minister get credit for her accomplishments. At the same time, she became the scapegoat for everything that went askew.

Then Harkness shared some of the discrimination she had experienced as a woman teaching religion in higher education. Women were ridiculed for not having theological minds, she told her audiences. This resulted in teaching positions in philosophy and religion often being closed off to women, as had been her own experience in the 1920s and 1930s.

At Oxford and Madras, Georgia had gained the vision that the "church is an all-inclusive Christian fellowship. Its strength rests upon its unity—a unity within which persons of differing gifts may work together in mutual respect." But within the past two decades she had experienced the deep wounds of sexism upon the Body of Christ.

It was a curious fact, Georgia stated, that at Union Theological Seminary in 1937 all senior honors, including a two-year traveling fellowship, went to women students. But what would these young women do with their training after they were finished with it? Ordination was not the crux of the problem, she continued, but the right to have a parish! Further, women's societies had a legitimate place in the church, but they were not the answer for the long run. Both pointed to the same issue: genuine inclusivity of women in the mainstream life of the people of God. The church clearly had a long way to go before unity was achieved among its basic constituency: men and women.

———

Georgia knew herself to be more of an activist than a mystic. In a spirit of confession, she told her readers that God had reached out to her with greater vividness and warmth in the hustle and bustle of her daily life, calling her to a deeper sense of reverence. "In the midst of increasing activities I have been led to find a richer communion in living silence and in the great liturgies of the church," she told her *Christian Century* readers. Harkness's mind changed in a final way during the 1930s in terms of worship.[34]

The awareness that she needed a more worshipful attitude toward God came to Georgia through her contact with students. As she taught daily and lectured throughout the country, she saw large numbers of students seeking to escape into themselves, to withdraw "from the difficulty of making decisions about social action in a world which seems almost at an impasse. This has deepened my realization," she confided to the public, "that what I would try to impart I must first seek to possess."

One door to more meaningful communion with God and her sisters and brothers opened for Georgia through her citizenship in a widening world. On her two sabbaticals at Union Theological Seminary, the types of worship services and the content of the preaching in the seminary chapel "left me with much—more, perhaps, than the refreshing winds of doctrine which are ever blowing there." Then, as she sat in silent meditation before the Taj Mahal after the Madras Conference, its exquisite beauty gave her a sense of the divine being "such as has never been stirred in me by any Christian art."

Further, the services of worship at St. Mary's Church were the focal point of the Oxford Conference for Harkness, as for many of the delegates and visitors. The sense of tradition, on this site where Christian worship had been held continually for nearly one thousand years, inspired her with awe. Even more overpowering, "one felt all contemporary differences to be merged in a common loyalty to Christ. The inclusive nature of the church was evident in the fact that those leading in worship, like the conference membership as a whole, were of the most diverse ecclesiastical traditions and national cultures." Differences in dress and speech celebrated the variety of God's household, "while the unity that binds together the Body of Christ was apparent in the use of hymns and prayers which transcend linguistic barriers."[35]

Most important to her own growth in faith, Georgia came to realize by the opening years of the 1930s that she lacked a "sense of silence" in her worship of God. Through a seemingly paradoxical but notable progression of events—writing a book on John Calvin, buying some nonessential material goods and a cottage on a beautiful lake in the Adirondacks, and beginning to write poetry—Harkness moved toward a more meaningful life of prayer and worship.

The idea for her book on the life and ethics of John Calvin came in January 1928. Georgia had a new "bug" to apply for a Sterling Fellowship for a sabbatical at Yale University. It was then that she wrote to Brightman asking him to recommend her for the Fellowship.[36]

Her idea for a project, if she could do what she wanted to do and had an eternity to accomplish it, would be to make a comparison of the social ethics of Jesus with that of every major type within historical Christianity. This comparison at least would include such movements as the early church, scholasticism, monasticism, Calvinism, Lutheranism, modern Catholicism, Fundamentalism, and liberal Protestantism. She would seek to discover how much of the dominant social ethical concepts of the movements was gained from Jesus, how much from economic and environmental factors, and "how much from the general cussedness of human nature." Georgia thought that by the time she completed this project she would be an educated woman—but "also that Gabriel would have blown his trumpet."

So, to cut her topic down to a manageable subject, she would focus on one aspect of her grand plan: the relationship of Calvinism to the capitalistic system. Her theory was that "Calvinism was a social and ethical movement quite as much as a religious one, protesting against the vices inherent in Catholic practice. Then having become victorious and prosperous it incorporated these same vices in its own social ethics, and has passed them down to us in a garb of Protestant respectability."

Accepting the Sterling Fellowship of $1,500 for the sabbatical at Yale, Georgia had a happy and fruitful time in New Haven. After the sabbatical, she continued work on her subject and developed it into a book-length manuscript, *John Calvin: The Man and His Ethics*, published originally by Henry Holt in 1931.[37]

A multifold movement was about to commence in Georgia's life. Her highly activist nature, manifest in exceptional physical, mental, and emotional energy, served her well in the years during which her career escalated rapidly. The tremendous productivity and ability to maintain an almost superhuman schedule of writing, teaching, and speaking were possible because of her inward drive. Further, her need to "be doing," to be striving and busy about the Lord's work, provided release to a nature that could be easily restless and bored. It also compensated for a lack of close relationships and social life.

However, as she ran herself ragged, Harkness discerned the shortcoming of her activist nature and her need for a closer personal relationship with God. Her consuming schedule and rapidly accelerating prominence created a barrier in her spiritual life. Georgia's personal correspondence indicates that writing on John Calvin served a therapeutic purpose to help release her from a long-held worship of the Calvinistic ethic that one earns his or her salvation by living the "good life" of frugality, piety, and proper works. Georgia thought until close to the time of publication that the book would be entitled "The Calvinistic Consciousness." This original title, which she herself had chosen, provides insight into the personal movement going on inside of her: She was in the process of shedding at least some of her "Calvinistic consciousness."

With a genuine sense of abandon, she wrote Brightman after Holt's acceptance of her manuscript that in the last six months she had "become a hedonist in practice, if not in theory. I have spent more money on non-essentials than in my whole previous experience, and in general have broken loose from most of the restraints of my Calvinistic conscience. My friends look at me aghast, and wonder if I have lost my mind. I sometimes wonder myself."[38]

Georgia had not become a hedonist, though her immediate acquisitions might indicate such a turn. She described her delight in her purchases and her personal happiness in these words to Brightman:

> In October I traded in my car for a DeSoto sedan, a beautiful maroon which is a great source of aesthetic delight to me. Then I felt so congested in my two rooms in Factory House that I

took another plunge, and December 1 I moved across the street to a four-room apartment. I have had great fun furnishing it. I got a good deal of the furniture at second-hand stores and painted it up, but I brought a four-poster, some chairs and some other antiques from our attic at home. I have an Oriental rug and a big stuffed chair which give me more satisfaction, aesthetic and physical, than I ever supposed mere material possessions could. At present I am in the process of buying a radio. My faculty friends had a kitchen shower for me, so I am pretty well supplied with the necessities of a domestic menage. Have also bought a new fur coat, a diamond ring, and various other non-essentials. So it isn't strange if my friends began to wonder if I have gone crazy. But everybody is keen about my apartment, which is the only really spread-out, home-like place on the campus. (To be exact, just off the campus.)

I have not been so happy, or so physically well, in years. Contentment, quiet, and the physical exercise my housework gives me, seem to have taken all the nervous kinks out of me. My classes seem to have shown more philosophical interest than they ever have before. So all in all, I spend most of the time, when I am not doing anything more important, thinking how happy I am.

As you may judge from this tale, I am more prosperous than ever before. I get $3100, plus $200 more for my extension class, had $225 last year in royalties, and took in about $100 for preaching. Having taken out a retirement and disability insurance I have decided I may as well spend my salary for things I want. Hence, the loosening of the shackles of my Scotch Calvinism. But all my purchases have been bargains. I'm still Scotch.[39]

Certainly Harkness's work was going well. She had received good reviews of *Conflicts in Religious Thought*. *John Calvin: The Man and His Ethics* had been accepted for publication, and her salary and additional revenue gave her a new feeling of financial prosperity. It is not known whether other things were happening in Georgia's personal life to enable her to experience better physical and emotional health than she had long known. But in her letter, she expresses a sense of release, an enthusiastic outpouring of happiness not often seen in her. And her purchasing fling should be seen as a new-found ability to enjoy material as well as spiritual blessings and a release from her worship "of the shackles of my Scotch Calvinism."

The most important acquisition that Georgia made in 1931, probably the most meaningful during her entire life, was an eight-room bungalow at Willsboro Bay, just outside the small town in which she had taught high school before going to Elmira. Located on Lake Champlain and in the Adirondack Mountains, her cottage was only eighteen miles from the family home in Harkness. From the large porch or the living room and dining room running across the front of the house, Georgia looked out on the lake across a spacious bay, with mountains in the background on each side. Several steps led down to a swimming area immediately in front of her house. It was only after acquiring her summer home that Georgia began to swim, rightfully proud of her adult learning experience and enjoying it immensely. Georgia described her property as a summer paradise set in the most beautiful and peaceful spot in the world. And she named it, appropriately, "Hate-to-quit-it"—the sign is still prominently displayed across the front of the house. By the second summer she had built a small bungalow for herself on the back of the house and soon after bought an adjacent cottage, enabling her to have many friends visit in the summer and to rent the bungalows at other times.

Here she relaxed, wrote books, scrubbed and painted the cottages inside and out, and entertained friends. Thrilled with her home, Georgia had 140 guests the first summer, "though my remnants of conscience force me to say that 85 guests came at one time, for a Sunday School picnic." She had "sleeping equipment" for sixteen, and often entertained from two to thirteen people at a time. "Hate-to-quit-it" evidences Georgia's need for friendships—and her own efforts to reach out for those relationships.

However, "Hate-to-quit-it" meant even more to Georgia. It provided space and time for the "sense of silence" in her worship of God, a place in which to cultivate the inwardness and mystical quality of her devotional life. In the years to come, the writing of poetry and spiritual meditations became a part of her spiritual expression, an outpouring of a different side of Harkness than was found in her academic writings. Through her poetry and prose meditations, she opened herself before the mystery of God, and her cottage on Willsboro Bay symbolized the quiet centeredness of her spiritual life. Even more particularly, Georgia came to find God's presence in nature, and her poetry contains many allusions to the scenes near her Willsboro Bay retreat home.

The writing of poetry became the most significant expression of Georgia's change of mind regarding worship. In November 1931, she made the "interesting and amazing discovery—that I can write verse." Georgia literally stumbled upon this new avocation, which she cultivated for the rest of her life. In the 1950s, after a reviewer of her recent book of poems and prayers, *Be Still and Know*, referred to Harkness as "something of a poet," she described the beginnings of her avocation. "This 'something' began when a poet friend came to Elmira to give a two weeks course in versification, and I joined the class—partly to swell the numbers and partly to see if I could find out what modern verse was driving at."

The friend was Molly Anderson Haley, and the class was held the first two weeks in November. "Hers was the method of creative 'group dynamics' before we heard the term so often, and I began to burble with both light verse and sonnets." Such a self-description by Georgia represents a lightness and abandon not often associated with her. From this initial invigoration, a little poetry club formed that "was a source of relaxation in those depression years when many lost their jobs and we all worried lest we should."

Georgia began to pour out poems as a release from her normal schedule of work at a rate similar to her writing of essays for church journals. She reported in August, nine months after composing her first verse, that she had written over sixty poems and that fifteen of them had been accepted by *The Christian Century*, *The Congregationist*, and other religious publications, for a total sum of $22.50! By 1935, a collection was gathered and printed, at her expense, under the title of her first serious poem, *Holy Flame*. She recalled in the 1950s that this "is the only one of my 17 books which I have ever had to submit a second time."[40] In fact, *Holy Flame* was submitted to seven publishers before finally being accepted, and it was continually returned because editors believed the poetry market to be doubtful.

The volume *Holy Flame* dealt with human experience and its relationship to God in a variety of aspects: biblical themes, the revelation of God in nature, in suffering, in the social struggle, and in the round of everyday life. Her poems reflected the same "warmly affirmative attitude toward God and the universe" as did her other writings. But poetry provided her the medium to grapple with the awe and mystery of God, so different from the methodical, clear-cut, declaratory style of her prose. Harkness's writing of prose and poetry reveals the reasonable and emotive qualities within her, two highly different sides of her being. It was particularly noted at the time of her writing that she was one of the few persons professedly devoted to scholarship and organized religion who "writes poetry that not only means well but is thoroughly good poetry."[41]

A look at three of her early poems helps to bring together who Georgia Harkness was and how her mind had changed by the end of the 1930s. "Stump Fence" was a recollection of her own cherished roots growing out of her meditation on Psalm 16:6, "The boundary lines have fallen for me in pleasant places; I have a goodly heritage." The poem traces the life journey of trees on the family farm in northeastern New York. Nurtured by the God of nature, they grew from seeds to infant saplings, to become towering pines, straight and majestically poised landmarks of the countryside. Settlers came and felled the trees to make a clearing, with the tree stumps used to make fences.

Side by side the settlers placed them,
Roots tip-tilted in the air.
Prone they lay, their glory humbled,
Shorn of grandeur, stark and bare.

Long ago the earth they conquered
Has received the pioneers;
But the stump fence stands unvanquished,
Guarding borders through the years.[41]

The stump fences on the Harkness homestead go back to the earliest days of settlement in the area. They would not be the effective means of "guarding borders" today and, like her ancestors, must be put to rest. But it would be a sad day to forget the stump fences and her forebears who provided the foundations on which we build. Georgia was telling her readers, "These *were* and *are* my roots."

A second short poem of three verses, "The Strength of the Hills Is His Also," is a description of the countryside near the Harkness home and "Hate-to-quit-it" after much of the snow has melted in the spring.

> Around me all is murky mud
> And springtime freshets flow,
> For here the frost is going out—
> But on the hills is snow!
>
> Across an opalescent lake
> They tower, jagged, high,
> Gray, lapis, azure, turquoise, mauve,
> Snow-capped against the sky.
>
> I look around at the muddy earth:
> I think of earthy things.
> I lift my eyes up to the hills:
> My spirit then takes wings!

Her poem is a response to the question of the psalmist: "I lift up my eyes to the hills—from where will my help come?" (Ps. 121:1). The juxtaposition of hills and mud provides a parable of human existence. Georgia was sharing her own reflection on the awe, mystery, joy, and strength that the mountains of the Lake Champlain area brought to her, and praying to God to help us "to remember that amid the mud and scum of things, there always, always something sings."

Finally, "Holy Flame" was the first serious poem that Georgia wrote, and it seemed "like a first baby" to her. She wrote it during the Depression and referred to it throughout her life for its applicability to the war years and cries for social justice throughout the second and third quarters of the century. "Holy Flame" reflects upon Isaiah's response to God's call: "I heard the voice of the Lord saying, 'Whom shall I send, and who will go for us?' And I said, 'Here am I; send me!' " (Isa. 6:8). For all its applicability to the call of other prophets, "Holy Flame" must first be read as the most significant expression of how her own mind and life had changed in the 1920s and 1930s.

> Isaiah mourned the passing of the king
> And to the temple came to muse and pray.
> Dark was the kingdom's future on that day,
> Beset with greed and every evil thing.
> No spokesman of the Lord was there to sting
> The conscience of the mob, or lead the way
> To gallant victories in Jehovah's fray
> With sin and strife, with self and suffering.
>
> God gave Isaiah then the vision high;
> His unclean lips were purged with sacred fire.
> Out of the smoke a Voice in challenge came;
> Unhesitant, he answered, Here am I.
> Again the days are dark, the outlook dire;
> Lord, touch Thy prophets now with holy flame.

VI. "For Such a Time as This"

From "Triumphant Religion" to the Dark Night of Her Soul *1937–1945*

Georgia was embarking on the spiritual pilgrimage of her life—not completing it—when she was almost fifty years old. Writing her essay on "How My Mind Has Changed" at the beginning of 1939, she was in buoyant spirits. Her vitality after the Madras Conference and her travels in India led her to believe that her bodily fatigue and heaviness of heart over the past two years were gone forever. However, she could not conceive the depths of spiritual estrangement, emotional depression, and physical disability that the late 1930s and early 1940s would hold for her.

In 1939, at age forty-eight, Harkness brought her faith journey together neatly and rationally for her *Christian Century* readers. Her mind changed in four ways in relationship to theology, social justice, worship, and the church during the previous decade. She stated her beliefs clearly and strongly. And in her poem "Holy Flame," she offered herself to God out of the sincere conviction that now she was equipped to "go forth"—whatever that call might mean!

Although she was not aware of it yet, Georgia was setting forth on a deeply inward spiritual journey, a dark night of her soul, that would extend for several years until the mid-1940s. In the summer of 1940, just sixteen months after she succinctly summed up her religious journey in *The Chris-*

tian Century, she wrote another essay that opens the door into her deeper inward spiritual pilgrimage. However, this later article, "For Such a Time as This," was not autobiographical. She was challenging the women of Methodism to respond to the challenge in Esther 4:14:

> For if you keep silence at such a time as this, relief and deliverance will rise for the Jews from another quarter, but you and your father's family will perish. Who knows? Perhaps you have come to royal dignity for just such a time as this.

The nameless Hebrew writer spoke these words through Mordecai to Esther in a "time of national catastrophe and racial persecution not unlike our own," Harkness wrote.[1]

Published in *The Christian Advocate* in July 18, 1940, "For Such a Time as This" was addressed to the "Women in the New Church," who were joining together to begin the Women's Society of Christian Service of the new Methodist Church. The formation of the new denomination in 1939–40 entailed both the dissolution of its predecessor organizations—the Methodist Episcopal Church; the Methodist Episcopal Church, South; and the Methodist Protestant Church—along with the inauguration of the inclusive church.

"For Such a Time as This" was representative of many of Harkness's writings that were published in church journals in the late 1930s and early 1940s. In this large body of brief articles, she challenged the clergy and laity of mainstream Protestantism to shoulder their prophetic responsibility by speaking out against the march of Hitler across Europe, as the shadow of World War II loomed throughout the entire world. Harkness called Christians personally and the church corporately to labor and pray for peace in our time: "We have something to say to a world that needs many things, but above all else needs prayer, prophetic utterance, and incisive Christian action. . . . We are come to the Kingdom for this day!"[2]

Georgia's strong words were addressed not only outwardly, to the church and to Christians, but also to herself personally. Mature both as an individual and as a Christian, she also must have asked herself the radical vocational question: Have you "not come to the kingdom for such a time as this"?

To many persons who knew Harkness by her distinguished reputation, it seemed clear that God was raising her up for this particular time in history. Her strong challenge for a Christian pacifist witness, her leadership in the international ecumenical church, and her pioneer role as a woman in a man's academic world of philosophy and theology offered notable signs. Certainly, Georgia's article on "How My Mind Has Changed" confirmed that identity.

Harkness herself could look back over the first half of her life with satisfaction. She was a "shy, green, and countrified" girl who had not been more than twenty miles from home before she went to college. Grounded in the discipline of philosophical idealism in college and graduate school, she internalized its meaning in her fifteen years of teaching philosophy at Elmira. Georgia lived successfully by practicing the faith of "triumphant religion," a belief that one's salvation is closely tied to the good works one does. She had well-earned God's favor.

Now, after twenty years in a steadily rising academic career, Harkness stood alone as the famed woman theologian in a field dominated by men. At the same time, she had the satisfaction of living her life in service to God. To succeed professionally as a lone woman in a man's professional world would continue to be an uphill climb. However, Georgia was still under fifty years of age, and there seemed no reason why her career and calling should not continue to advance together on the same course.

Harkness had convinced the world around her that she was a woman of almost invincible physical, mental, emotional, and spiritual strength. However, she was beginning to seriously question whether she had fallen far short of the goals of triumphant religion, and, in turn, of her God-given call "for such a time as this."

———

The language of triumphant religion came primarily from Georgia's academic study of philosophy, not from her evangelical background. It symbolized the quest for an ideal of philosophical objectivity to enable the person to "live religiously," which underlay her writing until she was almost fifty years old. Harkness's commitment to triumphant religion is stated definitively in her two books published in 1937, *Religious Living* and *The Recovery of Ideals*, and a third book, *The Resources of Religion*, which was written two years earlier. These volumes provide a fitting summary and benediction to her vocational journey and long-held identity until this critical turning point.

In *The Recovery of Ideals,* Harkness wrote that her basic religious concern was to discover the "true grounds on which one may believe in and live by moral and spiritual ideals." The book's main purpose was to "suggest the outlines of a constructive philosophy of life" growing out of those ideals.[3]

An ideal, Harkness stated simply, is "a conviction that something ought to be held before the mind with sufficient power to motivate effort to bring it to pass." Most people settle or aspire in life, she wrote, to lesser levels of idealism of "prudential adjustment," to live out of a proper mean, do nothing to excess, and to maintain a socially respectable character. The Christian, however, should aspire to the highest idealism of triumphant religion, the level of active saintliness demonstrating the dynamic union of social action and social passion, sympathy for all persons and courage to serve the needy.[4]

Georgia succinctly stated the purpose of ideals and their centrality to triumphant religion in these words:

> It is through ideals that we discover direction and power both to resist temptation and to overcome limitation. If our ideals are as inclusive as they ought to be, we find through them not only personal mastery but the impetus toward the creation of a society where none need be inhibited by artificial barriers from living at his best. The function of the ideals is both individual and social. In the power to live by ideals, whether directed against sin or chaos, lies salvation.[5]

To live religiously, Harkness also wrote in 1937, "is both a quest and an achievement" to live out of the highest ideals of triumphant religion. As a person's life is turned outward, to seek the good of others, his or her inner life is enriched and deepened. "To find one's way into living religion is the most important thing any person can do," she stated unequivocally.[6]

God and Jesus Christ played a part in the individual's quest to live by the highest ideals and to gain salvation. As would be expected, Harkness understood the nature of the deity in 1937 much more out of a philosophical perspective than a stance of Christian faith. God was the organizing mind, who brought system and order to what otherwise would be chaos. The Divine Being was also the source and goal of ideals and the object of supreme worth. In what Harkness understood to be the most profound insight of the Christian faith, she defined God as the cosmic companion who suffers with us.

Seeking to live a moral life, the person of ethical sensitivity is sometimes confronted with the awareness, she wrote, "that having done all he can do, he is still an unprofitable servant. 'The evil which I would not, that I do' is the perennial cry of the baffled spirit."

However, God delivers us from evil to the paradoxical assurance of victory in Christ, she wrote. The same person, so bound by evil, also "says with calm assurance: I can do all things through Christ." The definitive statement of her faith in 1937 is well-summarized in these words from *The Recovery of Ideals*: "Living in Christ, one could look the world in the face, do a mighty work, and know that nothing could daunt the soul."[7]

While still working out of a stance of philosophical idealism, she knew the essential language of her evangelical Christian background rooted in the incarnation, crucifixion, and resurrection of Jesus Christ. However, her articulation of that faith lacked the power of inner conviction that sometimes comes after a person's beliefs go through the fires of deep inward testing. To keep up with her escalating schedule in the late 1930s and to survive its pressures, Georgia had no choice but to "look the world in the face, do a mighty work, and know that nothing could daunt the soul." Despite the inner strain, she held fast to the precept of triumphant religion that "I can do all things through Christ."

Georgia's success in living triumphantly reached a crest in January 1937, when she completed her manuscript on "How to Find Religion," her lectures for the Hazen Foundation Conference, which would be published under the title *Religious Living.* In a letter written to Edgar Brightman on January 24, she described the "great burst of energy" that enabled her to write the book in two weeks and one day, with the last chapter written in a twenty-hour spurt, and then go immediately to Lynchburg to speak and give six addresses in Harlem, plus read the proofs and organize the appendix for *Recovery of Ideals.*

Her last sentence to Brightman was crucial: "I think perhaps I had a 'reason for living' during that period."[8] This statement, written at the end of January 1937, provides the first indication of her inward questioning, the earliest sign of the onset of spiritual depression that would strike to the heart of her life's goal of triumphant living.

Immediately after her surge of energy and purposefulness in early January, the crucial turning point occurred in Georgia's spiritual journey. Her pace of work came to a sudden halt when her father became seriously ill. At the beginning of February, Georgia returned to the family home in Harkness to nurse him through his final illness.

In writing her autobiographical sketch for the Pacific Coast Theological Group years later, Georgia described the life-shaking significance of being with her father during the final two months of his life and of receiving his last words to her on his death bed on April 1:

> Those two months of intimate fellowship with a great soul, who had lived so quietly but richly, and who now faced death as calmly as one would walk into the next room, meant much to me. I am well aware of the sentimentality often attached to "last words." Nevertheless, I cannot faithfully recount my spiritual autobiography without telling something which he said to me within an hour of his death, and which I took as a

directive from an eternal realm. Asking me how many books I had written (by that time seven), he said, "I think they must be good books. Wise men say they are. But I wish you would write more about Jesus Christ." This word, reinforced by the fact that after that time I was mainly teaching the Bible or theology rather than philosophy, marks a definite turn in my writing and thinking toward a more Christ-centered approach to religious truth.[9]

In almost his dying words, Harkness's father asked her to recover the roots of her Christian faith, which had been instilled in his daughter from the time she was a few weeks old, and to "write more about Jesus Christ." Georgia's father had played a god-like role in her life, and she knew that this "directive from an eternal realm" did not simply mean writing *more* about God's son. Her father's words meant that she needed to say something different about Jesus Christ. In coming to "a more Christ-centered approach to religious truth," the foundations of triumphant religion were shaking under her feet. She would soon realize that her belief in the personal and social conquest of earthly evil through faith in Jesus Christ could no longer be sustained.

The death of Warren Harkness began to release the hold of triumphant religion over his daughter. In his prodigious activity for the good of others in his church and community, Georgia's father was her model of triumphant living. She sought to emulate his example and to live out the high expectations he set for her and that she, in turn, embraced for herself. Further, because Warren had to maintain the family farmstead and give up his dream of teaching and venturing into the wider world, Georgia strove to fulfill his dreams through her own life. In significant measure, her life was an extension of her father's until his death. Her contributions and prominence in the national and international arenas, in a sense, mirrored his service on the local scene. A life of service to God, the church, and other persons always shaped her Christian commitment. However, after her father's death, Georgia's motivations altered radically, and she began her journey toward spiritual maturity.

The greater depth in Georgia's spiritual journey after her father died did not occur because of an immediate conversion in her academic and faith perspectives from philosophical idealism to a more Christ-centered approach to theology. Rather, his death initiated a lengthy process of inner change in her vocational motivations. During the first period of that process, which extended for two and one-half years from the spring of 1937 until the fall of 1939, a series of events occurred in Georgia's life that caused her to move back and forth from emotional depression to psychic exhilaration. These public events form a backdrop to the private trauma that was building within her.

Georgia identified the late months of 1939 as the actual onset of her "dark night of the soul." This second period continued from October 1939 until mid-1944, when she wrote one of the most important books of her life, *The Dark Night of the Soul*.

The initial period of vocational change began shortly after her father's death. A different perspective is gained on these events of the late 1930s when they are seen in relationship to her spiritual depression. Georgia returned to Union Theological Seminary on her leave from Elmira shortly after her father's death. She intended to immerse herself in her manuscript on Christian ethics and to complete it. Understandably, she experienced herself "too tired to bring it to completion."[10]

The summer of 1937 brought relief. As a consultant to the Oxford Conference, she became caught up in the mission of the international ecumenical movement and was uplifted by the adventure of her first major ecumenical gathering. Her speech on the place of women in the church created a stir out of proportion to its length of four minutes, and she enjoyed the publicity her words brought. However, the side effects of being run ragged by attempting to keep up with school work and speaking invitations took a heavy toll of physical and emotional weariness.

In the fall of 1937, Georgia became a member of the faculty of Mt. Holyoke College in South Hadley, Massachusetts, an opportunity she had long hoped would open for her. Despite the tremendous personal and professional investment she had put into teaching and community involvement at Elmira for fifteen years, and the satisfaction gained from teaching and friendships there, she was restive during her entire tenure there. Further, institutional financial strain and struggles between the faculty and administration during her last years at Elmira led all faculty members who could make a move to increasingly look for openings in other institutions.

Correspondence between Georgia and Edgar Brightman documents that she was seeking continually to find another position. The Seven Sister Colleges looked especially inviting. More than once during the 1920s and 1930s, positions at Radcliffe, Smith, and Mt. Holyoke came onto the horizon, only to fade before her eyes.

The opportunity to become a member of the department of religion at Mt. Holyoke seemed a fitting move at this juncture in Georgia's vocational journey. As she had written in *The Christian Century,* she was becoming a theologian during the 1930s while she was teaching and seated in philosophy at Elmira. The move to Mt. Holyoke was essential to bring together her daily work life with her professional identity. Hired by Mary Woolley as Associate Professor of the history and literature of religions, Georgia's courses officially seated her in theological studies. Among classes that she taught the first year were Introduction to the Christian Religion, History of Christian Thought, Contemporary Religious Movements, Present-Day Applications of the Teachings of Jesus, and Religious Problems and Leaders.[11]

Further, to teach at a more prestigious institution meshed with her personal desire and with her increasing national and international visibility. Finally, the move from Elmira to Mt. Holyoke enabled Georgia to maintain her lifelong commitment to the advancement of women. Both schools made a special claim to pioneering in women's education. In 1837, Mt. Holyoke became the first seminary to provide young women with the equivalent of high school training. Then later, in 1888, Mt. Holyoke gained college status. Following Elmira's lead as the first college for women, several outstanding women's institutions of higher education, including Barnard, Bryn Mawr, Goucher, Hood, Hunter, Mt. Holyoke, Pembroke, Radcliffe, Randolph-Macon, Smith, Vassar, Wellesley, and Wells, were founded at the turn-of-the-century.[12]

Harkness remained at Mt. Holyoke for only two years, however, because of both circumstances internal to her relationship with the college and the fact that she was soon invited to become a member of the faculty at Garrett Biblical Institute. Georgia summed up her feelings regarding her two years at Mt. Holyoke in these words:

> In the Fall of 1937 I went to Mt. Holyoke to teach in the department of religion, just as a great woman, Dr. Mary E. Woolley, was retiring from the presidency. Had she remained, I think I should have been happier there. My relations with the students were thoroughly happy, and in spite of the New England reserve, which I felt more than I had at Boston, I had good friends among the faculty. I found, however, that within my department my public contacts were viewed with suspicion, and tensions developed which need not be narrated here. The upshot was that after two years, I was glad to accept the invitation of Garrett Biblical Institute to join that faculty as Professor of Applied Theology.[13]

Harkness was one of the last faculty members hired by Mt. Holyoke's president, Mary Woolley, who was almost a legend on the campus when she retired in 1937, the year in which Georgia came onto the faculty. When Woolley became president in 1901, at age thirty-eight, she was one of the youngest college presidents in the United States. She shared commonalities with Harkness. Woolley was the first woman to enter Brown University in 1891, the year Georgia was born. Immediately after graduation from Brown in 1895, she was named an instructor in biblical history and literature at Wellesley College and by 1899 was promoted to professor. Assuming the presidency of Mt. Holyoke two years later, she established herself as a leader in liberalizing and upgrading women's education. Woolley committed herself to building a strong faculty by drawing women and men from leading graduate schools. Harkness's appointment capped her successful effort before Woolley retired.[14]

Woolley and Harkness, each working out of religious conviction, supported similar radical causes beyond the college campus. Particularly notable was their mutual involvement in causes for international peace and their pacifist stands. Both held the distinction of being the first woman in delegations that were otherwise composed totally of men. Woolley, for instance, was appointed by President Hoover, after pressure from women's organizations, to the Conference on Reduction and Limitation of Armaments held in Geneva in 1932. In her liberal, optimistic Social Gospel emphasis of Christianity, Woolley's words could have been spoken by Harkness: "Some day there will be 'a Kingdom of God on earth.' The last thing for us to do, is to stop working for it."[15]

Woolley planned to retire in 1933 at age seventy, but alumnae petitioned her to remain in office until the centennial celebration of 1937. With Woolley's retirement and the appointment of the first male president, Roscoe Gray Ham, in that year, the times were turbulent at Mt. Holyoke.

When Harkness came onto the campus, the entire Mt. Holyoke community—students, faculty, administration, alumnae, and trustees—was split over Ham's selection. His appointment said to many that only a man could be found to lead a woman's college. To them, it negated all for which Mt. Holyoke stood! With her esteem and even veneration of Mary Woolley, Harkness would have been of this persuasion. Woolley herself was so infuriated by Ham's appointment that she never returned to the campus after her retirement.

Faculty who were disaffected with Woolley criticized her involvement in international and politically radical causes, such as pacifism, on the eve of the Second World War. Closely tied to this reaction was the criticism that she was away from campus more than many believed acceptable. Ham, himself, sought to curb faculty involvement in controversial off-campus movements. Harkness would have drawn similar negative response from faculty critical of Woolley's broad social and political activism.[16]

═══════

Despite the tensions in her professional life at Mt. Holyoke, Harkness found satisfaction during these years as she moved into the inner circle of the international ecumenical movement. Her contributions at Oxford in 1937 and at Madras the following year led to her invitation to the Geneva Conference of the Board of Strategy of the Provisional Council of the World Council of Churches in July 1939. These conferences created in Harkness, at least for a short time, a triumphalistic vision of the possibilities for change that the church could make in the world, a hope that the global church could lead nations to put away their dreams of earthly power gained through military might.

At Geneva, the Board of Strategy met to consider the relationship of the churches to the international crisis with the hope that something could "yet be done to avert war in Europe . . . through a more vigorous demonstration by the churches of the power of reconciliation." The original intention had been to call a large conference, but, because German and Japanese delegates could not participate in it, the decision was made "that a small group of allegedly competent people might get farther."[17]

Georgia spelled out to Edgar Brightman the ramifications of the conference in terms of her personal participation and her hopes for the churches. "I am the only woman delegate. The responsibility nearly overwhelms me . . . it took some persuading before I decided to go. However, I approve of Roswell's [Barnes] insistence that there ought to be a woman in the group." The purpose of her presence, as was true on countless occasions, was to be the one representative of the "women of the church" alongside the twenty-nine men on the Board of Strategy!

She also summed up to Brightman her guarded optimism in 1939 of what the churches might be able to accomplish as agents of pacifism: "Inasmuch as the church seems to be the only functioning international organism, I have rather high hopes that the meeting may amount to something. At least if the churches cannot avert war I doubt if anything can."[18]

Excited by the prospects of the Geneva Conference and her role in it, Georgia then came to her real point of the letter. "Now for more personal matters," she wrote excitedly, telling Brightman about her major professional change that lay on the threshold. After teaching seventeen years in institutions for women students only, Georgia had been invited to join the faculty of Garrett Biblical Institute, a major seminary for graduate study to prepare men for ordination in mainstream Protestant churches. Located in Evanston, Illinois, on the campus of Northwestern University, Garrett was an institution of her own denomination, the Methodist Church, although it drew students from a wide range of denominations.

As students of the Chicago Training School, women also attended Garrett to prepare for Christian education work in local churches and for deaconess service in home and foreign missions. This feature was attractive to Harkness as a means of continuing her deep commitment to the professional training of women. But the opportunity to prepare church leaders for ordination was another confirmation that Georgia "Stood Number One." While other women had taught Christian education courses in seminaries, Harkness would be the first full-time woman professor of theological studies—including Christian thought, Bible, church history, and ethics—in a Protestant seminary in the United States.

Georgia ecstatically described her experience of teaching a course in the 1939 Garrett Summer School, which led to the invitation. "I doubt if I ever before made as many warm friends in four weeks as at Garrett." Her class of seventy-five students, more than one-half of the summer enrollment, gave her "a fountain pen and—believe it or not—a compact with the Seminary seal on it! The day of sex equality has arrived," she told Brightman gleefully.[19]

Her course was so appreciated that President Horace Greeley Smith received pressure from several sources to hire her.

He told her that the invitation had come at the request of Dr. Harris Franklin Rall, Professor of Systematic Theology, who would be Harkness's closest colleague, "some of the Trustees, some of the faculty, and not a few of the students." In looking back at the way in which the president phrased his words, it may be that Smith was seeking to distance himself from the appointment even when he invited her.

President Smith first asked Harkness to come at the rank of Associate Professor and a salary of $3,600, with the understanding that she would be promoted to Professor of Applied Theology, at $4,250, after one year. Georgia was prepared to accept the invitation on those terms. Brightman may have urged her to insist on a full professorship from the beginning, for the announcement of her appointment the next month stated that Harkness would begin in January 1940 as Professor of Applied Theology. This timetable enabled her to spend the fall of 1939 writing her book *The Faith by Which the Church Lives*, her Mendenhall lectures at DePauw University. Her invitation to deliver this major lectureship again marked Georgia as the first woman to speak in this annual series.[20]

In a letter to Edgar Brightman written on August 17, Georgia first shared her excitement: "My going to Garrett . . . is now all fixed up and is being announced in the *Advocate* this month or next." However, she continued by revealing the more private side of her life at that time: "Have been in such a lethargy since I got home that I shouldn't think my head would ever work again to write a book or teach theology—but it probably will."[21]

The months from August through October 1939 were a period of both exhilaration over her new teaching position and the onset of her dark night of the soul. At the end of October, she wrote in more detail of her personal condition. "I have been ill, or at least semi-well, most of the time since I got back from Europe in early August." She described the ups and downs of her physical and emotional state in a manner that would be repeated several times over the next four years: "In the last two or three weeks have recovered my former vigor. I don't know what ailed me for the doctor never found out. I lost all my pep and was in the hospital a couple weeks running a low fever every evening. It is fortunate that I was not planning to teach, for the rest has done me a lot of good."[22]

In 1952, when Georgia wrote her autobiographical sketch for the Pacific Coast Theological Group, she summed up the extended years of her "dark night" from 1939 until 1944.

> The next chapter I should gladly omit, but it is too crucial to do so. In the fall of 1939 my health, which up until this time had been invulnerable, began to crack. An illness resembling undulant fever, though as yet undiagnosed, put me in the hospital for awhile, though I got well enough to write the Mendenhall lectures for the next Spring and to begin teaching at Garrett first. My energy had been depleted by the strains of leading a double life, both public and intramural, at Mt. Holyoke and trying desperately not to neglect either set of duties. For several years thereafter, though I learned to say no to most of the invitations, it was a struggle to find energy enough for my work. This problem was rendered the more acute by the fact that in the Spring of 1940, an apparently minor injury to my spine precipitated several years of nagging pain and baffled all the specialists on whom I spent my money. This combination of low energy, a "thorn in the flesh" and frustration at "suffering many things at the hands of many physicians" plunged me into insomnia and acute depression. It was in these years that I learned what appeared in 1945 as *The Dark Night of the Soul*. The book was written as an alternative to having a nervous breakdown, and in those dark years God taught me much that I could not otherwise have learned. I do not wish to repeat them, but neither do I wholly regret them.[23]

Harkness's summary statement is in keeping with the more detailed descriptions of her depression that are found in letters written during the years of her dark night, including those to Brightman, along with one letter to friends at Christmas and another to Horace Greeley Smith. Four particular themes emerge from Georgia's descriptions of her condition in personal correspondence and public writings from the fall of 1941 until the fall of 1944: first, the complexity of physical and emotional causes; second, the need to reduce her outside speaking engagements and to get more rest; third, her continued satisfaction in teaching at Garrett Biblical Institute; and fourth, underlying and critical spiritual needs. The four themes interweave as her journey over these years unfolds.

Harkness believed that her story was "pretty completely stated in the New Testament in Mark 5:26." Like the woman with the flow of blood, Georgia had suffered many things at the hands of her physicians, spending all she had, yet never finding what ailed her. Often she was buoyant after an appointment with a specialist, believing that the cause had been found and that the cure was imminent, only to have other symptoms appear.[24]

After a genuine breakthrough diagnosis at the Mayo Clinic in the late fall of 1941, she wrote a letter to many friends who had been concerned about her illness: "During the past two years I have been prescribed for by three general practice physicians, three orthopedists, two gland specialists, two psychiatrists, a consulting psychologist, two osteopaths, a naprapath, a physiotherapist, a chiropodist, an oculist, two dentists, and a neurologist. All are experts and supposedly the best of their kind in the vicinity."

Five minutes after the Mayo doctors began her examination, Georgia continued, they discovered infected tonsils. Though half the doctors to whom she had gone previously had looked in her throat, none saw any tonsils and assumed that they were atrophied. However, the Mayo "bacteriologist with one poke on each side discovered that they were embedded and full of pus." While the Mayo physicians found other symptoms and agreed with previous doctors that menopause and nervous exhaustion also were contributing causes of her physical and emotional instability, they prescribed removal of her tonsils within the next month. Jubilant that she would soon be well, she wrote in her Christmas letter to friends, "By Easter, I am going to be a new woman."[25]

Georgia went to Palmerton, Pennsylvania, for Christmas with a brother and sister-in-law, Everett and Margaret, and had her tonsils removed. At the order of her Mayo doctors, she then spent the winter months in summer climates, getting rest and relaxation. By Easter, she was not a new woman, but she was considerably improved and returned to Evanston in late March.

On April 6, 1942, Harkness wrote to Edgar Brightman that most of the time, while on her vacation, she could not sit, stand, or lie down comfortably. She felt better since back to Evanston, "partly because getting to work has taken my mind at least partially off my pains." Work was stimulating and rewarding to Georgia, and the Garrett environment seemed the perfect setting. As she had stated to Brightman on another occasion, "I am loving my work at Garrett. The opportunities here are great. I see enough that needs to be done to stir my crusading zeal. I see no reason why I should ever wish to move again."[26]

Georgia also felt better because she had "a new orthopedist who seems to know some more than the other two dozen specialists to whom I have thus far been subjected." His diagnosis was a deep-seated case of sacro-iliac arthritis, which affected her back and feet. Indeed, the orthopedist's judgment was correct. Her back problem could not be cured, and for years to follow Harkness carried with her a pillow that she sat on everywhere she went to gain some relief from the pressure.[27]

Discouraged at being tossed to and fro by so many doctors, Georgia said wryly that she doubted that "any of them know much and I have decided I shall probably get well *if* and *when* the Lord wills!" She ended her letter to Brightman, including Easter greetings to his wife and family, with these words: "My soul gained through the withdrawal, probably more than my body. I shall probably not hereafter be able to do nearly as much writing and speaking as formerly, but I take a new and deeper delight in my Garrett teaching."[28]

Though Georgia's condition improved somewhat, the dark night was not over. Rather, it was still closing in upon her. Almost exactly one year later, on April 17, 1943, she wrote a two-and-one-half page, single-spaced, typewritten letter to President Horace Greeley Smith, asking him to relieve her of teaching responsibilities the following fall, if her condition did not improve. "Though my back is somewhat better than formerly, I feel as near to the edge of nervous collapse as at any time since the Fall of 1940." She then listed and gave a paragraph explanation of the eight reasons, as she saw them: streptococcus infection, glandular imbalance, nerve exhaustion from three years of nearly continuous pain, insomnia and too many sedatives, a complex or fixation making her feet oversensitive, too little relaxation, too much work, and finally, emotional conflicts. Her concluding point moved from emotional to spiritual causes, and bears quoting in full:

> All my emotional conflicts center in my inability to get well, or do what I could if I were well. Among them are
>   (a) humiliation at having to cancel engagements or ask favors,
>   (b) disgust with myself at doing only a mediocre job of teaching,
>   (c) mental decay from not being able to read enough to get new ideas or keep up with what is happening,
>   (d) shame at my egocentricity in being so absorbed in my body and its pains when the world is in so much greater anguish,
>   (e) spiritual defeat at not being able to trust God and live triumphantly. I feel as if my personality were disintegrating, and instead of being able to live and work with enthusiasm and zest as I once did, I endure existence. And this is no way for a Christian to be![29]

Such a candid disclosure to her employer, who held great power over her, says much about Georgia's nature. She would not have asked for a quarter's leave without highly justifiable reasons. Further, her words are a cry of agony, most poignantly revealing the depth of despair she was experiencing.

———

Georgia's psychological and physical problems fed upon and exacerbated each other. She was emotionally conflicted because she could not get rid of her physical illnesses. And her bodily ailments heightened her inward tension and fear. Worried and anxious about many things, Harkness was unable to put her physical and emotional problems into perspective and get outside of herself.

Worst of all, God seemed to withdraw from her. As her personal preoccupation mounted, Georgia realized that she was burrowing more deeply inside herself, feeling separated and isolated from God. In both her private and public writings, she described herself countless times as being spiritually defeated, bereft of God's presence in her life. The underlying cause of her dark night of the soul was spiritual depression, a sense of being cut off from God, of seeking but not finding the source of strength and support she needed most. Harkness was perfectly clear about the deepest reality of her life. At its heart, her dark night of the soul was a spiritual crisis. "And this is no way for a Christian to be!" she wrote out of the depth of her pain—physical, emotional, and spiritual.

Not surprisingly, the most overt way she dealt with the dark night of her soul, the manner in which she developed her own therapy, was by writing about her experience. She described her condition unreservedly to her closest confidant, Edgar Brightman, as was natural in the light of her previous correspondence. As in her letter to President Smith, it is amazing that Harkness could write so frankly and be so vulnerable to the vast public audience that read her books and articles. In all of her voluminous published writings of almost forty books and hundreds of articles, she is nowhere more open and passionate than in several essays, published from January 1942 until January 1944, and in *The Dark Night of the Soul*, written in the summer and fall of 1944, after she was beyond the severely debilitating effects of her spiritual depression.

These publications are best described as pastoral theology written out of Georgia's personal experience. In a letter written to Brightman on September 26, 1944, she described to him the condition of her health at this time, in which she was emerging from her long spiritual depression, and its connection to her writing of *The Dark Night of the Soul.* "As to nerves, energy and general health, I am better this fall than I have been in five years—in fact, practically cured. I see very little difference as to my coccyx"—the small bone at the base of the spinal column, consisting of several fused rudimentary vertebrae, which created her insolvable back problems. She was getting somewhat used to her "thorn" and believed that it had some compensations, she told him. "For one thing, it absolves me from sitting at meetings as much as I should otherwise think I ought to."[30]

However, her back problem had a wider significance in relationship to her new book, *The Dark Night of the Soul,* which would be published by Abingdon Press in early 1945. "It is not biographical though I should never have written it except for the coccyx," she told Brightman. "It deals with the religious aspects of nervous depression with some intimations as to what Christian faith can and cannot do for a person caught in the dark."

Georgia disclaimed the autobiographical content of *The Dark Night of the Soul.* However, when it and her preceding articles from 1942 through 1944, particularly five that were published in *The Christian Century,* are read in conjunction with her private correspondence with Brightman, Horace Greeley Smith, and friends, the autobiographical content of her published writings becomes clear. Equally significant is Georgia's reason for writing publicly about such a personal matter. Her words in her autobiographical essay to the Pacific Coast Theological Group that *The Dark Night of the Soul* "was written as an alternative to having a nervous breakdown" need to be read along with her statement of the book's purpose, in its introduction: "It is written primarily for those who have tried earnestly, but unsuccessfully, to find a Christian answer to the problem of spiritual darkness. . . . It is these unhappy ones, who not only continue on in the 'dark night' but are plunged still deeper into it by the corroding effects of failure, who are the chief object of our concern."[31]

Harkness identified the book's title as the same as that important, but by then little-read, volume by the sixteenth-century Spanish mystic St. John of the Cross. "Its theme is the sense of spiritual desolation, loneliness, frustration, and despair which grips the soul of one who, having seen the vision of God and been lifted by it, finds the vision fade and the presence of God recede."[32]

Countless persons experience spiritual bereftness or "dryness" in this as in any day, not just the mystics of the past, she continued. However, modern literature of religious therapy and psychology of religion has given little attention to the subject, and "this book stems from the conviction that the theme needs to be reopened." Harkness, who now was pioneering at the mid-twentieth century in applying theology to the daily personal issues of individuals' lives as well as to the social problems of the nation and world, decided to confront this one herself. "This study presents no final wisdom. . . . I should have preferred that the book be written by one who has had training in clinical psychology, but it has seemed better to write than to wait. The field is open, and there is room for many."[33]

Harkness wrote pastoral theology in the early 1940s, not as a licensed psychologist or psychiatrist but as a Christian layperson who knew the inseparable connection of a person's emotional and physical condition to her or his spiritual pilgrimage. In December 1941, as her correspondence with Brightman and her Christmas letter to friends document, she had suffered many things at the hands of physicians without finding out what ailed her. Encouraged by a possible breakthrough in the diagnosis of Mayo doctors, she wrote the first article, which was published in *The Christian Century* on January 14, 1942, "If I Make My Bed in Hell," reflecting on the relationship of evil to spiritual health. She also placed this article as the first chapter in *The Dark Night of the Soul*.[34]

The last word on the problem of evil from the perspective of Christian faith, she wrote, "is not to be found in a theoretical explanation but in the promise repeatedly validated in Christian experience: 'My grace is sufficient for you; my strength is made perfect in weakness.' But is it?" Georgia bluntly questioned. Is God's grace always experienced as present and as sufficient? This is the perennial and agonizing cry of faithful believers throughout the ages who have suffered and sought in vain for God's sustaining presence. Harkness succinctly described her own spiritual condition, and that of nameless others:

> Sometimes persons of deep spiritual sensitivity, earnestly desiring to trust their lives to God's keeping, find they must cry out as did our Lord, "My God, why hast thou forsaken me? . . ."
>
> Mind you, I am not talking about those persons who pray in vain to have some suffering removed, some bad situation in their homes or in the larger community corrected. What we are here considering is the more subtle and more terrible torment of sheer inability to find power in God to bear the pain or meet the situation. If one says that this never happens or that a person is really not a Christian when it happens, one reveals (pardon me for saying so) either blindness or bigotry. Or perhaps both.
>
> It is not the callous sinner who lives in this kind of hell, but the sensitive soul who is caught by the unresolved conflict of his insight and his impotence.[35]

Harkness offered no easy pious assurance to the person who experiences "this the deepest hell . . . [whose] reason tells him there are things in life to live for, but to his emotions life is meaningless and the future black." In this and future essays, however, she sought to discern ways, all of which had affinity to her own journey, in which the individual could cope with his or her spiritual depression and move toward the light beyond the dark night of the soul. Foremost, she believed, when one feels cut off from God it is a curious and paradoxical time in which to trust God more, not less. The assurance is that "this is still our Father's world." God remains in charge and will find us, even though we cannot find God.[36]

This abiding belief sustained Georgia through the traumatic periods in which she felt that God had withdrawn from her life. It was an assurance that defied reason, a dearly bought faith. From the saints and mystics of medieval and modern times, whom she began to study during her journey into the dark night of the soul, Georgia gained primary examples of intense personalities, not unlike herself, who struggled with similar seasons of spiritual barrenness. Such individuals as St. John of the Cross, Madame Guyon, George Fox, St. Teresa of Avila, John Bunyan, Evelyn Underhill, and John Woolman were among those witnesses whom she drew upon in *The Dark Night of the Soul* who were perplexed, but not unto despair, knowing that when "God is there in the dark, any darkness can be endured."[37]

As a person practices the spiritual virtue of patience, waiting for God's grace to be given in more positive ways, the redemptive character of the dark night of the soul becomes visible. Georgia's discernment reveals that she was coming to grips with her long-held faith in triumphant religion and living. To believe that God's grace is sufficient for all our needs releases a person from the strain of subjective activism and the effort to save oneself, she wrote in the summer of 1943, just three months after telling the president of Garrett Biblical Institute that she felt "spiritual defeat at not being able to trust God and live triumphantly."[38]

"Nothing burneth in hell but self-will," Georgia pondered, as she studied the words of the anonymous sixteenth-century theologian whose *Theologia Germanica* had been published by Martin Luther in 1516. The writer, unlike orthodox theologians of his day, placed the experiences of heaven and hell in this life, as well as in the next. Harkness, reading the work as a part of her own spiritual discipline, came to understand its ageless truth that our peace lies only in "the burning away of dross within ourselves," the self-aggrandizement found even in the pride of doing God's work.[39]

Now, Georgia could look back at her former spiritual goal, the striving to live triumphantly, as the "pride in being well thought of as a servant of God, satisfaction in being able to do well the works of God." It constituted a deep level of self-centeredness in which a person quested "for spiritual blessings through communion with Him, not for the love of God but for one's own satisfaction."[40]

By the time she wrote *The Dark Night of the Soul* in 1944, she had come to a new understanding of triumphal religion.

Before she worked out of a faith that human beings gained their own spiritual victory, that salvation lay in the ability to live out of high ideals. Through the redemptive experience at the heart of the dark night, Georgia now knew that the victory was in God's gracious giving of divine grace—and in human acceptance.

Central elements in Harkness's emerging theology can be drawn from *The Dark Night of the Soul:*

> The Christian gospel is not that we save ourselves by finding God. It is that God finds us and saves us when we let him. . . . It is the Christian's rightful faith that, however dark the night, God's love surrounds us. . . . When we are assured that God ceases not to love us, we can watch in patience through the night and wait for the dawn. . . . If with all our hearts we truly seek him, we can know that *God finds us* and gives rest to our souls. . . .
>
> There is one assumption without which this quest cannot be undertaken. This is that there is a way forward out of the dark. One can launch forth with much tentativeness and keep going if he believes that the goal is sure. . . . Such assurance we can have through the God revealed in Jesus Christ. It is the ultimate conviction of Christian faith that there is no situation in life where spiritual defeat is final. We may be defeated, but God cannot be. It is the message of Christianity—and has been ever since the first Easter morning—that though God's victory may be deferred it cannot be lost. . . . Across the years he speaks in Christ to say to darkened spirits in our time, "Let not your heart be troubled, neither let it be afraid." In his light we can see light.[41]

Harkness had journeyed a lifetime from 1937, when she wrote that "living in Christ, one could look the world in the face, do a mighty work, and know that nothing could daunt the soul." She addressed *The Dark Night of the Soul* to people who knew the depths of emotional depression, helping those whose souls were dark to gain religious resources to find meaning in life.

Georgia received ten times the number of letters from persons reading "If I Make My Bed in Hell," when the first chapter of the book was published in *The Christian Century,* than she had ever received regarding anything else she wrote. That article summed up their condition and helped release them for new life, they said. Harkness was an authentic witness to her words, because her dark night had been a search for purpose when the conquest of life by triumphal religion finally fell short.

"The Christian faith imparts meaning to life," she wrote in *The Dark Night of the Soul*. "A living faith that is centered in the God revealed in Christ takes our chaotic, disorganized selves, with their crude jumble of pleasures and pains, and knits them together into a steadiness and joy that can endure anything with God." Harkness was experiencing life in this new way as she emerged from her long spiritual depression. And she interpreted her own new life as the promise at the heart of the Christian faith. The meaning to which Georgia pointed lay in the cross: that "sin can be forgiven, pain overcome, by the victory of God—a victory that is both within and beyond this earthly scene. The lives of countless Christians in this and every age bear witness to power through faith that in Christ we see what life is for."[42]

Georgia journeyed deeply within herself on her spiritual pilgrimage during the early 1940s—leading her to more profoundly understand what life is for. Coming to grips with the spiritual depression at the heart of her physical and emotional problems, she realized that her inward relationship with God had been neglected. She did not confront the fragility of her personal response to God until she was forced to do so by the continued downward movement of the dark night of her soul.

Of all the mystics and saints who became her close spiritual companions, Brother Lawrence, the cook in a French monastery three centuries ago, who "did nothing more spectacular than to live a simple, radiant life of fellowship with God," was a primary mentor to her. Harkness reflected on the spiritual significance of his sixteen letters and four conversations, brought together in his classical devotional piece, *The Practice of the Presence of God*, in her last article in *The Christian Century* on how a Christian confronts spiritual depression, published on January 26, 1944.[43]

Brother Lawrence, like Georgia, went through a long period of spiritual dryness and defeat, his dark night continuing over ten years. Accepting that he might spend the rest of his life in this state of disquiet, he found himself "changed all at once; and my soul which til that time was in trouble, felt a profound inward peace, as if it had found its center and place of rest."

In her personal letters, Georgia had written candidly about her own spiritual condition as being fraught with disquietude and nervous tension, which she described in *The Christian Century* as "the curse of our time, even among Christians." Worry and frustration, due to her inability to find the underlying causes of her physical ailments and emotional trauma, heightened her level of stress and anxiety. She questioned whether it was even possible "to have such 'an uninterrupted composure and tranquility of spirit' . . . pressed as we are by many matters." Georgia realized that anxiety erected a spiritual barrier in a person's relationship with God that made it impossible for her, as well as others, to find profound inner peace.

By letting his end goal, to do everything for the love of God, determine how he lived his daily life, Brother Lawrence experienced profound inner peace. Georgia discerned that his vocational understanding was applicable to her condition, even though his life-style and environment were much simpler than hers. She internalized the deep spiritual insight that only as she responded to God with the whole of her self—meaning her inner spiritual life as well as her outward professional commitments—could she genuinely live out a calling from God.

Georgia now was able to journey outward, where she also confronted what life is for in a new way.

CHAPTER TWELVE

"Remember Me Not of That Woman!"
1943–1949

Georgia's journey into the world was transformed by the dark night of her soul, just as her inner spiritual life was radically changed. Student that she was, she had read well her Reformation forebears, including Martin Luther, John Wesley, and the Puritans. In John Calvin, she had confronted most directly their belief that a person's vocation lay in his or her particular calling to work in the world. Through her extensive work on his life and ethics several years earlier, Georgia came face-to-face with the seduction of work, and particularly the encroachment of career on the calling of a Christian in a capitalistic society.

Both the Roman Catholic and Protestant traditions held that all Christians had a general calling to respond to God with the whole of their lives. Over the years, the Roman Catholic emphasis was placed more on the heritage of the saints and mystics, that the inner spiritual life defined the vocational response of the serious Christians. The withdrawal of monks and nuns from the everyday secular work world personified what it meant to live the religious life.

Protestants, on the other hand, too narrowly equated vocation with work, the honest labor of any Christian in the world. Georgia's faith told her that she had received specific gifts for teaching in higher education in both secular and seminary settings. However, because work became synonymous with vocation in the Protestant mind, Harkness fell into the same snare as had many of her fellow Christians.

In good American fashion, she lived more immediately by adhering to the secular work ethic. Benjamin Franklin long ago expressed this American consciousness succinctly: An individual's vocation was vested in her or his occupation, and by keeping one's nose to the grindstone, success followed. Despite serious experiences of sexual discrimination in Georgia's academic life, this careerist mentality had worked for her. She had grown professionally, and by the time she came to Garrett Biblical Institute, she was making it in a man's professional world.

Georgia would not have acknowledged, nor perhaps even recognized, that she had embraced this classic American work ethic. She knew that the primary commitment of her life was to her calling from God. But, as true for countless American Christians, the careerist work ethic had insidiously undermined and encroached upon her calling from God, particularly evidenced in her continual restlessness throughout her tenure at Elmira to find another teaching position and in the unlimited amount of time she put into her work. Further, while Georgia was widely acclaimed and sought after for public engagements, close personal relationships were missing in her life. The lack of deep companionship also caused her to seek greater fulfillment and to vest more of herself in her professional commitments.

To respond to God with all of her life meant, primarily, that as her inward spiritual commitment deepened she gained proper direction for her outward journey. This general calling of all Christians penetrated through the dark night of her soul to Georgia's heart, and led her to question her particular calling to her work. Her devotional reading of *The Practice of the Presence of God* by Brother Lawrence was pivotal in her serious inner evaluation.

The maturity of faith that Georgia gained in later mid-life is best understood through the interweaving of her general and particular callings from the time she was fifty to sixty years old while she taught at Garrett Biblical Institute. In the 1940s, Georgia's inward spiritual pilgrimage enabled her to better understand what it meant to live the whole of her life as a response to God. In turn, it led her on an outward vocational journey related to her personal needs and to her work. She learned that it took more than work to respond to God with the whole of her life!

———

Georgia spent 182 pages of *The Dark Night of the Soul* discussing the relationship of the inner spiritual life to religious depression, seeking to help others find inner comfort and strength. On the final two pages, she shifted her focus, calling her readers to journey outward to relate to their close neighbors in need. "To help suffering, struggling souls find the way to God is a work to be done, not by ministers only, but by all Christians. . . . If one can do nothing else to help a troubled soul, one can treat him with understanding, sympathy, and Christian love."[1]

The "old" Georgia, the herald of triumphant living prior to her inward spiritual pilgrimage, would not have recognized the calling that she placed before her readers in the final paragraph of the book:

> In these days of despair, the most important thing that anyone can do is to refuse to be desperate and to help others to find power in God, who is our refuge and our strength. To comfort those who mourn, to give to them beauty for ashes, the oil of joy for mourning, the garment of praise for the spirit of heaviness—who has a greater task? Let no Christian think lightly of his calling.[2]

She had opened the book by expressing thanks to persons who supported and encouraged her in writing *The Dark Night of the Soul.* Two of these people particularly related to her out of the calling to bring comfort and strength to those burdened with the spirit of heaviness, helping her to find new life beyond her spiritual depression. One was Ernest Fremont Tittle, her "beloved" pastor of the First Methodist Church of Evanston, the "cathedral church" of Methodism in the Midwest. The other was Verna Miller, who became Georgia's closest companion and with whom she shared a home for the next thirty years.

Verna was an administrative secretary with a firm in Chicago. She was also a musician, playing the piano well. Attracted to the preaching of Ernest Fremont Tittle, she began to attend the First Methodist Church of Evanston in the early 1940s. This was also the time that Harkness moved to Evanston and came to the church. The two women were close in age, about fifty years old.

Murray and Dorothy Leiffer hold unique awareness of the special relationship between Georgia and Verna during the years of Harkness's "dark night," and of Tittle's part in introducing the two women.[3] The Leiffers had an office together next to Harkness's study while she was a member of the Garrett faculty. Murray taught social ethics and sociology of religion at Garrett for many years, and Dorothy offered courses in recreational leadership.

Shortly after Harkness died in 1974, Verna told the Leiffers about a significant early encounter she had with Georgia. She recalled that at the time, probably in 1943, Georgia was experiencing serious depression. At a church social gathering, Ernest Tittle spoke confidentially to Georgia, telling her, "You ought to go over and get better acquainted with that young woman over there. It is possible that living with her would be very helpful to you." A few minutes later, Georgia came over and talked with Verna. As they conversed, Georgia told her that she was tired and felt somewhat worn out. Verna invited her to her home and prepared some tea. She urged Georgia just to relax and rest a little, to take a nap while she prepared supper. "So Georgia followed that advice, stayed a bit for the evening meal, and apparently they hit it off quite well," Murray remembered from Verna's account.

Ernest Tittle saw her personal need, Murray continued: "He was obviously quite sure that it was not good for Georgia to be living too much detatched from other people. . . . When she first came here she kept much to herself." Tittle recognized Georgia's shyness and difficulty in making friends. "Georgia needed to have somebody who appreciated her and she grew to feel that it was great to have somebody who thought as much of her as Verna did. . . . Her relationship to Georgia was one of mothering, and Georgia needed that very much."

Another perspective on Georgia's and Verna's relationship is provided by Jan Shipps, now Professor of history and religious studies at Indiana University-Purdue University in Indianapolis.[4] When Jan was nineteen years old in 1950, she and her husband, Tony, moved to Evanston, Illinois, and lived in a rooming house owned by Harkness. They were from Alabama, where Tony had been teaching in a small public school. After one year of married life, Tony and Jan relocated so that he could enter the Graduate School of Northwestern University.

"We got on the Trailways Bus and rode to Chicago with everything we owned . . . we had some suitcases, a foot locker, and a couple of duffel bags, and that's all we had," Jan reminisced in 1991. After checking their belongings in a locker at the bus station in downtown Chicago, they took "the elevated train" to Evanston and proceeded to the Graduate Student Housing Office, where they rented a room in a rooming house owned by Harkness.

Georgia and Verna lived in a nice apartment complex, and Harkness owned the rooming house as an investment. After being interviewed by Georgia and Verna, the Shipps "made arrangements to rent this room and indicated that our things were at the Trailways Bus Station downtown. She and Verna said, 'Well, we will take you down and get your stuff,' " Jan remembered. "They were very pleasant, just really very nice people that were taking pity on these country folk that didn't know what was going on. But they were really astonished when they saw all of our stuff, the foot locker and the suitcases, and so forth. So getting it all in the car with four adults, and getting back to Evanston was quite a 'to-do,' even in one of the big cars of the 1950s!"

After their venturous journey from the Trailways Bus Station in the Chicago Loop to the rooming house on the edge of the Northwestern campus, Jan's and Tony's main relationship was with Verna. "It was clear that Georgia and Verna were very close friends and that Verna was kind of a business manager. She would come and collect the rent and visit, and provide a kind of oversight to be sure that we were okay. It was clear that she was handling the business of this, and that their relationship was that of a partnership." Jan remembered Verna staying to visit for a while when she came for the rent and enjoying the conversation. While they were both cordial, Verna was more engaging and easier to relate to personally. "Georgia seemed more reserved, more forbidding in appearance."

Jan Shipps's impression was borne out by students on the Garrett Biblical Institute campus during the 1940s. Dorothy Jean Furnish, now Emeritus Professor of Christian Education at Garrett-Evangelical Seminary, was working toward a Ph.D. in the Joint Northwestern/Garrett graduate program.[5] She remembered her as composed, well-organized, and highly articulate when delivering lectures in her classes. But when Harkness stepped down from the platform and talked to students informally in the hall or in her office, she was shy and awkward. She wanted to relate personally to students but found herself uncomfortable in unstructured situations.

Verna, on the other hand, was much more relaxed in social settings. Her carefree manner in mixing with people provided a needed complement to Georgia's social discomfort and awkwardness. Dorothy Jean remembered Verna and Georgia having students into their home for dessert. "Seminary pie" was a favorite recipe. During these years, Verna did most of the hostessing, both in preparing and serving the coffee and food.

By nature, Georgia and Verna were very different people. However, they fulfilled deep personal needs for companionship and caring in each other's life. "Let no Christian think lightly of his calling," Harkness wrote in concluding *The Dark Night of the Soul*. This comfort, which persons in relationships of trust bring to each other, must have been expressed very personally by Verna Miller, who saw Georgia through the traumatic period of her dark night of the soul before they shared life in brighter days. If vocation is response to God out of the fullness of one's life, the value of intimate personal relationships is at the heart of the general calling of all Christians. That quality characterized Georgia's and Verna's companionship from the beginning of their friendship.

===

Georgia's journey outward also necessitated a major reevaluation of her particular calling to work. A part of Harkness's spiritual pilgrimage throughout the 1940s lay in redefining for herself and for the world what it meant for her to be a theologian. On May 20, 1941, one and one-half years after she began her appointment as Professor of Applied Theology at Garrett Biblical Institute, Harkness received the distinction of being one of fifty-six "notably successful pioneers" chosen by the General Federation of Women's Clubs to receive a scroll of honor. In a way shocking and sobering to Georgia, the award spelled out a public perception of her identity as a theologian at the beginning of this crucial decade.

The Golden Jubilee Meeting of the General Federation of Women's Clubs was held in Atlanta in late May 1941. The awards were presented on May 20, the day on which the retiring president, Mrs. Saidie Orr Dunbar, made a stirring speech advancing the social ideals Harkness held so ardently. "We stand here, at the close of fifty years, challenged as never before to do some very straight thinking about America's position in a war torn world." She called the women to evaluate the United States national defense program, its relationships with other nations, and "the necessity of adjusting Democracy for human welfare, through safeguarding our social and educational institutions."[6]

The award from the General Federation of Women's Clubs provided the "outward recognition that, by the canons of the world, I had 'arrived,' " Georgia stated later in her autobiographical essay to the Pacific Coast Theological Group. The persons honored constituted a distinguished list of "Who's

=== 235

Who Among American Women" of the day. Among them were political leaders Frances Perkins and Jeanette Rankin, and women's rights activist Carrie Chapman Catt. From social service and education came Helen Keller, Evangeline Booth, and Mary Woolley. Representing the world of entertainment were Mary Pickford, May Robson, Kate Smith, and Ethel Barrymore. Dorothy Canfield Fisher was selected for her literary distinction and Anne Morrow Lindbergh for her aviation achievements. Georgia was duly proud to be included in such a group.

However, the interpretation that a popular church journal gave of her identity numbed Georgia's joy. "The other person in the field of Religion to be honored was Dr. Hilda Ives of New England Congregational fame, and an article in *Advance* regarding this incident spoke of us as 'Dr. Hilda Ives, great organizer and worker in the church, and Dr. Georgia Harkness, abstract theologian and retiring mystic.' "[7]

Harkness would not have seen herself as an "abstract theologian and retiring mystic." No one who read her passionately stated arguments for pacifism, world peace, and other social issues close to her heart in *The Christian Century* and similar publications could apply such a designation to her. However, another side of Georgia, the philosophical idealist, came across in the books she had written to date, such as *Conflicts in Religious Thought, The Resources of Religion,* and *The Recovery of Ideals.* The image of "abstract theologian and retiring mystic," could easily be drawn from these books.

During the 1930s, Georgia moved professionally from philosopher to theologian, but not until coming to Garrett did she gain the title of a theologian. In fact, Harkness was seeking her professional identity, deciding what kind of a theologian she wanted to be, when she joined the faculty of Garrett Biblical Institute as Professor of Applied Theology in 1940.

The title of Professor of Applied Theology was created for Georgia when she was hired at Garrett. It was appropriate for her, defining the application to practical ministry that had characterized her professionally since she began teaching at

Elmira in 1922. The term embraced Harkness's work in religious education and her strong advocacy of social justice issues, including women's rights, peace, race relations, and economic justice, which she saw as inseparably connected.

However, in the academic world of religion, a systematic theologian was a professional of full stature in the field. This person interpreted and interrelated in an ordered and formal manner the basic doctrines of the Christian faith.

When Harkness joined the faculty, Harris Franklin Rall was the distinguished and beloved Professor of Systematic Theology at Garrett Biblical Institute. He had come to the school in 1915 and was probably the most widely known member of the faculty during the second quarter of the century. Rall's contribution to Garrett was inestimable. He was deemed the major proponent of modernism on the faculty because of his approach to biblical higher criticism, in his many books on theology, and his active participation in the Methodist Federation for Social Service, which he helped to found in 1907.

Georgia espoused his rigorous brand of liberalism, growing out of the Social Gospel and in his advocacy of the ministry of the laity. It was against the background "of Biblical and creedal literalism, often joined with a 'die-hard' social conservatism in matters of racial and economic justice, that Dr. Rall for a half-century did valiant service in the cause of Christian truth as he had come to see it," Harkness wrote at the time of his death in 1964, many years after his retirement from Garrett."[8]

When Georgia came to the seminary, Dr. Rall was approaching seventy years of age, and administrators and faculty believed that he might retire at the end of that academic year. While she was negotiating her contract with President Horace Greeley Smith during the summer of 1939, she wrote two letters to Edgar Brightman, expressing her belief and anticipation that she would be selected to succeed Rall when he retired. She jubilantly shared with Brightman on July 10, 1939, her first word of the invitation to come in "Applied Theology" to Garrett. Then she continued in a confidential tone, "Dr. Smith did not say definitely that I would be Dr. Rall's successor but I think this is what it amounts to."[9]

In the second letter of August 17, 1939, Georgia again interpreted what she believed to be President Smith's unstated intention for her future at Garrett Biblical Institute. As if to justify her appointment in applied theology to herself as well as Brightman, she wrote, "It wouldn't do to call my field Systematic Theology because then the public would think I was selected to be Dr. Rall's successor."[10]

During the first several months of 1940, Harkness's letters to Brightman were filled with her happiness of being on the Garrett faculty. "We have a glorious group of students here," she wrote on January 24, near the end of her first month. "They seem to me somewhat lacking in intellectual verve, but perhaps this is because I misjudge them. . . . In any case the potentialities are great." On May 28, Georgia evaluated her first winter and spring terms on campus: "I am loving my work at Garrett. The opportunities here are great. I see enough that needs to be done to stir my crusading zeal. I see no reason why I should ever wish to move again."[11]

No mention was made by Harkness in her letters to Brightman the following year regarding a replacement for Rall in the theology field. Her correspondence during 1941 primarily concerned the worsening of her physical and emotional health and the inability of doctors to make a helpful diagnosis. Anticipating that the discovery of her infected tonsils by Mayo physicians would lead to a full cure, she expressed hope to her friends at Christmastime that "by Easter, I am going to be a new woman!"[12]

Then turning to her professional life at Garrett, Harkness wrote: "I continue to take delight in my Garrett teaching. Believing as I do that the Church is now the only real source of stability in the world, I thank God daily for the opportunity of having a part in training its leaders. Our boys and girls are of all sorts but are in earnest, and it is a spiritual tonic to be with them."

Georgia made no further comment to Edgar Brightman about the appointment to be made in systematic theology to replace Harris Franklin Rall until May 13, 1944, almost three

238

years after she had previously mentioned it. She was clear by then that the chair in systematic theology would not be offered to her, but she wrote of that reality only indirectly and in the most professional manner. Rall was teaching only two out of three quarters each year, and he probably would retire within two years, she reported to Brightman. "Whether another new person will be brought in when he retires, or whether the person who comes now will carry the work with Dr. Whitchurch and me, is yet to be decided."[13]

Harkness gave no indication to Brightman of whether she had been considered to receive Rall's chair, or whether she knew anything about the consultation between the president and the board of trustees on the appointment. She simply continued that "the Trustees wanted someone with a reputation already established, and we on the faculty want somebody who has proved his ability to teach." Her personal choice was Nels Ferré, then on the faculty of Andover-Newton Theological Seminary and a former student of Brightman at Boston University. "My prediction is that he is one of the coming 'big men' in our field," she forecast correctly! "In any case there is a real job here now, with a great opportunity, a full-sized permanent and independent chair, and a good-enough salary," Georgia wrote, committed to seeking a highly qualified colleague with whom to work.

By the spring of 1944, when Rall announced that he would retire one year hence, the search for his replacement became intense. Over the next year, Harkness and Brightman discussed possible candidates openly and candidly, with Brightman giving his honest estimate of their strengths and weaknesses. It was a difficult time to fill such a major appointment because, as Georgia put it, "all the people I can think of whom I should like to see here are already so well established in their own institutions that I doubt if they want to leave." Georgia's professional concern was that the best possible person, with whom she would work in very close conjunction, be hired. She told Brightman of one person who had taken "an unconscionably long time" to give Garrett an answer before deciding to continue in his present appointment. "It seems strange there should not be some promising candidate for so great an opportunity, but a large question mark confronts us at this point."[14]

Harkness made considerable input into the consultation process and gained significant evaluation from Brightman regarding Gerald McCulloh, the candidate who was selected by early 1946 to replace Rall. McCulloh was a young man who had taught briefly at Hamline University and was then serving as the pastor of a church in St. Paul, Minnesota. He had done work toward his doctorate at Boston University but completed his degree in Scotland because he "was not quite sure of making the grade with us," Brightman wrote on December 10, 1945. Brightman evaluated him as "vivacious, musical, cordial, a good mixer, adaptable to all sorts and kinds of people, he is a grand personality. . . . What would need to be looked into closely is his scholarship." Georgia graciously thanked Brightman "for your fine frank statement about McCulloh" when she responded four days later, indicating that she would share with President Smith "what you say about his possible academic limitations."[15]

President Smith hired Gerald McCulloh to replace Harris Franklin Rall, and McCulloh assumed the newly established Henry Pfeiffer Chair of Systematic Theology. However, he remained on the faculty only until 1953. McCulloh then moved to the staff of the Methodist Board of Higher Education, where he remained until his retirement in 1977.

The selection of McCulloh, rather than Harkness, to become Professor of Systematic Theology was a major turning point in Georgia's academic career and had a critical effect in her formation as a theologian. Interviews with some of her closest confidants while she was at Garrett Biblical Institute and in the years to follow—Henry Kolbe, Mary Durham, and Murray and Dorothy Leiffer—help to construct this pivotal episode in her professional and personal life.

Dorothy Leiffer recalled that Georgia at times would come into her office and cry, simply saying that "sometimes it is hard to be here." Murray tied these expressions directly to her interaction with Horace Greeley Smith. Though Smith had hired Harkness, he backed off in supporting her after she had been on the faculty a short time. "She was never confident of her relationship to President Smith," Murray Leiffer explained.

> Horace Smith was never too sure of his relationship with women, even though he was a married man, and Edith and he loved each other and were most complementary in the idea of each supplementing and strengthening the other. . . . On more than one occasion he would show both exceeding deference toward women, and I would not say a feeling that they are subordinate, but that men and women played separate roles. . . . He remarked to me on more than one occasion that Georgia would like to have it both ways: She wants to have every privilege that goes with being a regular full member of the faculty on par with all the others, but she also wishes to have special deferences shown to her. . . . It was a lack of clarity of definition of being a woman on an all male or predominantly male faculty and how she adjusted to that role, in part.[16]

Mary Durham saw the problem in President Smith's inability to accept a woman in a peer relationship with men. Georgia did not share the strain she experienced with Smith directly with the Leiffers, her professional colleagues. However, she unburdened herself more intimately to Mary Durham, a trusted confidante outside the Garrett community. Durham graphically portrayed the way in which Smith's attitude toward Georgia changed in the early 1940s.

> She came down to my house and just unburdened herself and cried. He said to her that she would never get more salary. She would just stay at the same salary although the men were being increased. He said that he hadn't wanted to have a woman on his faculty and didn't like having a woman on his faculty. . . . You just felt so badly because there was always a little essence of loneliness in Georgia. . . .
>
> I don't think that any of the faculty had any animosity to Georgia. They enjoyed her. She was one of them. I think it was only the president, but that is hard to take when it is the president, when he says you won't get any better salary and so forth. And when he controls all that. . . .
>
> I think that being a woman was the base. He would have accepted the pacifism in a man perhaps. He had a bunch of

them, like Rockwell Smith and Murray Leiffer, on the faculty. But her popularity, I think, was one of the troubles with the president. The boys apparently always wanted her courses.[17]

Georgia had the security of tenure, so there was never a question that she might lose her position at Garrett. But President Smith could keep her from receiving salary increases that he was giving to other faculty members. While the faculty as a whole was of high caliber and several were distinguished, Georgia had the widest national and international reputation of any of her colleagues.

Further, Smith had the final jurisdiction regarding the hiring of faculty. Murray Leiffer indicated that to his knowledge the issue was never raised that Georgia might become professor of systematic theology. If the president had given Georgia some implied but unspoken expression that she would receive the position when Rall retired, the dream lived only in Georgia's mind. Henry Kolbe's observation confirms her early comments to Brightman that she anticipated receiving the position and that she was deeply hurt in not being granted it.

Kolbe, now deceased, was a student of Harkness in his Bachelor of Divinity program, became her first Ph.D. candidate, and returned to the seminary a third time in 1951 to teach Christian ethics. Kolbe assumed courses that Harkness had taught and carried on much of her theological tradition when Georgia resigned to become a member of the faculty of Pacific School of Religion in that year. They remained friends until her death. Martha Scott, who interviewed Kolbe when writing her doctoral dissertation on Georgia Harkness in 1984, summed up his judgment: "Georgia Harkness was clearly overlooked. She assumed that President Smith understood 'applied' theology to be inferior to 'real' theology or systematics. She took this personally, judging that a woman could be an applied theologian because it was inferior. However, when it came to systematics, even a man with no teaching experience was better than a woman. She never quite forgot it."[18]

The immediate implications of Georgia's outpouring to Mary Durham point to heavy-handed sexism in the way

Horace Greeley Smith exerted his presidential power over her. And the wider reflections of persons who knew Smith and Harkness confirm the injustice involved and her feelings of hurt.

Georgia obviously held unrealistic expectations regarding her professional future at Garrett. She may have read too much into Smith's ambiguous expressions to her when she was hired. From the beginning, he probably felt unsure about his own pioneering stance as a seminary president in hiring a woman in a full-time tenured faculty position. Further, as time elapsed, her escalating national and international reputation and her increasing popularity on campus bore on him in ways he did not anticipate initially. In Smith's mind, Harkness must have constituted such a threat to the long-established order of male dominance that he drew back his original support of her.

Whether Smith would have named Georgia to succeed Harris Franklin Rall if she had been a man is only speculation. But one wonders, considering the major concern of the trustees and the president to gain a person of established national stature. Further, the candidate hired would become the first person to hold the newly established Henry Pfeiffer Chair of Systematic Theology, increasing the need to gain a professor who already had earned distinction. The prolonged search to fill the chair failed to produce that candidate. The most that could have been hoped in hiring Gerald McCulloh was that he held such promise.

Georgia may have been overly sensitive to the way Smith, as an authority figure, related to her. Some persons who knew her believed that her ego ruffled too easily. However, she was moving in uncharted territory as almost a sole woman in a male-dominated profession. Murray Leiffer reported that President Smith claimed Harkness wanted it both ways, expecting to receive special privileges because she was a woman but at the same time desiring to be treated like "one of the boys." Leiffer saw the problem in the lack of definition of how a lone woman could function in a man's world.

Though she maintained a professional stance and never mentioned it in public or professional settings, the denial of the professorship in systematic theology came as a heavy blow to Harkness. As her past history demonstrates, Georgia had a strong need both for a God-given, useful purpose in her life and for public affirmation. Her feelings of rejection and humiliation regarding her professional status at Garrett could only have intensified the downward movement of the dark night of her soul.

That Harkness did not become Henry Pfeiffer Professor of Systematic Theology at Garrett Biblical Institute had positive, long-range consequences in her life and in the institution's, despite its immediate negative effects. One of Georgia's strongest inner qualities was resilience. When it was clear that the position would not be hers and that a serious search was at hand for a candidate outside the institution, she unstintingly sought the best possible replacement for Rall in systematic theology. Further, she began to reconceive her professional identity of what it meant for her to be an applied theologian. In significant measure, the consequential upward turn out of the dark night of her soul was due to the way in which Georgia gained a new vocational vision of her work.

At no point in Harkness's life is the therapy of writing more dramatically evidenced than during the late 1930s and the 1940s. Through her journal articles, published by the time she came to Garrett Biblical Institute, Georgia established the vital connection of applied theology to social justice. However, her entire university education in philosophy, and particularly her dissertation on the social ethic of T. H. Green, trained Harkness to think systematically about the nature of God and the created order. Then, on his deathbed, Georgia's father asked her to "write more about Jesus Christ," words that she received as "an edict from the eternal realm." Publication of *The Dark Night of the Soul* in 1945, and her preceding articles in *The Christian Century* and other journals, marked her crucial upturn in coming to terms with the spiritual grounding of her emotional depression.

In her unique way, Georgia put together these strands of theology, social justice, and spirituality to become an applied/systematic theologian of the *laos*, the whole people of God. Three books, published by Abingdon and Abingdon/Cokesbury in the succeeding years of 1947, 1948, and 1949, as well as a host of articles on related subjects during the latter half of the decade, constitute a declaration of Georgia's mature identity as a theologian. Her books *Understanding the Christian Faith, Prayer and the Common Life,* and *The Gospel and Our World* demonstrate the movement in her life from a philosophical idealist to an evangelical liberal theologian.[19] And as a seminary professor for the last twenty-two years of her teaching career, her purpose was to train clergy to communicate to laypersons, relating in nonacademic language to their world and their needs.

The first of the trilogy, *Understanding the Christian Faith,* was published in 1947 and remained in print for over forty years, longer than any other book Harkness wrote. In the opening page of the introduction, she defined the theological purpose that guided her until she died in 1974. "In the churches it is the layman, not the theologian in the seminary or even the minister, who is the ultimate consumer for whom churches exist."[20] With these words, Harkness became one of the first professional Christians of the mid-twentieth century to commit herself to reevaluating and revaluing the place of the laity in the church and their purpose in the world.

Theology "is a systematic attempt to understand what God is and does, how he is related to the world and to ourselves," she continued. "Everywhere are persons—some who are Christians, others interested inquirers—who would seriously like to know what a Christian may believe about God, and Christ, and prayer, and sin, and suffering, and salvation, and death, and destiny. It is for these that this book is written." The book's purpose was to set forth "the basic Christian convictions for the *lay,* and not for the *lame,* mind."[21]

The major problem confronting the church at the mid-twentieth century was the widening chasm between the church and the world, between what is preached and professed in the churches on Sundays, and the vital interests and activities of the laity during the week. In tones familiar to the evangelical heritage of her childhood, Georgia asked confrontational questions in *The Gospel and Our World:* "What are the churches trying to say? Has the Church a message with which really to confront the world? Does the layman or the student hear in the church what can 'speak to his condition'? Does the Christian gospel have in it that which can arrest and alter life? In short, has the gospel any power?"[22]

Harkness was convinced that the gospel had power. But the churches, and particularly the ministers, were not doing the job they were called to do. In evangelical tones, she cut to the core of the problem: "What then ails our churches? Inadequate numbers, unhealthy divisions, meager financial support, unprophetic leadership, lethargic congregations— all these and many more symptoms of ill health are found. But at the root of them all lies the fact that the very thing for which the Church exists—the proclamation of the gospel— is being in our time so feebly done."[23]

Powerful communication of the gospel—"the most important task under God that any person can undertake"—was seriously lacking in the churches. Because people did not understand the basic principles of Christian belief, the faith could not speak effectively to their needs nor mobilize them to address the needs of the world.[24] The primary purpose of Harkness's vocation as a mature theologian, and as enunciated in all three books, was to communicate the Christian faith powerfully and radically. She also committed herself to write in language that was not technical and that the non-professional theologian could understand.

Harkness was calling the churches to make a closer connection between theology and evangelism. The Christian faith was something both to be believed and to be lived, she contended. As theology, the faith constituted all the inherited body of Christian belief that needed to be reexamined and reinterpreted for personal and societal needs in every age. As evangelism, the faith meant the power of God to bring salvation to both individuals and the world, to reconcile them both to God. Theologians too often had been abstract and afraid to speak simply, while evangelists too often had addressed their message to people's hearts and not to their minds.[25]

Harkness saw herself in the late 1940s as a theologian seeking to help people understand Christian beliefs systematically in order that their lives and the life of society might be changed. Belief and action were separate aspects of the Christian gospel, but they needed to interact radically. Georgia knew she was equipped to appeal to people's minds, so that they could understand the reasonable truth of the Christian faith. As they comprehended the faith intellectually, their wills and their life commitment in turn would be changed.

From this stance, Harkness cogently stated her theological position as an evangelical liberal:

> Open always to more truth from whatever source it comes, suspending judgment when necessary till relative certainty emerges, resolved to live by the truth one has and to let others differ if their insights lead in another direction, one combines tolerance with decisiveness, open-mindedness with Christian conviction. Such an attitude leads both to knowledge and to power. The greatest word ever spoken about the pursuit of truth is the word of Jesus, "Ye shall know the truth, and the truth shall make you free."[26]

Liberalism, she pointed out, "rightly emphasizes breadth of vision, with humility, tolerance, openness to new truth as fundamental." Georgia did not believe that philosophy, theology, the Bible, Christian experience, and science approached truth in inherently contradictory ways. She trusted in their ultimate harmony. Out of this conviction, she stated that her book *Understanding the Christian Faith* "is not for the curiously critical. It is for the open-minded seeker who, not expecting all mysteries to be revealed, is willing to live by the light he has while he seeks for more."[27]

Georgia clearly recognized both the strengths and the deficiencies of the liberal tradition. Its strength, as evidenced in the Social Gospel, lay in pointing out the range of social sins and arousing "something of a conscience over such matters as mass exploitation, child labor, race discrimination, preventable disease, and indiscriminate killing in war, which our fathers less often thought of as sin."[28]

However, as liberalism widened the scope of sin to the evils of society, its emphasis on personal rebellion against God receded into the background. Neoorthodoxy correctly called liberals to task for their complacency. But while neoorthodoxy refocused on the personal state of pride and rebellion, it gave little attention to the specific sins for which individuals are accountable. Further, neoorthodoxy gave inordinate attention to God's judgment without adequately recognizing divine grace and the acts of love persons need to perform to bring in a better world. "The only corrective," Harkness stated persuasively, "is the preaching and teaching of a broader, deeper, more incisive doctrine of sin, and with it the ever-present resources of God for its mastery."[29]

As an applied/systematic theologian, Georgia's explicit purpose was to address the inner life of the individual and the outer life of society. Lack of a clear understanding of the Christian faith had meant, first, that "many people can no longer pray because to them a personal God means an old man with a beard (visually conceived as a mixture of Moses, Santa Claus, and Father Time), and this God of their childhood has evaporated with nothing in its place but an impersonal principle."[30]

Prayer and the Common Life could be described both as a systematic theology of prayer, methodically laying out the foundations, methods, and fruits of prayer, and as a devotional guide on how to live the life of prayer. Many people do not know how to pray, how to offer "up our desires unto God, for things agreeable to His will."[31] Georgia's purpose in the book was simply to describe different kinds of prayer and ways of praying, in order to help people learn how to direct their wills, in the ordinary round of their daily lives, to God's purposes.

However, basic instruction in learning to pray was meant to enable the reader to live a *life* of prayer, or in the language of vocation, to live one's whole life as a response to God. Without prayer, there was no likelihood that a person could resolve the competing desires and anxieties in his or her life, a truth to which no one could better witness than Georgia herself. As one grew in the life of prayer, or in seeking God's purpose for one's life, that person also was led toward the promise of spiritual victory, the ability to claim God's grace as the sufficient and sustaining power for a meaningful existence.

As an applied/systematic theologian, Georgia always related to the condition of society, as well as the inner needs of the individual. Again, she addressed the issue in terms of a lack of clear understanding of the Christian faith, which "stands in the way of an effective attack on the evils of our society. Laymen make the greater part of the political, economic, and social decisions on which human destinies depend. There are enough Christian laymen in the world to establish 'peace on earth, good will among men' if laymen understand the Christian gospel and act upon it."[32]

In helping people understand the foundations of their faith, Harkness sought for them to apply their theology to their ethics, to their judgments on the most vital social issues of the day: "The control of atomic energy, treatment of vanquished enemies, peace-time conscription, the settlement of labor disputes, the right of the Negro to fair conditions of employment." Because ministers failed to apply principles of the gospel to such issues as these, the laity who worked in the secular world fell prey to opinions generated in the newspaper, the radio, and casual conversation.[33]

Faithful to her heritage of the Social Gospel, Harkness worked for social salvation, "the coming of the Kingdom of God in our day," by bringing spiritual resources to bear upon the needs of society. The Christian could not separate inward piety from outreach for the welfare of the world. In *Prayer and the Common Life,* she developed the social implications of the life of prayer.

Without the spiritual and moral resources which prayer exists to heighten, the action required for dealing with such issues is likely to go on being as limited and as misdirected by self-interest as we now see it. . . . A major reason why the world is now on the brink of the abyss . . . is that there has been no general openness of life to direction and power of God, and hence no general acceptance of responsibility for doing "the things of peace."[34]

Until now, Harkness contended, this understanding of the centrality of spiritual direction to the life of society, as well as to the individual, had been stated almost exclusively by religious leaders. As World War II ended, that call "for remaking the human spirit" was also being stated by scientists, journalists, statesmen, and even military leaders.

The words of General Douglas MacArthur, spoken in Tokyo Bay in reflection upon the bombing of Hiroshima, bore powerfully on Georgia's pacifist witness: "We have had our last chance. . . . The problem basically is theological. . . . It must be of the spirit if we are to save the flesh." Similarly, she dwelt upon the statement of Albert Einstein when he chaired the Emergency Committee of Atomic Scientists: "Science has brought forth this danger, but the real problem is in the minds and hearts of men."[35] This summons reached to the core of Harkness's hope, as an applied theologian of the evangelical liberal persuasion, that as people understand the Christian faith their hearts and minds will be moved to bring the gospel to bear upon the world.

She never raised a fundamental question regarding the liberal tradition. If people know the intellectual truth of the faith, will they naturally live out of those convictions? Georgia posited that as minds are changed, actions also will be changed as well. Real life experience calls this philosophical ideal into serious question.

———

One of the most important consequences emerging from Georgia's spiritual pilgrimage during the 1940s was the inner peace she gained both with her professional identity as an applied theologian and with her personal life as well. Don Williams, a student of Harkness who graduated in 1948, summed up the satisfaction she expressed in her characteristically logical manner and with a twinkle in her eye, that "she had the most important job in the world."

> If the world is to be saved, it will be by the influence of the Church, and the strongest part of the Church . . . is the American Church. She felt that the Methodist Church led the Christians of America in its influence for social good and, within the denomination, the training offered by its seminaries was the critical point. Of these seminaries, Garrett Biblical Institute was the largest. Theology is the heart of the curriculum, and applied theology the place where this discipline comes to bear on the needs of the world. Therefore, the professor of Applied Theology in Garrett held the most important job in the world![36]

But Karl Barth, the giant of systematic theologians of the twentieth century, could not so affirm Georgia Harkness and her vocation as an applied theologian. She loved to tell the story of their fateful encounter at the 1948 organizing meeting of the World Council of Churches:

> With a few other men, Karl Barth chose to participate in the section on the Life and Work of Women in the Churches. At the beginning of the discussion Sarah Chakko, the Chairman, asked me without warning to state its theological basis. I said briefly that in the O.T. it is stated that both male and female are created in the image of God; in the N.T. Jesus assumed always that men and women were equal before God, and in our Christian faith is the chief foundation of sex equality. Barth claimed the floor; said that this was completely wrong; that the O.T. conception of woman is that she was made from Adam's rib and the N.T. that of Ephesians 5, that as Christ is the head of the Church, so man is the head of woman. Then followed a lively interchange in which I did little but to quote Gal. 3:28, but the room buzzed. Barth convinced nobody, and if I have been told he was trying to have some fun with the women, his joke back-fired. A year later when a friend of mine asked him if he recalled meeting a woman theologian from America, his cryptic reply was, *"Remember me not of that woman!"* [37]

Barth's words demonstrated the inherent weakness of systematic theology when beliefs are stated abstractly, even by

$=251$

brilliant thinkers, and not applied directly to personal and social conditions. One of the ways in which Garrett-Evangelical Theological Seminary wrote the practice of theology into its institutional commitments was by establishing a lasting tribute to its pioneer woman professor. The Georgia Harkness Chair in Applied Theology, held now by Rosemary Ruether, was endowed in 1975. The chair particularly distinguishes a quality that women may bring to seminary teaching today by closely relating theological inquiry to issues of social justice, pastoral care, and the practice of ministry.

For Georgia herself, Barth's recollection simply confirmed what she already knew: She had found her rightful vocation of work by applying theology to the critical life issues of the day "for such a time as this"!

VII: "A Hardy Perennial"

CHAPTER THIRTEEN

"To Plant My Roots Anew" *1950–1961*

*L*ate in 1950, Harkness had another historic encounter with distinguished male colleagues. She was the one woman on the Commission of Christian Scholars appointed to consider the moral implications of obliteration bombing and the use of hydrogen bombs for mass destruction. This encounter and the one with Karl Barth pointed to the same underlying reality: One visionary woman spoke a word of prophetic truth to the premier male theologians of the Western world.

If one picture tells a story better than a thousand words, it is the photograph of this Commission, selected by the Federal Council of Churches of Christ in America, when it met for a weekend in the fall of 1950 at the Princeton Inn. The photo of the "Dun Commission," as it was called for short, shows Georgia Harkness standing in the front row surrounded by nine men.[1]

On Harkness's right is Reinhold Niebuhr, of Union Theological Seminary in New York, and immediately in back of her are Robert Calhoun of Yale Divinity School and Paul Tillich of Union. To her left are Angus Dun, Bishop of the Washington, D.C., Diocese of the Episcopal Church and also the Chair of the Committee, and John Bennett of Union Seminary. Other distinguished ecumenical church leaders who complete the picture are Chester I. Bernard, Edwin Aubrey, Peter K. Emmon, and George F. Thomas. Almost as tall as the men and of stocky frame, Harkness was "appropriately" dressed in her man-tailored suit and "sensible" shoes. Even though she stands out in the picture because she is the lone woman and is wearing a skirt, she also seems to "fit" among the group's membership. The picture captures the fundamental reality of Harkness's professional life: She was one woman, well-rooted but standing alone, in a male academic world.

The Committee's report was entitled "The Christian Conscience and Weapons of Mass Destruction," and its presentation was virtually the last act of the Federal Council before it merged with the National Council of Churches. The document was issued at the end of 1950, just six months after the United States entered the Korean War, which would drag on until 1953. John Bennett, Professor of Theology and Ethics at Union Theological Seminary in 1950 and its president from 1963 until 1970, wrote the report. Forty years later, bright and alert at age ninety-one, Bennett looked back on the scene of the Dun Commission's meeting. It was early in the Cold War, and people in the West were afraid that the Soviet Union might invade Western Europe using conventional weapons. "One of the big issues we discussed was whether or not the churches should say that no nuclear weapons should ever be used as a first strike."[2]

On this most crucial issue of the use of nuclear weapons for first strike, the Committee report read:

> Unhappily we see little hope at this time of a trustworthy international agreement that would effectively prevent the manufacture or use of weapons of mass destruction by any nation. This should not prevent us from the search for such an agreement, perhaps as a part of a general disarmament program, and for a restoration of mutual confidence that would make an agreement possible and effective.
>
> As long as the existing situation holds, for the United States to abandon its atomic weapons, or to give the impression that they would not be used, would leave the non-com-

munist world with totally inadequate defense. For Christians
to advocate such a policy would be for them to share responsibility for the world-wide tyranny that might result. We
believe that American military strength, which must include
atomic weapons as long as any other nation may possess
them, is an essential factor in the possibility of preventing
both world war and tyranny.

If war should come out of the tragic and precarious situation in which we stand, what should Christians decide con-
cerning the use of weapons of mass destruction? Here again
we find *no absolute law* that can be binding in all conceivable circumstances. If atomic weapons or other weapons of
parallel destructiveness are used against us or our friends in
Europe or Asia, we believe that it could be justifiable for
our government to use them in return with all possible
restraint.[3]

The Commission's action, John Bennett further clarified,
was not designed to "speak *for* the churches, but to speak *to*
the churches." Eight members of the Commission agreed
that the churches should sanction "the alternative of using
nuclear weapons" if the United States military and govern-
mental commanders saw this action as necessary. Georgia
Harkness and Robert Calhoun stood outside this consensus.
"I think they were the only two members of the commission
who were absolute pacifists," Bennett stated.[4]

The final report recognized Harkness's and Calhoun's
position as a minority view on the Commission in these
words:

We believe that God calls some men to take the way of non-
violence as a special and high vocation in order to give a clearer witness to the way of love than those can give who accept
responsibility for the coercions in civil society. We rejoice
that God has called some of our brethren in the universal
Christian fellowship to bear this witness and are humbled by
the faithfulness of many in bearing it. Without minimizing
the moral heroism it can require, we are even envious of the
greater inner simplicity of that non-violent way.

But most of us find ourselves called to follow a course
which is less simple and which appears to us more responsible because more directly relevant to the hard realities of our

situation. And we believe it is the way in which most Christians must go. . . .

In the last resort we are in conscience bound to turn to force in defense of justice even though we know that the destruction of human life is evil. . . . Today, two great dangers threaten mankind, the danger that totalitarian tyranny may be extended over the world and the danger of global war. Many of us believe that the avoidance of both may involve us in policies which carry the risk of global war.[5]

From the vantage point of 1990, John Bennett continued to reflect upon the position held by his two colleagues on the Commission, Georgia Harkness and Robert Calhoun. "I thought I was an absolute pacifist myself. But I thought that the surest way of preventing the use of nuclear weapons was to prevent a war. And I believed that having a deterrent, which would involve the possible use of nuclear weapons against an opponent with conventional weapons from the East, would provide the surest safeguard against another global conflict."[6]

However, Bennett later interpreted this as a short-sighted position to be held by a leader in the church and a Christian ethicist. "By the 1970s, I would have taken the same position that Georgia and Bob Calhoun did. I would have said that no one should have the responsibility for initiating a nuclear war regardless of the issues, regardless of the cause involved. I would still say that."

Only one year after the Commission's report was issued in 1950, Harkness took "A Second Look at the Dun Report" in *The Christian Century*. She maintained that it "is not possible to give a precise blueprint for Christian action." To be consistently ecumenical, the Commission should have stated that a variety of views are held by Christians but "no Christian consensus." Georgia continued by responding to her colleagues on the committee and to the churches at large out of an unqualified prophetic stance of non-violent direct action. Christians can agree on one underlying ethical principle: "It is possible to say unequivocally that loving concern for persons—not 'us' or 'our friends' only but all persons—is for the Christian an absolute duty." There are many things that Christians can do to express that concern for all

God's people. But when they propose means of combatting an international aggressor, let that be "called military expediency and not Christianity."[7]

―――

At the time of the Dun Commission's meeting, Georgia and Verna Miller were settling into their new life in Berkeley, California. After serving as Professor of Applied Theology on an otherwise all-male faculty at Garrett Biblical Institute for eleven years, Georgia assumed the same position, again among all men, on the faculty of Pacific School of Religion. She retired from there in 1961 at age seventy. Her imagery captures the profound significance to her of this move—geographically, professionally, and personally: "I decided to tear up my roots in Evanston and plant them anew in Berkeley."[8]

As late as October, 1949, Harkness was firmly committed to remaining at Garrett Biblical Institute. In a letter she wrote to Edgar Brightman, the last one extant in the Brightman papers at Boston University, she sought to clear up the rumor that she was ill and was leaving Garrett. Though her back problem probably always would be "a thorn in the flesh," her general health was excellent and her back bothered her less than it once had.[9] The small pillow that Georgia carried to sit upon wherever she went was a trademark by now!

After giving the Earl Lectures at Pacific School of Religion in February 1949, out of which grew *The Gospel and Our World*, Harkness was invited by President Ronald Bridges to join the faculty. "I considered it very carefully," she told Brightman. However, "I received here [at Garrett Biblical Institute] such a barrage of protest from the President and my colleagues that they and my own good judgment persuaded me to stay here. I am going out to P.S.R. for the Winter Quarter. I originally thought of this as probably a trial period, but it is now clear in my mind that I shall be returning here, probably to remain until I retire."

Her decision was short-lived. While teaching at PSR during the winter of 1950, she was again asked to become a member of the faculty. "She wanted to stay on at Garrett," Murray Leiffer recalled. However, the time away from a cold Evanston winter persuaded her that her health would be better served if she were in another climate during the winter quarter. Leiffer continued that Harkness

> hoped that Garrett would let her continue as a full-time or at least as a regular member of the faculty on the basis of teaching in the autumn and spring. This was a matter for faculty discussion. Dr. [Horace Greeley] Smith talked with me about it and a question of precedence came up. It was agreed that we would be glad to have her stay if she would also be available for winter quarter when we tended to have our heaviest enrollment. But if she did not wish to be here in the winter quarter then it would be better for her to come back as a visiting professor.[10]

Because the Garrett president and faculty feared in 1950 that a reduced schedule might set a questionable precedent regarding other faculty who might desire special contracts, Harkness decided to become a member of the faculty of Pacific School of Religion. President Smith could have taken Georgia's request as a means of developing a more flexible policy toward senior faculty who were nearing retirement. Instead, he probably viewed it as Harkness's means of seeking preferential status.

If Georgia felt personally hurt, she did not acknowledge it publicly. She left Garrett on cordial terms and returned many times to teach, not only during the summer school but also during other quarters, and to present the distinguished Rall Lectures. That she gave her large collection of private and public papers to Garrett Seminary, and that Murray and Dorothy Leiffer catalogued the fourteen-box collection, attests to her life-long bond with the theological school and the Leiffers.

Georgia more candidly laid out her reasons for making the move in a long personal letter to Everett and Margaret, her brother and sister-in-law in Pennsylvania, on March 26, 1950. Writing from her apartment at 1864 Sherman Avenue in Evanston, she explained that "I thought it through from every angle and decided I should go":

(1) there is nowhere near so much theological or religious leadership out there as in the East or Middle West, the people are hungry for it, and I think I could do something of a pioneering missionary job,

(2) life at the school is much more leisurely than here, with lighter teaching schedules, fewer students to teach, less folderols to eat up the time, more chance to get some writing done, and I will be expected to teach only two quarters out of the three of the school year so it would be sort of like a perpetual sabbatical in my spare quarter,

(3) everything is so beautiful and the climate so balmy and invigorating that we both felt like new women out there. I did not see much difference in my back but I had so much pep and so little fatigue that I felt as if years had rolled off me, in spite of the fact that I made a lot of speeches and kept pretty busy.[11]

More than thirty years earlier, while an undergraduate student at Cornell University, Georgia took the Student Volunteer Movement pledge that if it were God's will, she would become a foreign missionary. In 1950, to "do something of a pioneering missionary job" was still the focus of Georgia's vocational vision. Her theological leadership was needed in the West, and the atmosphere in which to exert that influence felt vital and refreshing to her.

Work remained at the center of her life. However, Georgia at fifty-nine years of age was beginning to conceive a fuller vocational understanding. She was no longer trying to prove herself professionally. Now, she consciously sought to create a more humane balance among her professional commitments to teaching, writing, and serving the ecumenical church. The opportunity to teach in a smaller seminary and to cut back her teaching load to two instead of three quarters each year with "more chance to get some writing done" and "less folderols to eat up the time" was inviting to Georgia.

If her whole life was meant to be a response to God, Georgia realized that she needed to mercifully scale down her professional responsibilities and care for herself. For the first time in her life, Georgia was not moving alone. "Verna will go to California with me, though it means quite a break for her in giving up her tenure and security," she continued to

Margaret and Everett. Even before they moved to Berkeley, Verna was warmly welcomed into the community of Pacific School of Religion. She was given strong hopes for a job in the Business Office of the School, but until something more permanent developed she would take whatever job she could find. "I hesitated to urge Verna to make the break and she has spells of thinking she won't but in general she wants to. She hates the job where she is and she loved Berkeley as much as I."

Georgia's enthusiasm for the new venture is found in her description of their new apartment:

> We were given our choice of any apartment we wanted in an apartment house for married students next to the School, and chose the one on the third floor because it has a marvelous view of the Golden Gate, the Bay Bridge, the lights of Berkeley in the evening, and the sunsets over the Pacific. We hope you come to see us! It is a little smaller than what we have here, but has four rooms with a good-sized living-room and bed-room facing the West, kitchen with dinette, and a smaller room which can be either a second bed-room or study. After we have been there a while and have a chance to look around, I think I will take what I get from my real estate here and buy a five or six room house, for I do not expect to move again and might as well be comfortable. Many of my friends have houses on the hill with marvelous views, and it just lifts one's soul to have this beauty to look out on. The two apartments I am selling should nearly buy one.

As a practical part of tearing up her roots in Evanston, Georgia offered for sale the two apartments and the rooming house she owned there. She expected little trouble in selling the apartments, since desirable housing was scarce. If the rooming house did not sell, she would keep it and hire someone to manage it. Since she did not intend to move again, it would be worth taking the time to find the most desirable home in which to settle permanently.

Toward planting her roots anew in Berkeley, she had turned in her "old Plymouth this past week, which was getting to the point of needing quite a little money for repairs, and bought a new hydramatic six-cylinder Pontiac." In wonder over her new car, Georgia explained that "it has a 'low' for going up and down hills, which Berkeley is full of, but otherwise the automatic shift will greatly simplify the driving. We expect to drive West in it!"

When weighed in the balance, there were more reasons to go to Berkeley than to stay in Evanston. "Dr. Smith offered me pretty near the world with a fence around it to stay here," she said, though she gave no indication what those benefits might have been. "But I can't work up any enthusiasm to stay or feel any great sense of regret at leaving. I will of course hate to leave a good many of my friends, but feel as if I already have a good many warm ones on the Coast."

Georgia undoubtedly remembered her initial excitement after teaching summer school at Garrett before joining the faculty more than ten years earlier. "Of course, I know the people out there won't continue to make such a fuss over me when my presence gets to be an old story, but I think the people there are in general more warm-hearted and less smug than here, as well as religiously more open to whatever one can give them."

———

Georgia blossomed in West Coast soil. At age fifty-nine, she had entered older adulthood, a period of maturation when a person should be fully developed in natural growth. A wisdom that comes with experience is reserved for later life and is recognizable in some individuals by their sixth decade. However, older adults can also conceive new life, when, in the words of James Fowler, "freed from the burden of justifying their lives with their works . . . they have the internal freedom to take new risks and to initiate new roles and projects."[12]

Significant persons who live in Berkeley and Claremont, California, in the 1990s, were closely connected with Georgia during the 1950s. They provide intimate and discerning insights into Harkness, both as a personal and a professional woman, and into the paradoxical qualities of gaining maturity and conceiving new life that characterized her while she was on the faculty of Pacific School of Religion.

"I'd say she was very much at peace with herself by then. Whatever struggles she had gone through, I think she probably had come to accept who she was," stated Helen Von Rohr, the wife of Georgia's former colleague at PSR, John Von Rohr.[13]

Helen's words pose this question: Who was Georgia Harkness after she planted her roots anew in Berkeley when she was almost sixty years old? From the memories of people who knew Georgia well during the 1950s, a highly consistent picture takes form.

"I encountered her right from the beginning as an aloof, analytical, rational scholar in a warm, caring, compassionate person," stated Wayne Rood, Emeritus Professor of Religious Education, who was on the faculty from 1952 until 1981. His two characterizations capture the essence and the paradox at the heart of Georgia's being.[14]

Rood told the story of a Presbyterian woman who came to PSR as a student "because she had read Dr. Harkness, and was deeply impressed with her spirituality. She had read *The Dark Night of the Soul*, no doubt. In class she found a very rational methodical teacher, whose lectures were systematic, organized, and learnable. Then the student said, 'By the time Dr. Harkness had finished dealing with a subject, there was no mystery left about anything.' "

Analyzing the student's response, he continued: "It says something about Georgia's whole scholarly method. You can learn the data and the details and give them back on an examination. I wondered when students would sometimes complain about her courses whether Georgia brought with her a functional stereotype of what a lecturer in systematic theology should be like." Rood felt that from somewhere Harkness had acquired an idea of what a systematic theology lecture ought to sound like, what a professor of theology should be dealing with, and how theology should be done. Her lectures were highly organized and never deviated from an outline form of 1, 2, 3, and a, b, c. While some students appreciated the clarity of her presentations, others described them as cold and rote. "That was the style when she did her graduate work, and still is with many teachers. And that was what Georgia was doing."

The titles of two of Harkness's most widely read books, *Understanding the Christian Faith* (1947) and *Toward Understanding the Bible* (1952), notably define her teaching methodology. Her overriding concern as a theologian was to clarify ideas and to enable laypersons, who were not professional scholars, to clearly and rationally grasp the central beliefs of the faith. Such an approach, as her former colleagues and students agreed, met important needs—but also held liabilities.

The experience of another former student, the Reverend Harry Pak, now senior pastor of the Claremont United Methodist Church in Claremont, California, helps to discern the strength and limitations of Harkness as a teacher and scholar in many of her theological writings. Pak came to Pacific School of Religion in 1957. "There were some smart-alecky students who felt that she was too simplistic. I had that opinion at first, too. Her theology was really homespun. It was only afterwards that you realized how profound she was."[15]

Pak described the contrast between Alexander Miller, his professor during his undergraduate days at Stanford, and Harkness. "Miller was dynamic. He would lecture walking around the classroom and gesturing and all of that, and on the other hand Georgia Harkness was kind of low key." Pak's insights confirm Rood's description that Harkness's teaching style got in the way of her contribution as a theologian.

However, Harry continued, "What she was saying would really fit into what you would be doing in the local church situation. She was teaching as if you would be teaching your laypeople in your local church. You knew the practical benefit of sitting through classes like that."

Other former colleagues of Georgia at Pacific School of Religion probed the strengths and weaknesses of Harkness's style of teaching and writing theological prose. "To my mother and my sister, both devout Methodists and active in church work, it was like going to heaven for me to have the opportunity to come and teach on the same faculty as Georgia Harkness. They thought that I had truly arrived," stated Charles McCoy, Professor of Theological Ethics, who came to PSR in 1959 as Professor of Religion and Higher Education. As sincere and serious laypersons, they had read her books, and she brought the faith to them as did no other theologian. "I would get Georgia to autograph her books and send them to my mother and sister, and I was an intermediary once for her to speak at the North Carolinian Wesleyan Service Guild."[16]

McCoy expanded on the significance of his mother's and sister's reactions: "Georgia has not been fully appreciated for her conviction that theology ought to be able to communicate to the intelligent layperson. She took the lead in making Christian faith available to women and to men of this sort. She wrote so she could be understood."

Like many others, Durwood Foster, Professor of Christian Theology, particularly noted *Understanding the Christian Faith*, which he had used with countless laity groups, for its solid and clear presentation of Christian doctrine. Foster valued Harkness's work even more personally, however, in steering him, as a young man, in his own vocational direction: "I first became aware of her when somebody put in my hands, back in college at Emory University, a book entitled *Conflicts in Religious Thought* [1929]. That book meant a great deal to me, at a time when I was in a sort of sophomoric muddle, trying to get my head together and make a transition from a Bible Belt kind of naive Christianity to something that would be responsible in terms of modern thought. And that book was the perfectly pitched source that I needed."[17]

The judgment of professional theologians in their more mature years was different. "I never found myself terribly moved by her speaking and her writing, in part because she did not have the charisma that goes with excitement in verbal presentation, but in part also because she boiled things down, in my judgment, to very simple forms, concepts, and expressions," recalled John Von Rohr, Professor of Church

266

History when Georgia was on campus, later dean, and now retired. However, he also affirmed the advantages of her style. John invited Harkness to give a series of lectures on theology to university and college faculty at a Danforth Foundation conference that he led one summer in the 1950s. "Here were laypeople who were being exposed at a higher level than they would normally have known, to theological ideas, and yet she presented her lectures in a way that was clearly understandable and very, very helpful."[18]

Von Rohr cited his "complaint as that of a pro in this area, which had to be seen against the real service she provided for a lot of laypeople in the churches. I think that professional theologians, perhaps more than any group, are subject to the temptations of self-righteousness, pride, and arrogance. My feleing is that many people who were technically proficient in the field of theology looked with a little disdain upon her."

As a Professor of Religious Education, Wayne Rood was a professional theologian who focused on interpreting the Christian faith to laypersons. In evaluating her books on theology, he described them as "something students could use. She gave them an outline to think by, to preach from. It was clear and it was Methodist. It fit right in with what they needed. Reinhold Niebuhr and Hugh Vernon White, Georgia's colleagues in theology at PSR, didn't do that at all! What you got from them this Tuesday would make an impact on you twenty years from now. That's my personal witness."[19]

In one word, he said, she was a popularizer. "I remember from that period, I was involved in the same stuff. I was trying to make theology workable for church school teachers by training teachers and giving a lot of workshops and lectures to lay folks up and down the coast. My concern was that what I considered to be the great traditions of theology become meaningful and useful for teachers. And that must have been her source, too, because she started out in our common field, religious education."

One way to understand Harkness as an academic is to recognize that all her life she was a religious educator. Perhaps her deepest purpose, and one of her great strengths, was to communicate to the laity. However, the laity of her age may have been more attuned to dealing with the rationalism of her approach than it is now. "I think her work would miss people now," Wayne surmised. "But that's their fault, not the fault of the position or the effort."

=====

Harkness published nine books during the 1950s. They represent the broad range that characterized her writing during her entire adult life; one type being theological prose written in the rationalistic intellectual style, and the other poetry and prayers for devotional use. One of those books was a reprint of her *Religious Living* from 1937, reissued in 1953 in a collection entitled *The Religious Life*, along with essays by Douglas Steere and Ernest Fremont Tittle. In three books—*The Sources of Western Morality*, *The Modern Rival of Christian Faith*, and *Christian Ethics*—she developed her own systematic ethic. Three others, *O Worship the Lord*, *Through Christ Our Lord*, and *The Bible Speaks to Daily Needs*, were devotional manuals.

The final two books, *Toward Understanding the Bible* (1952) and *Foundations of Christian Knowledge* (1955), were treatises on theology. In style, purpose, and content, they bear out her colleagues' evaluations. The primary concern of both books is epistemology, in the technical language of the professional philosopher or theologian, or *how* one comes to understand the Bible and Christian faith. However, Harkness uses the word *epistemology* only once in either book, for both are directed, primarily, to intelligent laypersons who would be turned away by academic terminology.

Toward Understanding the Bible is subtitled "A Key to the Scriptures for the Layman." Harkness describes it as a preparatory statement. "This little book is not designed to answer all the complex questions of biblical interpretation . . . its usefulness will largely be determined by the extent to which the reader goes beyond it to the Bible itself."[20] The book is outstanding as an instrument enabling countless laypersons to open the Bible intelligibly.

Harkness is primarily concerned to introduce her readers to the tools of critical historical scholarship. Her key question is: What is meant by "the word of God," how is the selfhood of God declared through the Bible? In a decade in which the voice of Fundamentalism rose to a high pitch in the United States, she sought to counter belief in verbal inspiration and infallibility of the Scriptures.

As a primary spokesperson for the liberal tradition, Harkness pointed to "the necessity of taking the Bible to a teachable mind. This means using the best available tools of scholarship and being willing if necessary to give up cherished former ideas if new truth appears. God cannot speak to closed or biased minds."[21] To impress on the reader that the collection of Scriptures is written by a multiplicity of "earthen vessels . . . channels of human fallibility mixed with high insights through which the message comes," Harkness introduces the geographical, social, and religious settings of the Bible, as well as the literary types of the writings represented in the sixty-six books.[22]

However, one overarching standard for interpreting the Bible emerges "that goes deeper than the best historical and literary criticism and which . . . is our true index. Said Paul to the Philippians, 'Let the mind be in you, which was also in Christ Jesus' (Phil. 2:5)." The reader knows whether the true "voice of God" is spoken through particular passages if "it accords with the life, the words, and mind of Christ."[23]

Harkness's expressions from the Evangelical side of her heritage then merge with her liberal tradition. "Paul comes nearest to the mind of Christ in Galatians 3:28: 'There is neither Jew nor Greek, there is neither slave nor free, there is neither male nor female; for you are all one in Christ Jesus.' The reason is that Jesus treats men and women equally as children of God and persons of supreme worth."[24] In selecting this particular scriptural passage as her key to the scriptures for the lay person, Georgia chose the text that Christian feminists who followed after her held central to all biblical interpretation.

In *Foundations of Christian Knowledge,* written three years later, Harkness again was concerned to address *how* one believes the Christian faith more than *what* to believe. She projected this book to a "confused but wistful world" and to people outside as much as inside the church, "if the rift between the secular and the Christian world is to be bridged by exponents of the Christian faith."[25] Again writing to laypeople, she felt encouraged that within the past decade a dozen or so scholarly books had been written for laity, whereas before that time it was impossible to find any. She listed her own contributions among those of noted male academics, including Edgar Brightman, D. C. Macintosh, William Ernest Hocking, Walter Horton, Elton Trueblood, and Henry Nelson Wieman.[26]

Besides being a well structured, rationalistic, and methodical theological argument, the book synthesizes "convergent but disparate" methods and ideas in order to bring together persons of diverse perspectives in the Christian fold. Theology, philosophy, and science provide complementary foundations of gaining Christian knowledge. These should not contradict but reinforce each other, bringing greater truth to interpreting the Bible and vesting the authority of the faith in secular, as well as sacred, sources.

Harkness was concerned further to bring together the wide spectrum of persons representing diverse viewpoints within the Christian congregations. Biblical authority is the essential foundation upon which all Christian knowledge must rest, she contended. But communication with Fundamentalists is impossible, because "they are trying, sometimes without much Christian love, to preserve their own cherished prejudices. . . . The fundamentalist mind is by nature dissident." However, "among the conservative, liberal, and neo-orthodox approaches there is enough in common so that in local churches, denominations, and the ecumenical movement Christians are working together in fellowship."[27]

In *Toward Understanding the Bible* and *Foundations of Christian Knowledge,* some of Harkness's most important purposes as a theologian stand out. She sought to offer laity meat, not pabulum. She did not flinch in presenting the most difficult truths that constitute the faith. She presented her material in a direct, straightforward manner, using non-technical language. But as she set forth the essential tenets of Christian belief and action, her language was not pious and her thought was not simplistic. Her concern, as always, was to reach the "ordinary saints" of the church. And she was convinced that no essential differences split men and women, or persons of different races and persuasions, if they would but reason together.

Wayne Rood suggests that church people of the late twentieth century might not find her work as engaging, even compelling, as did laity of the 1950s. Adult religious education materials today do not take a straightforward, direct rationalistic approach to understanding the Christian faith, but are developed in terms of experiential learning, small-group involvement, and participatory activities. However, that does not necessarily fault Harkness's effort. The strength of her approach was its emphasis on content. Teaching methodology that balances presentation of content with experiential learning may offer the optimum learning opportunity.

In the final two chapters of *Foundations of Christian Knowledge,* Georgia turned to the mystery of Christian knowledge as we experience it through the inner light of the Holy Spirit, the spiritual or devotional life, and the mystic's way. Harkness knew well that rationalism could take a person only so far in understanding and living the Christian faith. She put this truth succinctly to any follower of the way:

> Beware against supporting that the Christian life in general can be vital and light-bearing in neglect of the devotional life. It can be conventionally moral, highly respectable, even to a considerable degree altruistic without it. But it cannot be the Kingdom-seeking, cross-bearing, richly fruitful life that God requires of the men of Christian faith. And without this quality, the light of faith tends ever to flicker as the winds of life blow upon it.[28]

Only as the inward life was cultivated could the spiritual commitment be gained to enable persons of diverse faith perspectives to overcome the disunity of the churches and affirm their oneness in the final authority of Jesus Christ. Harkness helped her brothers and sisters discern that the Christian life depended upon both rational knowledge and the inward spiritual experience of Christ's presence.

> The Vision of God must be recaptured afresh in every generation, caught from the past through the light shed by torches of long ago and carried from generation to generation by the Christian community. It must flame anew in every age through a living synthesis of faith and reason, a personal encounter wherein God in Christ becomes real and is again made flesh to dwell among us. The Word of God must be a living language, or it is not any word at all.[29]

═══

Harkness knew that such a "Vision of God" and personal encounter with God were part of the mystery of the Christian faith. She passionately experienced those mysteries in her inward spiritual journey, and they pervaded her poems and devotional writings, which from the 1930s until her death in 1974 were published simultaneously with her rational theological treatises. Her poem "The Agony of God," included in *The Glory of God: Poems and Prayers for Devotional Use* (1943), points to the suffering of God in seeing the pain of the people—and to the call to the privileged to enter into the world's need. It is a compelling statement, bringing together Georgia's personal spirituality with her social responsibility.

> I listen to the agony of God—
> I who am fed,
> Who never yet went hungry for a day.
> I see the dead—
> The children starved for lack of bread—
> I see, and try to pray.
>
> I listen to the agony of God—
> I who am warm,

Who never yet have lacked a sheltering home.
In dull alarm
The dispossessed of hut and farm
Aimless and "transient" roam.

I listen to the agony of God—
I who am strong,
With health, and love, and laughter in my soul.
I see a throng
Of stunted children reared in wrong,
And wish to make them whole.

I listen to the agony of God—
But know full well
That not until I share their bitter cry—
Earth's pain and hell—
Can God within my spirit dwell
To bring His kingdom nigh.[30]

The Glory of God is much like the other devotional books that Georgia published. It is a small pocket- or purse-size book containing fifty poems and prayers on a variety of specific subjects related to nature, personal and corporate worship, special occasions and needs, and particular groups of people. Wayne Rood said about it:

> I used them in my own leadership of public prayers. For twenty or twenty-five years, when I pastored churches on an interim basis while teaching, I would start preparing my worship service with these prayers. They cover all the subjects that we need, and that a lot of people don't have prayers about—for those in love, for children, for mothers, fathers, wives, students, teachers—here we go—for soldiers and sailors, conscientious objectors, unemployed, those of other races, our enemies. Georgia's prayer life was not a supplement to her rational intellectualism; it was a simultaneous parallel ground. These strains were not so separate that they caused her intellectual or emotional problems. They gave balance.[31]

In their personal relationships with Georgia, her colleagues experienced the mystery of the "warm, caring, compassionate person" who is revealed in her poems and prayers. Wayne tells a story of his daughter, Sue Rood Cox, and Georgia Harkness.

Sue Rood Cox, who is now married, encountered Georgia for the first time when she was five years old and was spending an afternoon or so up here at the school with me. It was about the time of the birth of her brother, and I was taking care of her. We had been in my office. Apparently we had a little party of it and had gotten some soft drinks and things from the machine. I sent her to take the bottles back, and she got lost in this great capacious building, something I hadn't anticipated, of course.

She panicked and was running down the hall, unable to find anything that seemed right. And around the corner came this awesome, ancient, white-haired female figure. Sue literally ran into her, backed up, and was terrified. But the woman knelt down to her level and asked her if she was afraid or lost. She finally said, "Who are you?" And Sue replied, "Sue. I'm Sue." The large woman, who seemed trustworthy, continued. "Well, and who is your father?" After Sue told her, Georgia immediately said, "Oh, I know him, and I will take you to him." So she stood up, took Sue's hand in hers, and led her upstairs. All the while Georgia was telling Sue about me. She wasn't talking about Sue or about herself, but she was making Sue comfortable.

Wayne continued that when Sue's baby brother was born, the faculty wives and Georgia and Verna had a shower, and Georgia presented a night dress that she had made herself. Everybody was polite but amazed. They just never supposed that Georgia did any of the customarily woman things at all.

Time and again, Georgia supported students, as well as a small child, who experienced life as outsiders on the seminary campus. One was a young man who was suspected of being a homosexual and was dismissed from school by the president. Georgia and Verna had just moved from the PSR apartment into their house at 10 Kerr Avenue, and she helped him support himself by giving him odd jobs around the house and on her car. "She saw him through at least a year, until he got himself reorganized and became a primary school teacher," Rood shared.

Harry Pak's wife, Carmen, also must have felt like an outsider when she graduated from Pacific School of Religion shortly after The Methodist Church voted that women could receive ordination with full Conference membership. "It was not possible for her to be ordained by our bishop, Gerald Kennedy. He discouraged her very strongly," stated Pak. "On the other hand, there was Georgia Harkness. She insisted to Carmen, 'No matter what you do, be your own person.' And Carmen did that. When our kids went off to school, she decided that she would begin the ordination process. She has been ordained since 1982, pastors a church, and we are a clergy couple."[32]

Durwood Foster, whose office was next to Georgia's, noted the large amount of time that she spent in counseling. "She was appreciated on this campus as a counselor to students who would go through dark shadows in their own struggles, either in marriage or in vocational self-doubts or whatever. She took up their cause and was a friend and mainstay to a lot of students who were in difficulty." Foster saw Georgia's counseling as a way in which students experienced her personal spiritual dimension. "Students whom we called on the carpet, who might have been terminated because of their grade point averages or for disciplinary reasons, she was especially solicitous to minister to them in their personal crises, but in realistic ways. If somebody was clearly out of his or her depth as a student, she would accept that fact and then try to interpret it to the student."[33]

In summing up, Foster stated that "Georgia was a senior person who had a real ministry to persons through her counseling along with her teaching." And in Wayne Rood's recollection, "It wasn't just the bright students in class who commended themselves to her. It was because they were who they were." Harry Pak directly tied her concern for students to her theological understanding: "I don't think Georgia Harkness could ever have become a neo-orthodox theologian because she placed such a high value on humanity. Coming out of a church that was persecuted through the Second World War under Japanese ocupation in Korea, it was natural for me to gravitate toward Karl Barth's position. But Georgia

Harkness encouraged me to look at his phrase 'total depravity of humanity.' She forced me to rethink that. Her life was a demonstration that humanity is not really totally depraved. There is something good and precious about humanity."[34]

The families of the PSR faculty experienced the paradox of a loving woman in a rational scholar, and very often were surprised if not amazed. "For all her gruff exterior, she was one of the most gracious persons I have ever known," recalled Helen Von Rohr. "She remembered about our children, and even after she left the School she kept track and was very comforting sometimes."[35]

There was much socializing among these families, visiting in each other's homes for dinner, during the 1950s. Verna always was included in any faculty and school functions, either on campus or in homes. They were remembered as always together, inseparable, having a "fine and wonderful relationship."[36]

Georgia and Verna entertained often. The supposition was that Verna did most of the cooking, but when entertaining guests Georgia was the primary chef and took at least half of the responsibility of clearing the table. John Von Rohr echoed the recollection of several: "We remember her as a fine cook, which surprised me a little bit because I thought she was always so busy with her theological research that she wouldn't have time for a recipe."[37]

The Von Rohrs especially remembered Georgia and Verna's home on Kerr Avenue. When they moved to Claremont in the late 1960s, Georgia gave the home to the Pacific School of Religion. The School rented it to the Von Rohrs for three years from 1971 until 1974 while they were between housing. "Out at the back, there's this wonderful vista of the bay and the Golden Gate bridge. The view was from the dining room, which Georgia had built. It had this marvelous window looking out over the bay. In the lower level, which had a little kind of mother-in-law's apartment, Georgia had her study. Nice fireplace there and a little kitchenette, and I can just imagine her working there."

Charles McCoy and Durwood Foster particularly recalled the professional and personal response they received from

Georgia and Verna when they came to PSR in 1959. Georgia was sixty-eight years old, and she cut back her schedule further to half-time, both to provide needed space for them and to ease herself into retirement. She wanted a part of her reduced salary to be made available for hiring McCoy in Religion and Higher Education, a field close to Georgia's heart from her many years of teaching undergraduates. Further, she turned over to Foster the entire year-long basic theology course. She and Hugh Vernon White, whom Foster replaced, had each taught one semester of the course. Georgia realized that greater continuity would be brought to Systematic Theology if Foster taught the two-semester sequence, and that she could devote greater time to her course on the devotional life as well as to other electives and to her writing.[38]

She also proposed them for membership into the Pacific Coast Theological Group, the group of forty or so scholars in the San Francisco Bay and Pacific Coast area, which regularly met to discuss theological topics and to share their autobiographical journeys. It began in the early 1940s, with support by the Hazen Foundation and under the leadership of John Bennett, when he taught at PSR, and others. Later, when Georgia was on the faculty, she was the only woman member of the Theological Group. With her encouragement, McCoy and Foster joined shortly after they arrived.

They, like others, remembered the small, but gracious, kindnesses that Georgia had extended to them. McCoy and his family met Georgia and Verna for the first time when they attended Trinity Methodist Church in Berkeley on the first Sunday after their arrival, and they all went to lunch together after the service. Foster remembered the basket of fruit Georgia brought to his family immediately after they arrived. Verna, too, was remembered with great fondness by the Pacific School of Religion community. "She was a character," recalled Helen Von Rohr with a laugh. "You never knew what she was going to say—and Georgia never seemed to mind or be embarrassed by what she might come out with." Obviously, Verna was a good antidote for the more serious and controlled Georgia. In Harry Pak's words, "She was the kind of person who simply said what she believed—really direct. Sometimes it was really humorous, the conversations that Georgia and Verna carried on when Georgia invited class members to a meal in their home. There were frank exchanges and very often in some practical matters Verna would put Georgia in her place."[39]

Whereas Georgia had a depth of faith and was a mystic, Verna had a more plain, common-sense approach to the politics of the church, Charles McCoy remembered. "She was often nearer to being right about the actual workings of the institution than either of us!" He, as did all the colleagues, knew Verna as "very devoted to Georgia and to Georgia's career. She knew that Georgia had a great place in The Methodist Church and in Christianity and supported her in it, although Verna was not particularly devout."[40]

Verna took a traditional caretaker, wifely role, though she spoke with vigor and authority, in her relationship with Georgia. Durwood Foster asked a profound question about them: "She seemed to be oriented to supporting and expediting Georgia's work in whatever way. You know, was she too much the servant and companion of Georgia? I guess I could look back on the relationship and wonder, 'Did Verna have a life of her own?' "[41]

═══

Most women and men of the church in the 1950s knew Georgia Harkness only publicly, not intimately as the few people who spoke in this chapter. In 1947, she had been named one of the ten "most influential living Methodists" in a national poll taken by *The Christian Advocate*. In the decade to follow, her name was as well known by the rank and file of the churches, as well as their leaders, as any person in the ecumenical movement. Though Georgia and Verna may have shared some domestic responsibilities with equity, there is no question that Verna was the business manager of the home. In a traditional "wifely" way she enabled Georgia to be released for public service and distinction.

Much of that service and distinction came from within The Methodist Church. Retired Bishop H. Ellis Finger remembers:

> Ten years out of Yale Divinity School and a thirty-five-year-old pastor of Oxford University Methodist Church in Oxford, Mississippi, I was one of three clergy delegates from the North Mississippi Annual Conference to the 1952 General Conference in San Francisco, California.
>
> My legislative committee assignment involved being in a sub-committee on Social Concerns chaired by Georgia Harkness, an experience to be treasured even till this day. We dealt under Dr. Harkness's guidance with the variety of difficult problems the people in the United States were facing in those days of social change.
>
> Her committee leadership was a backdrop for my Presidential administrative opportunities and challenges the next twelve years, 1952–1964, at Millsaps College, Jackson, Ms., in the heat of civil rights, racial, and social problems in Mississippi.[42]

Harkness's most consequential contribution to The Methodist Church came in the lengthy struggle for women's ordination, which finally led to the granting of full clergy rights and Conference membership for women on May 4, 1956. She had worked for equity for women in the church since publication of her first article in a national adult church publication in 1924. More specifically, Georgia had championed full clergy rights for women since the 1944 General Conference. Though she had spoken and written on the issue countless times in the past, Georgia was intentionally silent that May 4, according to Thelma Stevens, her life-long friend and worker for social justice. Hundreds of memorials supporting full Conference membership for women were received by the Conference, in large part due to the work of the Women's Society of Christian Service and the behind-the-scenes strategy of Harkness, Stevens, and others. Georgia was confident that the church finally was ready to make its affirmative decision. She proved correct when the presiding bishop announced, "It is carried."[43]

The General Conference knew whose work had been most consequential in the long and arduous struggle. Lynn H. Corson, a clergy delegate from New Jersey, rose and called the assembly to express its thanks:

> Mr. Chairman, this is a day of particular triumph and significance to one of the members of this group who for many years has been looking forward to this moment when full clergy rights for women would be voted by this General Conference. I refer to Dr. Georgia Harkness. (applause)
> I think that it is a matter only due her as a courtesy from the General Conference to express the appreciation of the conference for the valiant fight she has waged for this cause for many years and express to her how we know that on this day she must feel peculiar satifaction in the knowledge that this fight has eventuated in final victory for her cause.
> Let us salute Dr. Georgia Harkness. (The audience arose and applauded.)

Of the vast work Georgia did in the ecumenical movement since the late 1930s, she is most widely known for her words to the hymn "Hope of the World," which was published in 1954. She based it on the theme of the Second Assembly of the World Council of Churches, meeting in Evanston in August 1954, "Jesus Christ, Hope of the World." Out of hundreds of hymns submitted in a search for modern ecumenical hymns sponsored by The Hymn Society, her text was selected as the winner. Bert Polman describes the context that the church, and Georgia Harkness, sought to address at this assembly: "In the wake of the Second World War and the Korean Conflict, the 'Cold War' had settled over the earth, and the then-new phrase 'population bomb' testified to an increasing ecological crisis. Torn internally by denominational strife and continued conservative/liberal controversies, the church attempted to speak and act with Christian convictions to a world which was thoroughly post-Christian in most of its public life."[44]

Harkness's mature theology of evangelical liberalism is nowhere more fully and succinctly expressed than in the words of this powerful and compassionate hymn, which was sung at the opening of the World Council of Churches assembly. It represents the heart of the social gospel in its prayer that the Spirit be given to the church to make it an instrument "to heal earth's wounds and end all bitter strife." But always the hope is in Christ's presence to forgive, reconcile, save, and direct the ministry of the church and to make it "faithful to thy gospel glorious":

Hope of the world, thou Christ of great compassion,
speak to our fearful hearts by conflict rent.
Save us, they people, from consuming passion,
who by our own false hopes and aims are spent.

Hope of the world, God's gift from highest heaven,
bringing to hungry souls the bread of life,
still let thy spirit unto us be given,
to heal earth's wounds and end all bitter strife.

Hope of the world, afoot on dusty highways,
showing to wandering souls the path of light,
walk thou beside us lest the tempting byways
lure us away from thee to endless night.

Hope of the world, who by thy cross didst save us
from death and dark despair, from sin and guilt,
we render back the love thy mercy gave us;
take thou our lives, and use them as thou wilt.

Hope of the world, O Christ o'er death victorious,
who by this sign didst conquer grief and pain,
we would be faithful to thy gospel glorious;
thou art our Lord! Thou dost forever reign.[45]

Though she had been a delegate to several international conferences over the past several years, a new ecumenical venture of teaching in the Far East came in 1956. As a result of a sabbatical from Pacific School of Religion in 1956–1957, she and Verna spent the year in the Philippines and Japan, where Georgia taught theology at Union Theological Seminary in Manila and at International Christian University in Tokyo. Besides working directly with students, she held ses-

sions with the faculties of the two institutions and with
laypersons and clergy in the area.

Japan International Christian University held its first
graduation in the early spring of 1957, and Harkness presented the baccalaureate sermon. Characteristically, she challenged the graduates to witness to both the light of learning
and to faith. "God does not require of us that we *be* that
great central light which shines only from His Son Jesus
Christ," but rather that each of us be "an interpreter, one
among a thousand," of its truth, she told the class of 1957.
She acknowledged that their task was harder than hers, for
each student from Japan and other Eastern nations was one
Christian among thousands who had not even heard of the
faith. Again, consistent with the all-embracing emphases of
her theology, she held up to them the bonds that brought
East and West together in Christ.[46]

Harkness received a host of public distinctions during the
1950s. Paradoxically, she was targeted by the Federal Bureau
of Investigation for surveillance in 1951 and was named
"Churchwoman of the Year" by the Religious Heritage of
America in 1958.

Religious leaders who engaged in political dissent during
the 1940s and 1950s were often victims of FBI surveillance.
The FBI file on Harry F. Ward, founder and longtime leader of
the Methodist Federation for Social Action, evidenced that
noted Christian clergy and laity were branded in the agency's
"secret war" against such lawful political dissenters. Harkness's name was among those included in the Ward file.

Ward himself was placed on a list of candidates for "custo-
dial detention" as part of a plan to incarcerate alleged security risks in the event of a national emergency. He was in the
high priority category on the list until 1949, and he
remained a part of the longer list until his death at age ninety-one in 1965. Among the religious organizations spied
upon by the FBI during the war were the United Christian
Council for Democracy, whose leaders included Reinhold

Niebuhr; the Episcopal League for Social Action; the Religious Freedom Committee; and the Methodist Federation for Social Action.[47]

The entry on Georgia Harkness in the Ward file in 1951, made by professional informer Louis Budenz, read:

> Advised that Dr. Georgia Elma Harkness . . . was clearly associated with the CP [i.e., Communist Party] and subsequently agreed to join. Informant stated that from 1943 to 1945 Dr. Harkness was a member of CP fronts; it was publicly known that she was a member of perhaps 10 such fronts and that she was influenced by Dr. Harry F. Ward to become associated with the front groups.

That Harkness advocated peace not war and that a substantial portion of her writing was on pacifism may have been enough to convince the FBI that she was a dangerous security risk. More specifically, during World War II she had opposed conscription of both men and women, military build-up, and defense spending. Further, in February 1941, Harkness inquired of the Treasury Department whether she could pay her wartime defense tax with a check designated for civilian use only. In response, the Treasury Department informed her that such tactics were unlawful.[48]

Georgia's opposition to the internment of Japanese Americans on the West Coast in the late 1940s, on the grounds of democratic rights, might have rated her suspect in the eyes of the FBI. She contended:

> The internment of 110,000 Japanese on the Pacific Coast, including more than 70,000 American citizens, will, I am sure, long remain a blot upon our democracy. It is a sobering fact that as war encircles the globe, Germany is the only country outside of the United States that has thought it necessary to intern any considerable number of its own citizens. I do not say that the treatment accorded to the Japanese in the relocation centers is comparable to the German concentration camp. Yet in the loss of economic security and professional opportunity, the uprooting of families and surrender of personal liberty that has been forced upon great numbers of our fellow citizens and loyal neighbors, there is something of which no American can be

proud. One wonders whether, in the history books of the future, we shall try as hard to forget it as we now do the Mexican War.[49]

A further public distinction came in 1958, when the Religious Heritage of America presented Georgia with the award "Churchwoman of the Year." Hardly a left-wing organization, the Heritage Society brought some 400 clergy and their wives together over the weekend of May 2–4 for its Eighth Washington Pilgrimage. The commissioners of the District of Columbia proclaimed the period "The Religious Heritage of America Weekend," citing their adherence to the basic purpose of the organization as "a mission of encouragement to men and women everywhere who believe that faith is the foundation of freedom."[50]

The large group visited the Supreme Court, where Justice Burton spoke on the religious foundation of the country; met with a group of senators and congressmen; and went to the Lincoln Memorial for a religious service. Others besides Harkness who were honored at the festive dinner were Cecil B. DeMille, as "Layman of the Year"; Dr. Joseph R. Sizoo, of George Washington University, as "Clergyman of the Year"; and Louis Cassels, Religious Editor for United Press, recipient of the "Faith and Freedom Award" in religious journalism. Letters of commendation to Harkness poured in from lesser-known, as well as prominent, pastors, laity, educators, former students, and friends throughout the world.

———

Georgia herself cited another distinction of the 1950s, a personal one, and in some ways the most important of all. After becoming settled in Berkeley, she wrote in her autobiographical sketch, presented to the Pacific Coast Theological Group:

> I came to Berkeley; I saw; it conquered. After a try-out period the following winter, I decided to tear up my roots in Evanston and plant them anew in Berkeley . . . so much do I rejoice in my school, my friends, my home, even my somewhat recalacitrant garden, that I am happier than I have ever been in my life before.[51]

CHAPTER FOURTEEN

"The Kingdom Is Nearer Than When We Believed" *1962–1974*

*D*istinctions continued to come to Georgia after her retirement from the faculty of Pacific School of Religion in 1961. She received an especially meaningful honor the following year when Elmira College, at its 104th Commencement on June 3, 1962, awarded her the honorary degree of Doctor of Letters. It symbolized the deep roots of her New York origins, of her family, and of the institution where she had her longest tenure of teaching. The smile on her face as she received the honorary doctorate radiates profound happiness.[1]

The citation read at the graduation ceremony contained the superlatives describing her contribution as a pioneer woman theologian. Her presenter cited "her distinguished scholarship in the field of theology, her genius in prose and verse for making theological ideas comprehensible to the layman and relevant to human living, her eminence as a churchwoman, and her devoted work as a teacher concerned with preparing young people for the highest in human living and for the best in religious leadership."[2]

Ten years later, Georgia received her most unusual distinction and the one she termed "the greatest." The date was April 21, 1972, and she was a lay delegate from the Southern California-Arizona Conference to the General Conference of

The United Methodist Church, meeting in Atlanta. Pauline Bobbitt, also a lay delegate from the Southern California-Arizona Conference, rose and addressed the session:

> This is a special day for one woman member of the Conference, and a delegate of the Southern California-Arizona Conference. Dr. Georgia Harkness has long been a champion and advocate for the liberation of all men and women. This is her birthday. We believe it would be fitting that Dr. Harkness be recognized at this time.[3]

After presiding Bishop Reuben Mueller invited Harkness to stand and "have a word for us," Georgia acknowledged that she could "hardly find words to express my gratitude and it is perhaps unusual for me to fail to find words," an opening that brought laughter throughout the house. "But above all the things that have come to me, you touch my heart deeply. This is the greatest." The 1972 assembly was her sixth General Conference, Georgia told the delegates, and she was eighty-one years old. "It might be said I'm *a hardy perennial*" (underlining mine).

This would be Georgia's last General Conference, for she died two and one-half years later on August 21, 1974. She wasn't as spry as in past years, and Pierce Johnson, her close friend and pastor at the Claremont United Methodist Church during those years, remembers giving her some assistance in walking. Her self-description as a "hardy perennial" conveys the essential Harkness better than those penned for any public citation. Over her eighty-one years, she had transplanted her sturdy roots from the Northeast to the Midwest to the far West. With each geographical move, and with changes within and without, Georgia kept sprouting, experiencing the fruits of generativity and conceiving new and fresh life.

———

Retirement meant an end to formal teaching responsibilities for Harkness at Pacific School of Religion. However, Georgia continued to preach and teach at laity and pastors' retreats, women's society meetings, on college campuses, and in local churches throughout the country and the world. She maintained, even accelerated, the pace of her writing, publishing one book each year until her death and keeping the same balance among theology, ethics, and spiritual devotional materials.

Georgia and Verna remained in their home in Berkeley until 1968. During these years they maintained their close friendships in the seminary community and their active participation in Trinity United Methodist Church. Then they transplanted themselves one more time to Claremont, a suburb of Los Angeles where the streets are lined with palm trees. After a few years in one home, they settled together at 927 Emerson Place by 1972 and remained there until Georgia's death.

A letter written to "Dear Friends Far and Near" at Thanksgiving time, 1972, gives an idea of their fruitfulness and contentment in older adulthood. "The story of our year will not require many words. We have taken three trips of some duration away from Claremont, and the rest of the time our lives have moved along quite uneventfully with the usual activities to keep us happily busy," they wrote. "We both remain in excellent health, troubled only by a few cricks in the bones such as one expects on growing older. For this, and for much else, we give God grateful thanks."[4]

In retirement, Georgia and Verna traveled together throughout the United States and the world. Most trips within the continental United States were taken in the big hydramatic Pontiac and successive cars. Verna feared to fly and worried about Georgia's flying alone. They also went to Hawaii, six times in all, and stayed at the Old Royal Hawaii Hotel. Among other enjoyments, they spent time with Harry and Carmen Pak and their children. Georgia and Verna frequently took the Paks to lunch at a beachside cafe. Harry invited Georgia to teach the adult Sunday school class at his church, and she did so whenever possible.[5]

The first of their three trips during 1972 was to Evanston and the East in May. Georgia was invited to speak at Garrett, providing "an occasion to revisit our old haunts and see such of our friends as are still there." Then they went on to Cape Cod to visit friends and to northern New York to see the Harkness relatives. "It was a happy time all around."

In early October they took a much shorter trip to Flagstaff, Arizona, where Georgia led a ministers' retreat. This also gave them the opportunity to spend several days with Verna's cousin, Adeline MacFarlane, in her lovely home in Tucson.[6]

Sandwiched in between these two excursions was a much longer jaunt—the Bible Lands Cruise in the Middle East. Georgia was the Bible lecturer for two successive cruises, so she and Verna were away for almost a month. On their way to New York, where they took a plane with thirty-three others in the group, they stopped to visit a grand-nephew and "his fine family" in Havertown, Pennsylvania. Two hundred fifty other people went from Los Angeles on a chartered plane, and Georgia and Verna joined them in Cyprus. "The Greek cruise ship was our hotel as we saw by bus daily the most significant places connected with Jesus in Israel and with Paul in Syria, Turkey and Greece. It was a very rewarding experience with wonderful Christian fellowship."

Describing their normal day's round in Claremont near the end of the letter, Georgia and Verna continued, "This about tells our story, save for the fact that Verna continues to enjoy her musical opportunities here and Georgia the School of Theology library and her writing. *Mysticism: Its Meaning and Message* was published in March and she is now working on a book on the kingdom of God—a perennial theme much passed over in recent years."

Georgia was persuaded to give the lectures again for the sixteen-day Bible Lands Cruise the following year in 1973. As tour host and Bible teacher, she made arrangements and corresponded with participants throughout the year. On the travel brochure, the cruise was described as "The Ideal Journey," combining "relaxing vacation, rich inspiration and thrilling travel . . . a happy combination of comfortable jet air travel and Greek ocean liner convenience."

The travelers were in the Holy Land just one month before the tragic Arab-Israeli war broke out. Lois Seifert, Director of Christian Education at Georgia's own Claremont United Methodist Church, described the tension that the political division of Jerusalem meant in terms of religious faith:

> We lived in Jerusalem two days, being a part of the mix of the old and the new, the Jew and the Arab, and Wailing Wall and the Moslem Temple. Not even the wisdom of Solomon could make a just division of that city which holds all that is so sacred in the national and religious history of these two people! For the Judeo-Christian, it seems right that the Jews should have free access to the Wall that remains from Solomon's Temple, and to the Rock that might have been the spot of Abraham's near sacrifice. But the Moslems too have built their faith into the Rock and the beautiful "Dome of the Rock" that now stands over it.[7]

Georgia died on August 21, 1974, almost one year after the 1973 Holy Land Cruise. She was working on her manuscript *Biblical Backgrounds of the Middle East Conflict* until just a few days before her death. Dr. Charles K. Kraft, her former colleague at Garrett Biblical Institute, completed the book by writing the last four chapters and bringing the story through the early 1970s.

Harkness's concern in her last book was to bring the basic facts of the biblical background and modern development of the Arab-Israeli conflict "to the attention of the general reader," the same audience for whom she had written almost all of her books. "If I could do even a little to promote understanding and thus alleviate intolerance and animosity, this would be reason enough for the undertaking." But she had another, more personal, reason. Serving as the Bible lecturer for a Bible Lands cruise to Israel and to the places connected with Paul and the early spread of Christianity had brought her a love of this whole area, both rich in its history and crucial to our spiritual heritage.[8]

Georgia sought to interpret the past and present turmoil in the Middle East and to help her readers understand the just cause of both sides. "One must have deep sympathy with the Israeli yearning for a secure homeland. . . . But one must also sympathize with the plight of the Palestinian refugees who feel that their homeland has been taken from them. Until this difficult problem is settled with some measure of justice for both sides, there can be no permanent peace in the Middle East."[9]

In the spirit of Harkness, Charles Kraft concluded the book by spelling out more specifically what he believed should be the basis of the attitude of North American Christians. Notably, he quoted a "Christian interpreter," Rosemary Radford Ruether, who became Georgia Harkness Professor of Applied Theology at Garrett-Evangelical Theological Seminary in September 1976. Ruether "urged a 'new start' in attempting to bring Christian thought to bear on present-day Middle East conflicts":

> A new start must be based on an unequivocal concession from the Arab side of the right of Israel to exist, and Israel too much come to see that it cannot survive by military counterattack forever. . . . Concerned Christians . . . must start by affirming the principle of the interdependency of . . . two causes (the development of new conditions for the Palestinians' existence and a commitment to Israel's secure survival). . . .
>
> In the prophetic tradition divine donation cannot simply be translated into a secular land claim. Israel can be called the Zion of God only by those willing to accept the implication of this faith: Israel is not called to be a nation like other nations but must strive for the higher ethic of love and justice that will make it a beacon light of redeemed human relations *for all nations*. Therefore, a secular land claim for the right of a state to exist "like other nations" turns biblical language into idolatry.[10]

Georgia Harkness, Charles Kraft, and Rosemary Ruether spoke in the Christian spirit of reconciliation, but never compromised the prophetic principles they considered essential to bring love and justice to bear on any situation. This message defined Harkness's mature Christian witness and applied theology. She sought to *be* an instrument of reconciliation and to equip other persons for that same purpose as "ambassadors of Christ." Georgia spelled out this purpose succinctly in another of her late books, *The Ministry of Reconciliation*, written in 1971.

When experienced in depth, Christian faith and love are the most powerful means of overcoming alienation and estrangement, hostility and enmity, among individuals. "With a wide-enough base of persons in whom Christian faith and love are joined with political discernment and insight, social hope could be much nearer to fulfillment than it now seems to be."[11]

Harkness advanced principles of social justice in this book upon which Christians could continue to build throughout the last quarter of the twentieth century. Exploring the civil rights and black power movements, she counseled white Americans to understand that many blacks were now recoiling from the goal of integration because of the "new mood of ethnocentrism—with the emerging sense of self-identity, racial pride in black achievements, and the desire not only to appreciate one's racial heritage but to fulfill one's racial potentialities . . . there may need to be a period of separation before integration in the form of a harmonious pluralism can be brought about."[12]

Georgia helped white American church people, many of very conservative social orientation, understand that the Christian gospel was the most radical instrument for the rights and equality of persons and for the reconciliation of individuals and groups. Further she was coming to value the need and the good in pluralism, a significant step in her own growth, which likely would have developed further had she lived.

Georgia's commitment to the liberation of women was essentially radical, as demonstrated in two of her books of the early 1970s: *Women in Church and Society* and *The Ministry of Reconciliation*. She still maintained that the church was the "last stronghold of male dominance." After winning full clergy rights for women, the pressure now had to be maintained to bring true equity both to clergy and to lay women in the day-to-day workings of the church. Continually, she held the church accountable to its roots of the gospel and to its failure to exemplify their radical implications.[13]

Her interpretation of the gospel message was more radical than her proposals for acting upon it. In these later writings, she counseled women to maintain their femininity (though she never stated what she meant by that), and to let men sometimes speak for women when they could be more influential than women themselves. This had been her strategy at the final debate for full clergy rights for females in 1956.

Harkness's writings left feminists who were coming of age in the 1960s and '70s wondering just where she stood on women's rights. The confusion was legitimate, for while she had been one of their earliest advocates she was not in support of all the new thinking. Speaking in an informal discussion setting to a group of women clergy and seminarians in the Claremont area on March 6, 1974—one month before her eighty-third birthday and six months before her death—she was asked directly whether she considered herself a feminist. She replied:

> I suppose I am. I have worked for years for larger recognition of the place of women in the church. I have long favored the idea that women should have greater places of leadership in all spheres than they do. I don't go as far as some of the women's liberation people do. I read that there just recently had been a conference on whether you could use a male pronoun to refer to God. Mrs. Betty Friedan and some others have been talking about that. I think it is perfectly silly that you should hesitate to speak of God as "He" or as "Our Father." From long tradition, that has come to be the terminology. It doesn't mean a male being, it means personality. If you don't call God "He," I certainly don't want to call God "She." And the only other pronoun is "It," and that depersonalizes God, which is contrary to the basic belief of a God of love, care, purpose, and concern. So, I shall continue to speak of God as "He" but some people get very agitated over that.[14]

In the years immediately preceding her death, Georgia read and heard feminists inside and outside of the church. Her deepest philosophical commitment was to the open-minded search for truth. Equally fundamental was her theological conviction of the full personhood of all human beings in Jesus Christ. Harkness had constructed much of her applied theology upon those foundations. Through the years, she had conceived radical implications out of these basic precepts. Her openness and even excitement to the ideas that Rosemary Ruether was raising (when Georgia heard her speak in the Claremont area in May 1974, only two months before her death) are evidence of her essential spirit.

Mary Elizabeth Moore helpfully describes Harkness as a builder.[15] Her foundations were strong. Like everyone else, she did not have her whole house constructed. Georgia was growing and changing in her own thinking, and she consistently challenged her audience to that same openness.

———

The statement that Harkness made in front of her last United Methodist General Conference in 1972 was one of the shortest speeches she ever made before that assembly. She said a great deal in a few words. More than simply describing herself as "a hardy perennial," Georgia expressed the joy she experienced that the Conference that morning had voted to establish the General Commission on the Status and Role of Women in the Church. Since its inception at the 1972 General Conference, COSROW has been an advocate, catalyst, and monitor to ensure the full participation and equality of women in the church at the General, Conference, and local church levels. Georgia's last words to the General Conference were these: "With the action taken this morning in regard to the place of women in the church, I can say that I believe *the Kingdom is nearer than when we believed*"[16] (underlining mine).

Harkness would have interpreted the Commission on the Status and Role of Women, as well as the Commission on Religion and Race in The United Methodist Church, as agents of "harmonious pluralism." They were official structures of the Church whose purpose was to advocate for the full humanity of marginal persons and to reconcile dissident groups with church and society. This spirit of reconciliation represented the coming of the reign of God, or in her words, the kingdom of God on earth. It marked the natural evolution of her commitment from the Social Gospel tradition within the Protestant and Wesleyan streams to the new Liberation Theology of the late twentieth century.

The "Kingdom is nearer than when we believed," but it has not arrived yet. Of course, she would never see God's reign coming in fullness on this earth. The church did not embody the kingdom, but its function was to help bring the signs of God's reign to fruition.[17] As "a hardy perennial," her thought had affinity to the imagery of a Social Gospel "father in the faith," Walter Rauschenbusch, to the work of the church in his own day:

> Perhaps these nineteen centuries of Christian influence have been a long preliminary stage of growth, and now the flower and fruit are almost here. If at this juncture we can rally sufficient religious faith and moral strength to snap the bonds of evil and turn the present unparalleled economic and intellectual resources of humanity to the harmonious development of a true social life, the generations yet unborn will mark this as the great day of the Lord for which the ages waited, and count us blessed for sharing in the apostolate that proclaimed it.[18]

However, Georgia's expectations of the presence of the kingdom in our day were less grandiose than Rauschenbusch's. Hers had been tempered by the realism of neo-orthodoxy and the realities of the war-torn world throughout the twentieth century. However, as she spoke and wrote to change attitudes of individual Christians toward belief in the dignity and equality of all persons, she also challenged the church to fulfill its kingdom-building role of cleansing the structures of its own institutions. In two notable examples, Georgia applied this theological commitment to the church's purpose regarding race and sexuality in the last years of her life.

Harkness believed that her denomination had institutionalized evil in the creation of The Methodist Church in 1939 through establishment of the Central Jurisdiction for all black members beside the five geographical divisions for white members across the United States. The entire concept of a jurisdictional system defied the unity in Christ which the church should represent. Her radical position was presented through legislation at the 1956 General Conference of The Methodist Church, calling for the jurisdictional system to be abolished.[19]

Georgia believed that elimination of the jurisdictional system could pioneer the church toward its self-proclaimed, but unlived, unity in Christ. The inherent contradiction lay in the governing structures of the national denomination. In reality, The Methodist Church was one black church and five churches of white Americans. Under her proposal, both black and white bishops and ordained clergy would be ministers of the entire church, subject to appointment in any area of the country, not simply within the specific jurisdiction in which they were presently located. The proposal was primarily designed to abolish the Central Jurisdiction and to break loose the closed system of the denomination in the Southeastern states where racist views and policies were the rule.

The legislation had no chance of passing because it would require the votes of clergy and lay delegates whose views were firmly entrenched in their racial and regional configurations. It did, however, challenge the Methodists to confront how far their pronouncements of "one in Christ Jesus" fell short of the reality.

The Central Jurisdiction was not eliminated until after another union in 1968, when The United Methodist Church was created out of the former Evangelical United Brethrens and the Methodists. The proposal for merger provided that geographical annual conferences, presently composed only of white members, had one quadrennium to merge voluntarily with all-black conferences of the Central Jurisdiction.

Georgia Harkness opposed the union, again out of the prophetic vision that racism must be eliminated from the structures of the new denomination before unification was effected. Formation of the new church contained a built-in conflict between the values of immediate union and racial equality. Recognizing that her opposition to the union would puzzle persons who knew her as a "warm supporter of the ecumenical movement and of Christian unity for many years," she held that the intention of persons of good will to integrate all structures of the new denomination should not be trusted.[20]

"The segregated Central Jurisdiction, which has existed in Methodism since 1939, is a clear contradiction of Christian morality," she stated unequivocally. "It was voted at the Methodist General Conference of 1964 *not* to carry this ubiquitous structure into the union. It appears about to be carried into it—not by name but by substance in the continuance of segregated annual conferences in some sections." Such an interim arrangement created a double injustice to black people, denying "to our Negro members their present opportunities of representation without commensurate gain in Christian fellowship." Harkness concluded with these strong words: "This injustice I cannot stomach and I hope my church cannot."[21]

Harkness voiced a further prophetic word to the Church in the late twentieth century in response to the legislation regarding homosexuality approved by the General Conference of 1972, which she attended. The Conference declared: ⟨

Homosexuals no less than heterosexuals are persons of sacred worth, who need the ministry and guidance of the church in their struggles for human fulfillment, as well as the spiritual and emotional care of a fellowship which enables reconciling relationships with God, with others, and with self. Further we insist that all persons are entitled to have their human and civil rights ensured, though we do not condone the practice of homosexuality and consider this practice *incompatible with Christian teaching.* (underlining mine)[22]

Harvey Potthoff, Professor Emeritus at the Iliff School of Theology, remembers standing with Georgia in the hall of the General Conference immediately after the Conference passed its verdict on homosexuality. She expressed deep pain that it had made such a pronouncement, which she saw to be incompatible with the deeper principles of Christian love and unity and the dignity of all God's people.[23]

After the General Conference, Harkness preached in her own church, expressing to the congregation the pain she felt.

Mary Elizabeth Moore summed up the essence of Georgia's sermon as the memory has been kept alive in the communities of the Claremont United Methodist Church and the School of Theology: "Harkness stood in the pulpit of her church and reminded the congregation that twenty years earlier the General Conference had ruled that a woman should not be allowed to preach—not be allowed into full connection. She told the congregation that the church had been wrong, and it had finally changed its mind. Twenty years from that moment would be 1992, and she predicted that the church would again realize it had been wrong; she predicted that the Social Principles would again be changed."[24]

Though Georgia never published a book or an article about homosexuality, she did express her views on the subject at some length in a letter to Paul Hulslander on May 18, 1974, shortly before her death. Her thoughtful position bears quoting in full:

Since your letter is mostly about homosexuality, I will give you my opinion on it, though I can speak no authoritative word on the moot question. I think it has be looked at from two angles: (1) Is it intrinsically evil, and therefore a sin? and (2) What should the Church do about it?

As for the first question, homosexuals have been far more sinned against than sinning in the way both society and the churches have treated them as moral lepers and outcasts. I regard it more as an undesirable practice than as a sin, and in the words of theologian Norman Pittinger, a state of being "different" rather than "deviant."

I do not at all approve homosexual practices in which young boys, or other immature young people, are made the victims of adults. That must be discredited on the grounds of "using" the innocent for the sexual pleasure of the adults.

When it is practiced between consenting single adults, I think it is their own business and less reprehensible than either heterosexual adultery or sexual intercourse outside of marriage. In either of the two latter, it is apt to break up a marriage or make a bad foundation for a later marriage, plus the possibility of an undesirable pregnancy. In a homosexual case, if one or both of the partners is married it might seriously affect their family life, but otherwise it does not need to have these effects.

Another factor in the case is that it is so hard to define precisely. A strong attachment between two persons of the same sex may be mutually supporting and have nothing sexy about it, yet the suspicion arises that they are homosexuals especially if they share a home together.

But as to the second question, what to do about it in churches, my answer would be homosexuals should be treated charitably and not excluded from the churches' fellowship. However, with the sentiment against it still as strong as it is, one had better not advertise his homosexuality if he wants to be a minister. Just as one may smoke or drink in moderation and still be an effective minister if it is not generally known, so until the current mores changes there are things that are not expedient in the light of one's total influence.

This is as far as I get with it, and definitely do not expect to write a book about it.[25]

Georgia may have hesitated to write such a book because it would call attention to her own cherished and highly supportive relationship with Verna Miller for over thirty years. In her sermon to the Claremont United Methodist Church, Harkness predicted that in 1992 the denomination would change its stand on the ordination of homosexuals to ministry. What The United Methodist Church will do regarding the issue remains to be seen. But Georgia's letter clearly sets out a passionate and reasoned statement regarding the experience of persons who are treated as outsiders, and of the need for the Church to reexamine itself in the light of its Christian principles.

In the two and one-half years from the General Conference of 1972 until her death in 1974, the "hardy perennial" continued to blossom. Pierce Johnson, her pastor at the Claremont United Methodist Church during her years in Claremont, as well as her close personal friend and spiritual colleague, recalled in the 1980s and early 1990s that she continued to attend church services and functions regularly. She taught classes and spoke her views frankly at meetings, but did not expect any deferential treatment. Georgia also served on the Commission on Social Concerns and the Pastor-Parish Relations Committee. Continuing a heavy schedule of speaking engagements, Harkness did not want interviewers to know that she was in her early eighties, for people might stop inviting her to speak and write.[26]

Pierce Johnson was "like a son, one of the 'sons of the Lord' she adopted along the way and made family." Georgia's spirituality was more traditional than his. Her spiritual forebears, with whom she shared deep affinity, were the classical Christian mystics. She drew meaningfully upon them in two of her last books, *A Devotional Treasury from the Early Church* (1968) and *Mysticism: Its Meaning and Message* (1973). In her late years, Pierce shared his spiritual explorations into Yoga and prayer, biorhythms, and billets with Georgia. She enjoyed his curiosity and courage for extending such boundaries, but had no interest in pursuing them herself.[27]

Hoping that she would live to be one hundred, Pierce encouraged Georgia to be active and to care for her health. He wanted her to join a Yoga class taught by a seventy-six-year-old woman. Georgia laughed, but watched her diet and rode an exercise bicycle daily. Georgia loved his stories of a one-hundred-seven-year-old Turkish wrestler and a ninety-year-old skier in Aspen, whom he vowed was "the best."

While she showed some signs of discomfort at the 1972 General Conference, Georgia valiantly tried to attend nightly after-sessions to draft legislation for peace in Vietnam. She also began to drag her left foot. Georgia never admitted to a slight stroke, and she did not appreciably slacken her pace.

During her last spring in 1974, Harkness preached at Garrett Theological Seminary and at the Northern Indiana Conference of The United Methodist Church. Even in early August, she made two trips to Alaska to speak, and she preached at a vespers service at Claremont Manor. One book, *Understanding the Kingdom of God*, was published in 1974, and the manuscript of her last one, *Biblical Backgrounds of the Middle East Conflict*, was close to completion.

The kingdom was nearer for Georgia, personally, than she believed, for in the midst of her regular round of devotional and active living, she died unexpectedly on August 21, 1974. Verna wrote Georgia's niece and her husband, Peg and John Overholt, expressing the celebration accorded at Georgia's memorial service on September 20: "Georgia often expressed the wish that if she went before me that she wanted her last service to be triumphant with laughter and no tears. We tried to make it that way." Important delegates from agencies of The United Methodist Church and from seminaries across the country came, and newspapers in Europe carried notices of her death. "I have been sent clips from all over the United States," Verna continued. "Many have said she was the most famous woman theologian in recent years and it will be a long time before her place is filled."[28]

In her letter to the Overholts, Verna paid the first of countless tributes extended to Georgia: "She loved the Hallelujah Chorus from the *Messiah* and I loved to watch her face whenever it was played or sung. . . . Needless to say it is very hard to go on without her. She was a saint in every sense of the word. The house has a thousand rooms even though friends are wonderful. I am making no plans—it is too soon and I seem to be going through a nightmare." Verna remained in Claremont and later entered a nursing home there, outliving Georgia by ten years.

Other tributes given at her memorial service state the essence of Georgia Harkness as a personal and professional woman as her friends and colleagues knew her. At least one of them can reflect the thought of many others. Paul Irwin, Professor of Christian Education at The Claremont School of

Theology, read part of a letter to Verna from Harland Hogue, Professor of Homiletics at Pacific School of Religion when Georgia was on the faculty, which included these words:

> The theological community has no one to take her place. No theologian of my acquaintance has her gift for taking the profoundest of issues and putting it in clear, understandable terms for the layman or laywoman. She was God's very unique contribution to our world, and literally all over the world. Her friends and former students were everywhere as you, Verna, well know better than anyone else. She will be missed.
>
> But this is only one feeling: the other is that of praise to God for Georgia Harkness! No one in my acquaintance combined such a genuine Christian commitment to God as revealed through Jesus Christ; a life of prayer and devotion; and a commitment to the great Christian social concerns which were so much a part of her own compassion. Open, forthright, candid, fearless in the face of any wrong, she was probably the one woman in the Methodist church that could tell the truth to the Bishops, and who would be listened to by them with profound respect. She could also stand in the World Council of Churches and tell Karl Barth the truth from the New Testament about the place of women.
>
> One of the rare and beautiful things about Georgia was her concern for "little" people: the unknown and often unloved. I know of instances when she helped students at PSR, and former students, those who sometimes had gotten into trouble. But though the world ignored or neglected them, Georgia did not ignore nor neglect them. In this mood I feel like singing the Doxology for Georgia! I counted her among my most treasured friends. She has been and will continue to be a blessing.[29]

Even though death came unexpectedly for Georgia, she was ready for it and had been for a long time. Her own reflections, written in her older adulthood, provide the best benediction to Harkness's life. In *The Providence of God* (1960), she stated that eternal life begins in our earthly days, where our richest satisfactions are gained "in loving service and the endeavor by God's help to 'grow in the face and knowledge of our Lord and Savior Jesus Christ.' May we not believe by faith that the life beyond death also holds something of this high endeavor." From another standpoint, however, "eternal life means fulfillment, the completion of meaning, the unraveling of earth's tangles, the disclosure of ends previously but dimly apprehended."[30]

The Christian's faith in God's gift of eternal life "gives a vision of glory in the midst of earth's darkest pain. Anything then can be endured, and the future confronted with faith and hope," she continued. The Christian who trusts in the providence of God does not need to fear death, whether it comes early or late in one's life, or whether it has long been expected or comes with suddenness. "Without morbidity or undue desire he may not only anticipate it calmly but look forward to it as a great adventure—the passage by God's leading into new realms of fellowship, usefulness, and joy."[31]

Finally, in the concluding paragraph of *Foundations of Christian Knowledge* (1955), she summed up the journey even more succinctly for herself and her friends, students, colleagues, and readers everywhere:

> When we have finished our theologizing, we shall not understand all mysteries. We are but human pilgrims following the pathways of knowledge, and to the end of the earthly way we shall still "know in part." Yet our faith in Jesus Christ our Lord can give us the *assurance* of things hoped for, the *conviction* of things not seen. And is not that, after all, the object of the quest?[32]

Notes

Section I. "These *Were* and *Are* My Roots"

1. "*The Woman in the Red Coat*" *1710–1852*

1. Material in this paragraph and those following is taken from "Days of My Years," unpublished autobiography of Dr. Georgia Harkness written for the Pacific Coast Theological Group during the 1950s, Georgia Harkness Collection: Garrett-Evangelical Theological Seminary, Evanston, Ill., p. 4. Hereafter cited as "Harkness Collection: G-ETS."

2. George Arnold, Harkness, New York. My thanks to Arnold and the Rev. Marion Moore-Colgan, pastor of the Keeseville and Harkness United Methodist Churches in these New York villages, who graciously made local and church history of Georgia Harkness and her ancestors available to me.

3. Harkness, "Days of My Years," p. 18.

4. Mary Ryan, *Cradle of the Middle Class* (New York: Cambridge University Press, 1981), p. 229.

5. See Carolyn Heilbrun, *Writing a Woman's Life* (New York: Norton & Company, 1988), pp. 25-27.

6. Material that follows is taken from the Harkness Family Papers, in the possession of Georgia Harkness's niece and her husband, Peg and John Overholt, of Kilmarnock, Virginia, who generously made it possible for me to study and draw upon them. Hereafter cited as "Harkness Family Papers: Overholt."

7. Harkness, "Days of My Years," p. 3.

8. "Harkness Family Papers: Overholt."

9. Harkness, "Days of My Years," p. 2.

10. Charles Downer Schwartz and Ouida Davis Schwartz, *A Spreading Flame: The Stories of the Churches of Troy Annual Conference* (Rutland: Academy Books, 1986), p. 208.

11. Ibid., p. 128.

12. Unpublished "Sesquicentennial History of the Harkness United Methodist Church," unnumbered, "Harkness Family Papers: Overholt."

13. Notable studies of the Finney phenomenon are Curtis D. Johnson, *Islands of Holiness: Rural Religion in Upstate New York: 1790–1860* (Ithaca, N.Y.: Cornell University Press, 1989); the classic Whitney R. Cross, *The Burned-over District: The Social and Intellectual History of Enthusiastic Religion in Western New York, 1800–1850* (Ithaca, N.Y.: Cornell University Press: 1950); and Donald W. Dayton, *Discovering an Evangelical Heritage* (New York: Harper & Row, 1976), pp. 15-24. For the Methodist phenomenon, see Russell E. Richey, *Early American Methodism* (Bloomington: Indiana University Press, 1991); Frederick A. Norwood, *The Story of American Methodism* (Nashville: Abingdon Press, 1974); Charles Downer Schwartz and Ouida Davis Schwartz, *A Flame of Fire: The Story of Troy Annual Conference* (Rutland: Academy Books, 1982); and Schwartz and Schwartz, *A Spreading Flame*.

14. Warren Harkness and others, unpublished "Collection of Articles on Local History," vol. 2, unnumbered. "Harkness Family Papers: Overholt."

2. "A Goodly Heritage" 1802–1903

1. Harkness, "Days of My Years," pp. 4-7; "Harkness Family Papers: Overholt."

2. Harkness, "Days of My Years," p. 3.

3. J. Warren Harkness and others, unpublished "Collection of Articles on Local History," vol. 2, unnumbered, "Harkness Family Papers: Overholt."

4. Ibid., "The Harkness Family of Hallock Hill," J. Warren Harkness.

5. Ibid.

6. Harkness, "Days of My Years," p. 5.

7. Newspaper obituary notice of Nehemiah Harkness and letter from Nehemiah Harkness to unidentified recipient, undated, "Harkness Family Papers: Overholt."

8. Material in this and the following paragraph is from Harkness, "Days of My Years," p. 12.

9. Material on Georgia's father is taken from Harkness, "Days of My Years," pp. 5-7; Newspaper Collection, Harkness Papers; and

from J. Warren Harkness, the unpublished "History of Peru," "Harkness Family Papers: Overholt."

10. Material on Georgia's mother is from Harkness, "Days of My Years," p. 7, and Georgia Harkness, *Grace Abounding* (Nashville: Abingdon Press, 1969), p. 28.

11. Childhood pictures of Harkness's siblings may be found in "Harkness Family Papers: Overholt."

12. Material in this and the following paragraphs is found in Harkness, "Days of My Years," pp. 8-11.

13. Harkness, *Grace Abounding*, p. 21.

14. Harkness, "Days of My Years," p. 3.

15. Helen Johnson, "Georgia Harkness: She Made Theology Understandable," *United Methodists Today*, October 1974, p. 55.

Section II: "I Stood Number One"

3. *"To Be as Smart as Hattie Harkness" 1903–1908*

1. Material in this and following paragraphs is taken from Harkness, "Days of My Years," pp. 11-15, and Harkness, *Grace Abounding*, pp. 39-40.

2. "Diary," Georgia Harkness, Keeseville High School, January 1–June 15, 1904, "Harkness Family Papers: Overholt."

3. "Diary," J. Warren Harkness, Oswego Normal School, May 26 to December 22, 1867, "Harkness Family Papers: Overholt."

4. "Diary," Hattie Harkness, Keeseville High School, 1896, "Harkness Family Papers: Overholt."

5. The following section is based on "Diary," J. Warren Harkness, unnumbered.

6. This section grows out of "Diary," Hattie Harkness, unnumbered.

7. This section draws upon "Diary," Georgia Harkness, unnumbered.

8. Harkness, *Grace Abounding*, pp. 39-40.

9. Harkness, "Days of My Years," p. 13.

10. Beverley Ann Bella, "The Common Touch Secret of Success," newspaper clipping (name of paper and date not identifiable), "Harkness Collection: G-ETS."

11. Newspaper clipping, March 15, 1893, "Harkness Family Papers: Overholt."

12. Harkness, "Days of My Years," p. 14.

13. Harkness, *Grace Abounding*, p. 40; Harkness, "Days of My Years," p. 12.

14. "Diary," Georgia Harkness.

4. *"I Was Shy, Green, and Countrified" 1908–1912*

1. See Charlotte Williams Conable, *Women at Cornell: The Myth of Equal Education* (Ithaca, N.Y.: Cornell University Press, 1977), pp. 45, 55.
2. Ibid., pp. 51, 98.
3. Ibid., p. 53.
4. Ibid., p. 74.
5. See Morris Bishop, *A History of Cornell* (Ithaca, N.Y.: Cornell University Press, 1962), p. 145.
6. Ibid., p. 150.
7. Conable, *Women at Cornell*, pp. 115-17.
8. Ibid., pp. 131-32.
9. Ibid., p. 117.
10. Ibid., p. 163.
11. Harkness, "Days of My Years," p. 15, for this and following paragraphs.
12. Georgia Harkness, *The Recovery of Ideals* (New York: Charles Scribner's Sons, 1937), p. viii.
13. James Edwin Creighton, *Studies in Speculative Philosophy* (New York: Macmillan, 1925), pp. 6, 19.
14. Ibid., pp. 145-46.
15. Ibid., p. 252.
16. Ibid., pp. 250-51.
17. Ibid., pp. 275-76.
18. Ibid., pp. 280-81.
19. Harkness, "Days of My Years," pp. 15-16.
20. Conable, *Women at Cornell*, p. 80.
21. Ibid., p. 88.
22. Ibid., p. 81.
23. Lynn D. Gordon, *Gender and High Education in the Progressive Era* (New Haven, Conn.: Yale University Press, 1990), p. 4.
24. Ibid., p. 5. Other revisionist studies of women students in higher education during Harkness's era are Patricia A. Graham, "Expansion and Exclusion: A History of Women in American Higher Education," *Signs* 3 (Summer 1978): 759-37; Lynn D. Gordon, "The Gibson Girl Goes to College: Popular Education in the Progressive Era, 1890–1920," *American Quarterly* 39 (Summer 1987): 211-30; Mary E. Cookingham, "Combining Marriage, Motherhood and Jobs Before World War II: Women College Graduates, Classes 1905–1935," *Journal of Family History* 9 (Summer 1984): 179-95; Roberta Frankfort, *Collegiate Women: Domesticity and Career in Turn-of-the-Century America* (New York: New York University Press, 1977); Mary E. Cookingham, "Bluestockings, Spinsters and Pedagogues: Women College Graduates, 1865–1910," *Population Studies* 38 (November 1984): 349-64; Joyce Antler, "After College, What?" New Gradu-

ates and the Family Claim," *American Quarterly* 30 (Fall 1980)": 409-34.

25. Conable, *Women at Cornell*, pp. 172-81.

26. Interview of Peg Overholt by Rosemary Keller, Kilmarnock, Virginia, April 27, 1991.

27. Harkness, "Days of My Years," p. 16.

28. John R. Mott, *The Addresses and Papers of John R. Mott: The Student Volunteer Movement for Foreign Missions*, vol. 1 (New York: Association Press, 1946). Biographies of Mott include those by C. Howard Hopkins, *John R. Mott* (Grand Rapids: Eerdmans, 1979); Robert C. Mackie, et al., *Layman Extraordinary: John R. Mott, 1865-1955* (New York: Association Press, 1965); and Galen M. Fisher, *John R. Mott: Architect of Co-operation and Unity* (New York: Association Press, 1952).

29. Mott, *The Addresses and Papers of John R. Mott*, p. xiii; Hopkins, *John R. Mott*, p. 27.

30. Hopkins, *John R. Mott*, p. 60; Fisher, *John R. Mott: Architect*, pp. 10-13; Mackie, *Layman Extraordinary*, pp. 91-92.

31. Hopkins, *John R. Mott*, p. 60.

32. Mackie, *Layman Extraordinary*, p. 92.

33. Harkness, "Days of My Years," p. 16.

34. Mott, *The Addresses and Papers of John R. Mott*, p. 67; Mackie, *Layman Extraordinary*, p. 228.

35. *The Cornell Class Book: 1912*; Harkness, "Days of My Years," pp. 14, 16.

36. Harkness, "Days of My Years," pp. 16-17.

Section III: "I Had My Own Life to Live"

5. *"A New Profession for Women . . . This Was My Calling"* 1912-1920

1. Harkness, "Days of My Years," p. 17.

2. Helen Johnson, "Georgia Harkness: She Made Theology Understandable," *United Methodists Today*, October 1974, p. 55.

3. The following paragraphs grow out of Harkness, "Days of My Years," pp. 17-18; a copy of Harkness's official transcript, courtesy of Registrar's Office, Cornell University; and an undated letter written by an aunt or uncle of Harkness. "Harkness Family Papers: Overholt."

4. Georgia Harkness, "A Change for the Worse—Then for the Better," *Junior Herald*, September 5, 1914, p. 866.

5. Harkness, "Days of My Years," pp. 14, 16, italics added.

6. George W. Tupper, "The Church and New Americans," *Department of Social and Public Service, Service Series*, Bulletin No. 32 (Boston: Unitarian Association, n.d.), p. 2; Alan M. Kraut,

The Huddled Masses: The Immigrant in American Society, 1880–1921 (Arlington Heights, Ill.: Harlan Davidson, Inc., 1982), pp. 20-21.

7. Charles Carroll, *The Community Survey in Relation to Church Efficiency* (New York: Abingdon Press, 1915), pp. 4-5.

8. Ibid., p. 3.

9. Walter Scott Athearn, *Character Building in a Democracy* (New York: Macmillan, 1925), p. 119.

10. Carroll, *The Community Survey*, pp. 5-6.

11. Athearn, *Character Building in a Democracy*, pp. 118, 136-37.

12. Walter Scott Athearn, "The Outlook for Christian Education." Address delivered at the International Sunday School Convention, Kansas City, Missouri, June 27, 1922. *Boston University Bulletin* 11, 23, August 10, 1922, p. 7. See also Walter Scott Athearn, *An Adventure in Religious Education: The Story of a Decade of Experimentation in the Collegiate and Professional Training of Christian Workers* (New York: The Century Co., 1930), pp. 33-34.

13. Athearn, *Character Building in a Democracy*, p. 22. See also Athearn, "Report of the History, Progress and Present Status of The Survey of Religious Education Conducted by The American Religious Education Survey Department of The Interchurch World Movement," August 20, 1920, foreword.

14. Athearn, *Character Building in a Democracy*, p. 33; Athearn, "Report of the History" p. 3.

15. Athearn, *An Adventure in Religious Education*, Preface.

16. George W. Tupper, *Foreign-Born Neighbors* (Boston: The Taylor Press, 1941). See also Tupper, "The Church and New Americans."

17. Tupper, "The Church and New Americans," p. 14.

18. Georgia Harkness, *The Church and the Immigrant* (New York: George H. Doran Co., 1921), pp. vii-viii.

19. Ibid., p. ix.

20. Ibid., pp. 79-80.

21. Ibid., pp. 100-101.

22. Georgia Harkness, *Understanding the Christian Faith* (New York: Abingdon-Cokesbury Press, 1947), p. 9.

6. *"The Spell of Dr. Edgar S. Brightman's Kindling Mind"*
1919–1923

1. Georgia Harkness to Edgar Brightman, September 10, 1921. Edgar S. Brightman Papers, Mugar Library, Boston University. Collection cited hereafter as "Brightman Papers: BU."

2. Harkness, "Days of My Years," p. 18.

3. Ibid. A listing of Harkness's grades in Ph.D. courses may be found in "Brightman Papers: BU."

4. Dianne Evelyn Carpenter, "Georgia Harkness's Distinctive Personalistic Synthesis" (Ph.D. dissertation, Boston University, 1988), pp. 35-36.

5. Harkness, "Days of My Years," p. 19.

6. Discussion of Harkness's mother is based on ibid., p. 7, and Harkness, *Grace Abounding*, p. 28.

7. Harkness, "Days of My Years," p. 18.

8. Paul Deats, "Introduction to Boston Personalism," in *The Boston Personalist Tradition in Philosophy, Social Ethics, and Theology*, edited by Paul Deats and Carol Robb (Macon, Ga.: Mercer University Press, 1986), p. 3.

9. Interview of Walter S. Muelder by Rosemary Keller, November 17, 1990. Other biographical material from "Edgar S. Brightman: Person and Moral Philosopher," in Deats and Robb, *The Boston Personalist Tradition*, pp. 105-10; Carpenter, "Harkness's Distinctive Personalistic Synthesis," pp. 49-55; and *Boston University War Record* (Boston: Earnshaw Press Corporation, n.d.), p. 221.

10. Deats, "Introduction to Boston Personalism," p. 2; Peter Bertocci, "Borden Parker Bowne and His Personalistic Theistic Idealism," in Deats and Robb, *The Boston Personalist Tradition*, pp. 55-80.

11. Edgar S. Brightman, ed., *Personalism in Theology: A Symposium in Honor of Albert Cornelius Knudson* (Boston: University Press, 1943), pp. 41, 43.

12. Deats, "Introduction to Boston Personalism," p. 2; *Personalism in Theology: A Symposium in Honor of Albert Cornelius Knudson*, edited by Edgar Sheffield Brightman (Boston: University Press, 1943), pp. 41n, 43.

13. Edgar S. Brightman, *An Introduction to Philosophy* (New York: Henry Holt and Co., 1925), p. 315.

14. Ibid., pp. 353-54.

15. Ibid., pp. 355-64.

16. Ibid., p. 320.

17. Edgar S. Brightman, *Religious Values* (New York: Abingdon Press, 1925), pp. 97-98.

18. A list of grades in all of Harkness's philosophy classes taken on her Ph.D. program is included in "Brightman Papers: BU."

19. Harkness, "Days of My Years," p. 19.

20. Nina Barrows to Irma Brightman, March 9, 1921. This and letters following in this chapter are in the archival collection of the "Brightman Papers: BU."

21. Nina Barrows to Edgar Brightman, March 25, 1921.

22. Nina Barrows to Edgar Brightman, August 22, 1921.

23. Georgia Harkness to Edgar Brightman, June 27, 1921; Edgar Brightman to Georgia Harkness, August 17, 1921.

24. Georgia Harkness to Edgar Brightman, August 12, 1921.

25. Discussion between Harkness and Brightman on this subject is taken from the following correspondence: Georgia Harkness to Edgar Brightman, August 16, 1922; April 26, 1922; and June 12, 1922; Edgar Brightman to Georgia Harkness, October 4, 1922.
26. Edgar Brightman to Georgia Harkness, August 17, 1921; Georgia Harkness to Edgar Brightman, August 22, 1921.
27. Georgia Harkness to Edgar Brightman, August 22, 1921; Edgar Brightman to Georgia Harkness, August 26, 1921.
28. Ibid.
29. Georgia Harkness to Edgar Brightman, February 10, 1923.
30. Georgia Harkness, "T. H. Green as a Philosopher of Religion," *The Personalist,* July 1924, p. 172; Georgia Harkness, "Robert Elsmere and Thomas Hill Green," *The Personalist,* April 1926, pp. 115-19.
31. Harkness, "T. H. Green as a Philosopher of Religion,: p. 173.
32. Ibid., pp. 173-74.
33. Ibid., p. 174.
34. Harkness, "Days of My Years, p. 20.

Section IV: "A Woman with a Ph.D. Must . . . Contend Against the Tradition"

7. "A Pacifist, I Think, Forevermore" 1922–1925

1. Edgar Brightman to Georgia Harkness, October 1922. Letters cited in this chapter are in the "Brightman Papers: BU."
2. Georgia Harkness to Edgar Brightman, October 20, 1923.
3. Georgia Harkness to Edgar Brightman: October 20, 1923; January 26, 1924.
4. Georgia Harkness to Edgar Brightman: January 26, 1924; May 2, 1924.
5. Georgia Harkness to Edgar Brightman, May 2, 1924.
6. Ibid.
7. This and the following paragraphs are based on Georgia Harkness, "The Ministry as a Vocation for Women," *The Christian Advocate,* April 10, 1924, pp. 454-55.
8. Georgia Harkness to Edgar Brightman, February 16, 1924.
9. Sherwood Eddy, *A Pilgrimage of Ideas: The Re-education of Sherwood Eddy* (New York: Farrar and Rinehart, 1934), pp. 184-85.
10. Sherwood Eddy, *Eighty Adventurous Years: An Autobiography* (New York: Harper and Bros., 1955), p. 128.
11. Ibid., p. 128.
12. Robert Moats Miller, *American Protestantism and Social Issues* (Chapel Hill: University of North Carolina Press, 1958), p. 250.
13. Eddy, *Eighty Adventurous Years,* pp. 27, 113.

14. Ibid., pp. 101, 104.
15. Ibid., p. 128.
16. This and the following paragraphs are based on Georgia Harkness to Edgar Brightman, September 21, 1924.
17. Eddy, *Eighty Adventurous Years*, pp. 104-5.
18. Harkness, *Grace Abounding*, p. 15.
19. See John Nevin Sayre, "The Story of the Fellowship of Reconciliation," New York, 1935, p. 3; Donald B. Meyer, *The Protestant Search for Political Realism, 1919–1941* (Berkeley: University of California Press: 1960), p. 50.
20. Meyer, *The Protestant Search*, p. 51; Miller, *American Protestantism and Social Issues*, pp. 250-51.
21. Georgia Harkness to Edgar Brightman, March 7, 1925.
22. This and the following paragraph are based on Georgia Harkness, "Germany and the War Peace," *Zion's Herald*, January 7, 1925, pp. 11-12.
23. Georgia Harkness, "Germany's Place in the Shadow," *The Christian Advocate*, January 22, 1925, p. 111.
24. Georgia Harkness, "What the War Has Done to France," *The Christian Advocate*, February 19, 1925, p. 243.

8. *"A Lack of Feminine Charm" 1925–1929*

1. Edgar Brightman to Georgia Harkness, Easter 1925. Letters cited in this chapter are from "Brightman Papers: BU."
2. Edgar Brightman to Agnes Rogers, January 7, 1925.
3. Georgia Harkness to Edgar Brightman, October 20, 1923; Georgia Harkness to Edgar Brightman, May 28, 1925; Georgia Harkness to Edgar Brightman, January 4, 1927; Georgia Harkness to Edgar Brightman, December 13, 1929.
4. Georgia Harkness to Edgar Brightman, May 2, 1924.
5. Georgia Harkness to Edgar Brightman, May 28, 1925.
6. Georgia Harkness to Edgar Brightman, November 5, 1923; Georgia Harkness to Edgar Brightman, November 24, 1923.
7. Georgia Harkness to Edgar Brightman, January 26, 1924.
8. Georgia Harkness to Edgar Brightman, November 24, 1929.
9. Georgia Harkness to Edgar Brightman, November 24, 1925.
10. Georgia Harkness to Edgar Brightman, August 22, 1923; Georgia Harkness to Edgar Brightman, October 20, 1923; Georgia Harkness to Edgar Brightman, February 28, 1924; Georgia Harkness to Edgar Brightman, March 7, 1925; Georgia Harkness to Edgar Brightman, April 16, 1925; Georgia Harkness to Edgar Brightman, November 24, 1925.
11. Georgia Harkness to Edgar Brightman, October 20, 1923.
12. Georgia Harkness to Edgar Brightman, August 6, 1925; Georgia Harkness to Edgar Brightman, August 28, 1925.

13. Discussion in this and following paragraphs is taken from Georgia Harkness to Edgar Brightman, November 8, 1925.

14. Georgia Harkness to Edgar Brightman, November 15, 1925.

15. This paragraph and following ones come from Edgar Brightman to Georgia Harkness, November 20, 1925.

16. Material in this and subsequent paragraphs is based on Georgia Harkness to Edgar Brightman, January 27, 1928.

17. Edgar Brightman to Georgia Harkness, January 29, 1928.

18. Interview of Peg Overholt by Rosemary Keller, April 27, 1991.

Section V: "A Spiritual Pilgrimage: How My Mind Has Changed"

9. "I Ran Myself Ragged" 1929–1939

1. Harkness, "Days of My Years," p. 24.

2. Ibid., p. 25. See also Georgia Harkness, "A Spiritual Pilgrimage: Ninth Article in the Series 'How My Mind Has Changed in This Decade,' " *The Christian Century*, March 15, 1939, p. 349.

3. Ibid., p. 348. Georgia Harkness to Edgar Brightman, February 4, 1939. Letters in this chapter are a part of "Brightman Papers: BU," unless otherwise cited.

4. Edgar Brightman to Georgia Harkness, March 9, 1925.

5. Georgia Harkness to Edgar Brightman, March 26, 1937.

6. Georgia Harkness to Edgar Brightman, February 4, 1939.

7. Harkness, "A Spiritual Pilgrimage," *The Christian Century*, March 15, 1939, p. 348.

8. Harkness, "Days of My Years," p. 21.

9. Ibid., p. 21.

10. Ibid., p. 22. Interview of Peg Overholt by Rosemary Keller, April 27, 1991.

11. Harkness, "Days of My Years," p. 22; Georgia Harkness to Edgar Brightman, September 10, 1931.

12. Georgia Harkness to Edgar Brightman, September 1939.

13. Georgia Harkness to Edgar Brightman, November 20, 1935.

14. Georgia Harkness to Edgar Brightman, November 20, 1936.

15. Harkness, "Days of My Years," p. 23.

16. Georgia Harkness to Edgar Brightman, January 24, 1937.

17. Georgia Harkness to Edgar Brightman, January 16, 1935.

18. Georgia Harkness to Edgar Brightman, February 7, 1935.

19. Georgia Harkness to Edgar Brightman, April 8, 1937.

20. Harkness, "Days of My Years," p. 24, italics added.

21. Georgia Harkness to Edgar Brightman, October 28, 1938.

22. Georgia Harkness to Dr. Christian Reinner, April 21, 1939. "Harkness Collection: G-ETS."

23. Edgar Brightman to Georgia Harkness, January 13, 1939.

24. Georgia Harkness to Edgar Brightman, February 4, 1939.

25. Georgia Harkness to Edgar Brightman, June 2, 1939.

26. This and the following paragraph are based on an interview of Louise Proskine by Rosemary Keller, Ithaca, New York, April 6, 1991.

27. Interview of Peg Overholt by Rosemary Keller, April 27, 1991.

28. Ibid. Also Georgia Harkness to Edgar Brightman, September 27, 1932.

29. Georgia Harkness to Edgar Brightman, September 27, 1932; July 2, 1933; September 26, 1934.

30. Georgia Harkness to Edgar Brightman, March 18, 1932; July 2, 1933; June 20, 1934.

31. Georgia Harkness to Edgar Brightman, July 19, 1933.

32. Georgia Harkness to Edgar Brightman, December 22, 1926; Georgia Harkness to Edgar Brightman, January 22, 1927; Georgia Harkness to Edgar Brightman, January 16, 1935.

33. Georgia Harkness to Edgar Brightman, August 18, 1932.

34. Georgia Harkness to Edgar Brightman, February 1, 1937; Georgia Harkness to Edgar Brightman, February 11, 1937; Georgia Harkness to Edgar Brightman, March 20, 1937.

10. "The Most Impregnable Stronghold of Male Dominance" 1929–1939

1. For this and following paragraphs, see Harkness, "A Spiritual Pilgrimage," *The Christian Century*, March 15, 1939, pp. 349-50.

2. Georgia Harkness to Edgar Brightman, March 7, 1925, this and next paragraph. Letters referred to in this chapter are in "Brightman Papers: BU."

3. Edgar Brightman to Georgia Harkness, March 9, 1925.

4. Georgia Harkness to Edgar Brightman, February 7, 1931. The endorsements of her book *Conflicts in Religious Thought,* may be found in "Brightman Papers: BU."

5. Georgia Harkness, *Conflicts in Religious Thought* (New York: Harper and Bros., 1929; Rev. ed. 1949), p. xiii.

6. Ibid., p. 9.

7. Ibid., pp. 14-19.

8. Ibid., p. 30.

9. Ibid., pp. 165-66.

10. Ibid., pp. 166-67.

11. Harkness, "A Spiritual Pilgrimage," p. 348; Georgia Harkness to Edgar Brightman, November 20, 1935.

12. Georgia Harkness to Edgar Brightman, November 20, 1935.

13. Georgia Harkness, *The Resources of Religion* (New York: Henry Holt and Co., 1936), p. 29.

14. Ibid., p. 35.

15. Ibid., p. 41.

16. Ibid., pp. 41-42.

17. Georgia Harkness, "A Spiritual Pilgrimage," p. 350.

18. Harkness, *The Resources of Religion,* pp. 44, 46.

19. Ibid., p. 51.

20. Harkness, "A Spiritual Pilgrimage," p. 350.

21. Georgia Harkness, "Wanted—Prophets!" *The Presbyterian Tribune,* October 14, 1937, pp. 9-10.

22. Harkness, "A Spiritual Pilgrimage," p. 350, for this paragraph and the following ones.

23. See J. H. Oldham, *The Oxford Conference* (Chicago: Willett, Clark and Co., 1937); Hugh Martin, *Edinburgh 1937* (London: Student Christian Movement Press, 1938); Leonard Hodgson, *The Second World Conference on Faith and Order* (New York: Macmillan, 1938).

24. Georgia Harkness, "Women and the Church," Address to the National Meeting Presbyterian Women's Missionary Societies, Buck Hill Falls, Pennsylvania, May 1938. In "Harkness Collection: G-ETS."

25. Oldham, *The Oxford Conference,* p. 2.

26. Ibid., pp. 116-20, this and following paragraph.

27. Harkness, "A Spiritual Pilgrimage," p. 350.

28. Georgia Harkness, "Was Madras Worthwhile?" *The Garrett Tower,* April 1939, pp. 1-2, 5.

29. Harkness, "A Spiritual Pilgrimage," p. 351.

30. Discussion of the treatment of students and women within the church is based on Georgia Harkness, "Remarks at the Oxford Conference—Summer, 1937," in "Harkness Collection: G-ETS."

31. Georgia Harkness, "Women and the Church," *The Christian Century,* June 2, 1937, p. 708, italics added.

32. Manuscript copies of speech and letter are in "Harkness Collection G-ETS."

33. The following discussion grows out of Georgia Harkness, "Women and the Church," *World Call,* December 1938, pp. 16-17.

34. Harkness, "A Spiritual Pilgrimage," p. 349, this and the following paragraphs.

35. Georgia Harkness, "Una Sancta," *Zion's Herald,* August 11, 1937, p. 1007.

36. Discussion of her fellowship is based on Georgia Harkness to Edgar Brightman, January 13, 1928.

37. Georgia Harkness, *John Calvin: The Man and His Ethics* (New York: Henry Holt & Co., 1931; Rev. ed. New York: Abingdon Press, 1958).

38. The following discussion grows out of Georgia Harkness to Edgar Brightman, February 7, 1931.
39. These paragraphs refer to Harkness, "Days of My Years," p. 22.
40. Advertisement for Georgia Harkness, *Holy Flame* (Boston: B. Humphries, Inc., 1935). In "Brightman Papers: BU."
41. Typewritten copies are found in the "Brightman Papers: BU" and in published form in Harkness, *Grace Abounding,* pp. 19-20, 51-52, 125-26.

Section VI: "For Such a Time as This"

11. From "Triumphant Religion" to the Dark Night of Her Soul 1937–1945

1. Georgia Harkness, "For Such a Time as This," *The Christian Advocate,* July 18, 1940, p. 686.
2. Ibid.; see also Georgia Harkness, "For Such a Time as This," *The Church Women,* 1941, p. 13.
3. Georgia Harkness, *The Recovery of Ideals* (New York: Charles Scribner's Sons, 1937), pp. viii, 13.
4. Ibid., pp. 49, 58, 62.
5. Ibid., p. 46.
6. Georgia Harkness, *Religious Living* (New York: Association Press, 1937), pp. 1, 35.
7. Harkness, *The Recovery of Ideals,* p. 190.
8. Georgia Harkness to Edgar Brightman, January 24, 1937. Letters exchanged between Harkness and Brightman referred to in this chapter are from the "Brightman Papers: BU."
9. Harkness, "Days of My Years," p. 23.
10. Ibid.
11. Mt. Holyoke Alumnae Quarterly, February 1938, p. 283.
12. W. Charles Barber, *Elmira College—First Hundred Years* (New York: McGraw-Hill, 1955), p. 107.
13. Harkness, "Days of My Years," p. 24.
14. Hugh Hawkins, "Mary Woolley," in *Notable American Women: 1607–1950: A Biographical Dictionary,* eds. Edward T. James, Janet Wilson James, and Paul S. Boyer, 3 vols. (Cambridge, Mass.: The Belknap Press, 1971), vol. 1, pp. 660-63.
15. Ibid.
16. Among sources on this period of Mt. Holyoke's history are Frances Lester Warner, *On a New England Campus* (Boston: Houghton Mifflin Company, 1937); Elaine Kendall, *Peculiar Institutions* (New York: G. P. Putnam's Sons, 1970); and Anne Carey Edmonds, *A Memory Book: Mt. Holyoke College—1837–1987* (South Hadley, Mass.: Mt. Holyoke College, 1988).

17. Harkness, "Days of My Years," p. 25; Georgia Harkness to Edgar Brightman, July 19, 1939.

18. Georgia Harkness to Edgar Brightman, July 19, 1939.

19. Ibid.

20. Ibid.; Georgia Harkness to Edgar Brightman, August 17, 1939.

21. Georgia Harkness to Edgar Brightman, August 17, 1939.

22. Georgia Harkness to Edgar Brightman, October 30, 1939.

23. Harkness, "Days of My Years," pp. 25-26.

24. Georgia Harkness to Edgar Brightman, December 6, 1941.

25. Georgia Harkness, Christmas Letter to Friends, "Just Before Christmas, 1941"; Georgia Harkness to Edgar Brightman, December 6, 1941.

26. Georgia Harkness to Edgar Brightman, April 6, 1942; Georgia Harkness to Edgar Brightman, May 28, 1940.

27. Georgia Harkness to Edgar Brightman, April 6, 1942.

28. Ibid.

29. Georgia Harkness to Horace Greeley Smith, April 17, 1943. "Harkness Collection: G-ETS."

30. Georgia Harkness to Edgar Brightman, September 26, 1944.

31. Georgia Harkness, *The Dark Night of the Soul* (New York: Abingdon-Cokesbury Press, 1945), p. 10.

32. Ibid., p. 9.

33. Ibid., p. 11.

34. Georgia Harkness, "If I Make My Bed in Hell," *The Christian Century*, January 14, 1942, pp. 45-48.

35. Ibid., p. 46.

36. Ibid., p. 47.

37. Georgia Harkness, "Perplexed But Not Unto Despair," *The Christian Century*, July 14, 1943, p. 821.

38. Georgia Harkness to Horace Greeley Smith, April 7, 1943.

39. Georgia Harkness, "Nothing Burneth in Hell but Self-Will," *The Christian Century*, February 18, 1942, pp. 216-18.

40. Georgia Harkness, *Religion in Life*, Summer 1944, p. 339.

41. Harkness, *The Dark Night of the Soul*, pp. 170-71, 10-12.

42. Ibid., p. 178.

43. "The Practice of the Presence of God," *The Christian Century*, pp. 111-13.

12. *"Remember Me Not of That Woman!" 1943–1949*

1. Harkness, *The Dark Night of the Soul*, p. 183.

2. Ibid., pp. 183-84.

3. Interview of Murray and Dorothy Leiffer by Rosemary Keller, September 8, 1989, La Jolla, California.

4. Interview of Jan Shipps by Rosemary Keller, April 26, 1991, at the American Society of Church Historians Meeting in Richmond, Virginia.

5. Interview of Dorothy Jean Furnish by Rosemary Keller, October 30, 1991, Northbrook, Illinois.

6. *Christian Science Monitor,* May 20, 1941, pp. 3, 10. (In "Days of My Years," Harkness states that fifty-three women received awards, while the paper names fifty-six.)

7. Harkness, "Days of My Years," p. 24.

8. Murray Leiffer and Dorothy Leiffer, *Enter the Old Portals: Reminiscences: Fifty Years on a Seminary Campus* (Evanston, Ill.: Garrett-Evangelical Theological Seminary, 1987), pp. 21-22.

9. Georgia Harkness to Edgar Brightman, July 10, 1939.

10. Georgia Harkness to Edgar Brightman, August 17, 1939.

11. Georgia Harkness to Edgar Brightman, January 24, 1940; May 28, 1940.

12. Georgia Harkness to friends, "Just Before Christmas," 1941; Georgia Harkness to "Dear Friend-of-the-Year," undated.

13. Georgia Harkness to Edgar Brightman, May 13, 1942.

14. Georgia Harkness to Edgar Brightman, May 18, 1944; September 26, 1944; January 4, 1945; June 6, 1945; December 7, 1945. Also, Edgar Brightman to Georgia Harkness, May 22, 1944.

15. Edgar Brightman to Georgia Harkness, December 19, 1945; Georgia Harkness to Edgar Brightman, December 14, 1945.

16. Interview of Murray and Dorothy Leiffer by Rosemary Keller.

17. Interview of Mary Durham by Rosemary Keller, August 19, 1990, Ithaca, New York.

18. Quoted in Martha Lynne Scott, "The Theology and Social Thought of Georgia Harkness" (Ph.D. dissertation, Garrett-Evangelical Theological Seminary, 1984), p. 44.

19. Georgia Harkness, *Understanding the Christian Faith* (New York: Abingdon-Cokesbury Press, 1947); Georgia Harkness, *Prayer and the Common Life* (New York: Abingdon-Cokesbury Press, 1948); Georgia Harkness, *The Gospel and Our World* (New York: Abingdon Press, 1949).

20. Harkness, *Understanding the Christian Faith,* p. 9.

21. Ibid., pp. 10-13.

22. Harkness, *The Gospel and Our World,* pp. 83, 22.

23. Ibid., p. 24.

24. Ibid., pp. 14-15.

25. Ibid., pp. 9-10.

26. Harkness, *Understanding the Christian Faith,* p. 49.

27. Harkness, *The Gospel and Our World,* p. 58; *Understanding the Christian Faith,* pp. 13-14.

28. Harkness, *The Gospel and Our World,* p. 74.

29. Ibid., pp. 75-76.

30. Harkness, *Understanding the Christian Faith,* p. 11.

31. Harkness, *Prayer and the Common Life,* p. 26.

32. Harkness, *Understanding the Christian Faith,* p. 12.

33. Harkness, *Understanding the Christian Faith*, pp. 12-13.
34. Harkness, *Prayer and the Common Life*, p. 14.
35. Ibid.
36. Leiffers, *Enter the Old Portals*, p. 66.
37. Harkness, "Days of My Years," p. 28.

Section VII: "A Hardy Perennial"

13. *"To Plant My Roots Anew" 1950–1961*

1. The photograph of the Dun Commission, which is included in the picture section, is used courtesy of John Bennett, now of Pilgrim Place, Claremont, California.

2. Interview of John Bennett by Rosemary Keller, Pilgrim Place, Claremont, California, September 8, 1990.

3. "The Christian Conscience and Weapons of Mass Destruction," Report of a Commission appointed by the Federal Council of the Churches of Christ in America. Draft as revised by the Commission, November 3-5, 1950. "Harkness Collection: G-ETS," courtesy of John Bennett, pp. 7-8. Hereafter cited as "Dun Commission Report."

4. Interview of John Bennett by Rosemary Keller.

5. "Dun Commission Report," pp. 3-4.

6. Interview of John Bennett by Rosemary Keller, this and following paragraph.

7. "A Second Look at the Dun Report," *The Christian Century*, October 17, 1951, pp. 1186-88.

8. Harkness, "Days of My Years," p. 29. For the history of Pacific School of Religion, see Harland E. Hogue, *Christian Seed in Western Soil* (Berkeley, Calif.: Pacific School of Religion, 1965).

9. Georgia Harkness to Edgar Brightman, October 21, 1949, this and following paragraph.

10. Interview of Murray and Dorothy Leiffer by Rosemary Keller.

11. Georgia Harkness to Everett and Margaret Harkness, Palmerton, Pennsylvania, March 26, 1950. "Harkness Family Papers: Overholt."

12. James Fowler, *Becoming Adult, Becoming Christian* (San Francisco: Harper & Row, 1984), p. 147.

13. Interview of John and Helen Von Rohr by Rosemary Keller, Walnut Creek, California, June 27, 1991.

14. Interview of Wayne Rood by Rosemary Keller, Pacific School of Religion, Berkeley, California, June 27, 1991, this and following paragraphs.

15. Interview of Harry Pak by Rosemary Keller, First United

Methodist Church, Claremont, California, September 7, 1990, this and paragraphs to follow.

16. Interview of Charles McCoy by Rosemary Keller, Pacific School of Religion, June 26, 1991, this and paragraph to follow.

17. Interview of Durwood Foster by Rosemary Keller, Pacific School of Religion, June 26, 1991.

18. Interview with John and Helen Von Rohr by Rosemary Keller, this and paragraphs to follow.

19. Interview of Wayne Rood by Rosemary Keller, this and paragraphs to follow.

20. Georgia Harkness, *Toward Understanding the Bible* (New York: Charles Scribner's Sons, 1952, 1954).

21. Ibid., p. 22.

22. Ibid., p. 29.

23. Ibid., p. 25.

24. Ibid., p. 26.

25. Georgia Harkness, *Foundations of Christian Knowledge* (New York: Abingdon Press, 1955), foreword and p. 16.

26. See ibid., pp. 154-57.

27. Ibid., pp. 103, 114.

28. Ibid., p. 130.

29. Ibid., p. 151.

30. Georgia Harkness, *The Glory of God: Poems and Prayers for Devotional Use* (New York: Abingdon-Cokesbury Press, 1943), p. 16.

31. Interview of Wayne Rood by Rosemary Keller.

32. Interview of Harry Pak by Rosemary Keller.

33. Interview of Durwood Foster by Rosemary Keller.

34. Interviews of Durwood Foster, Wayne Rood, and Harry Pak by Rosemary Keller.

35. Interview of John and Helen Von Rohr by Rosemary Keller.

36. Interviews of Durwood Foster and Harry Pak by Rosemary Keller.

37. Interview of John and Helen Von Rohr by Rosemary Keller, this and following paragraph.

38. Interviews of Charles McCoy and Durwood Foster by Rosemary Keller, this and following paragraphs.

39. Interviews of John and Helen Von Rohr and Harry Pak by Rosemary Keller.

40. Interview of Charles McCoy by Rosemary Keller.

41. Interview of Durwood Foster by Rosemary Keller.

42. Letter to Rosemary Keller from H. Ellis Finger, November 14, 1991.

43. *Daily Christian Advocate,* May 4, 1956, p. 534, this and following paragraph.

44. Bert Polman, "Hope of the World," *The Hymn,* April 1991, p. 37.

45. *The United Methodist Hymnal* (Nashville: The United Methodist Publishing House, 1989), p. 178.

46. Georgia Harkness, "Witness to the Light." Baccalaureate sermon at first graduation, Japan International Christian University, March 17, 1957. "Harkness Collection: G-ETS," courtesy of Mamie Lee Finger.

47. *Social Questions Bulletin, Methodist Federation for Social Action,* March–April 1983, pp. 1-2, this and following paragraph.

48. Letter to Georgia Harkness from United States Treasury Department, February 2, 1941. "Harkness Collection: G-ETS."

49. Georgia Harkness, paper "The Racial Issue and the Church," n.d. "Harkness Collection: G-ETS."

50. Bulletin of the Eighth Washington Pilgrimage of the Religious Heritage of America, and scrapbook of letters of commendation to Georgia Harkness.

51. Georgia Harkness, "Days of My Years," p. 29.

14. *"The Kingdom Is Nearer Than When We Believed"*
1962–1974

1. Picture included in the book courtesy of Elmira College Library Archives.

2. Bulletin of the graduation service and citation, Elmira College, June 3, 1962. "Harkness Family Papers: Overholt."

3. *Daily Christian Advocate,* The General Conference of The United Methodist Church, April 22, 1972, pp. 334-45, this and following paragraph.

4. Georgia Harkness and Verna Miller to "Dear Friends Far and Near" Thanksgiving 1972; courtesy of Lois and Harvey Seifert, Claremont, California.

5. Interview of Harry Pak by Rosemary Keller.

6. Georgia Harkness and Verna Miller to "Dear Friends Far and Near," this and following paragraph.

7. Lois Seifert, "Bible Lands Revisited," letter to friends, December 1973.

8. Georgia Harkness and Charles F. Kraft, *Biblical Backgrounds of the Middle East Conflict* (Nashville: Abingdon Press, 1976), p. 13.

9. Ibid., p. 10.

10. Rosemary Radford Ruether, "Anti-Semitism and the State of Israel: Some Principles for Christians," *Christianity and Crisis,* November 26, 1973, pp. 240-44. See also Harkness and Kraft, *Biblical Backgrounds of the Middle East Conflict,* pp. 202-3.

11. Georgia Harkness, *The Ministry of Reconciliation* (Nashville: Abingdon Press, 1971), p. 14.

12. Ibid., p. 113.

13. See Georgia Harkness, *Women in Church and Society* (Nashville: Abingdon Press, 1972) and *The Ministry of Reconciliation*, pp. 116-22.

14. Audiotape, group of women clergy and students, Claremont area, March 3, 1974. Courtesy of School of Theology of Claremont Library.

15. Mary Elizabeth Moore, "To Search and to Witness: Theological Agenda of Georgia Harkness." Unpublished paper presented at the American Academy of Religion, November 23, 1991.

16. *Daily Christian Advocate*, p. 335.

17. Georgia Harkness, *Understanding the Kingdom of God* (Nashville: Abingdon Press, 1974).

18. Walter Rauschenbusch, *Christianity and the Social Crisis* (New York: Macmillan, 1907), p. 422.

19. *Daily Christian Advocate*, The Northeastern Jurisdictional Conference of The Methodist Church, June 13 and 16, 1956, pp. 43-44, 68.

20. *Journal of the Last Session of the General Conference of the Evangelical United Brethren Church, Last Session of The Methodist Church*, and *The Uniting Conference of The United Methodist Church and the General Conference of The Methodist Church*, vol. 1 (Nashville: The United Methodist Publishing House, 1968), pp. 524-31, 536, 537.

21. Georgia Harkness, "Letter to the Editor: Methodist-EUB Union," *The Christian Century*, April 20, 1967, p. 501.

22. "Social Principles," *The Book of Discipline of The United Methodist Church 1972* (Nashville: The United Methodist Publishing House, 1973), p. 86.

23. Conversation between Harvey Potthoff and Rosemary Keller, January 28, 1992, The Iliff School of Theology, Denver, Colorado.

24. Moore, "To Search and to Witness," pp. 16-17.

25. Georgia Harkness to Paul Hulslander, May 18, 1974. "Harkness Collection: G-ETS."

26. Interview of Pierce Johnson by Rosemary Keller, September 6, 1990. See also Martha Lynne Scott, "The Theology and Social Thought of Georgia Harkness" (Ph.D. dissertation, Northwestern University, 1985), pp. 49-50.

27. Letter to Peg and John Overholt from Verna Miller, August 31, 1974. "Harkness Family Papers: Overholt."

28. Ibid.

29. Harland Hogue to Verna Miller, August 31, 1974. "Harkness Family Papers: Overholt."

30. Georgia Harkness, *The Providence of God* (Nashville: Abingdon Press, 1960), p. 185.

31. Ibid., pp. 186-87.

32. Georgia Harkness, *Foundations of Christian Knowledge*, p. 153.

Books Written by Georgia Harkness

Be Still and Know. Nashville: Abingdon-Cokesbury Press, 1953.
Beliefs That Count. New York: Abingdon Press, 1961.
Christian Ethics. New York: Abingdon Press, 1957.
The Church and Its Laity. New York: Abingdon Press, 1962.
The Church and the Immigrant. New York: George H. Doran Co., 1921.
Coming to Life: A Study of the Gospel of John, Guide. Cincinnati: Board of Mission, United Methodist Church, 1968.
Conflicts in Religious Thought. New York: Harper and Bros., 1929.
The Dark Night of the Soul. New York: Abingdon-Cokesbury Press, 1945.
The Faith by Which the Church Lives. Nashville: Abingdon Press, 1940.
The Fellowship of the Holy Spirit. Nashville: Abingdon Press, 1966.
Foundations of Christian Knowledge. Nashville: Abingdon Press, 1955.
The Glory of God. Nashville: Abingdon Press, 1943.
The Gospel and Our World. New York: Abingdon-Cokesbury, 1949.
Grace Abounding. Nashville: Abingdon Press, 1969.
Holy Flame. Boston: B. Humphries, Inc., 1935.
John Calvin: The Man and His Ethics. New York: H. Holt & Co., 1931.
The Methodist Church in Social Thought and Action. New York: Abingdon Press, 1964.
The Ministry of Reconciliation. Nashville: Abingdon Press, 1971.
The Modern Rival of Christian Faith. New York: Abingdon-Cokesbury Press, 1952.

Books Written by Georgia Harkness

Mysticism: Its Meaning and Message. Nashville: Abingdon Press, 1973.

O Worship the Lord. New York: National Council of Churches in the U.S.A., 1952.

Our Christian Hope. New York: Abingdon Press, 1964.

Prayer and the Common Life. New York: Abingdon-Cokesbury, 1948.

The Providence of God. New York: Abingdon Press, 1960.

The Recovery of Ideals. New York: Charles Scribner's Sons, 1937.

The Religious Life, comprising these Hazen Classics: *Religious Living,* by Georgia Harkness; *Prayer and Worship* by Douglas V. Steere; *Christians in an Unchristian Society* by Ernest Fremont Tittle. New York: Association Press, 1953.

Religious Living. New York: Association Press, 1937.

The Resources of Religion. New York: Henry Holt and Co., 1936.

The Sources of Western Mortality. New York: Scribner Press, 1954.

Stability Amid Change. Nashville: Abingdon Press, 1969.

Through Christ Our Lord: A Devotional Manual Based on the Recorded Words of Jesus. New York: Abingdon-Cokesbury Press, 1950.

Toward Understanding the Bible. Cincinnati: Women's Division of Christian Service, Board of Missions and Church Extension, Methodist Church, 1952; New York: Charles Scribner's Sons, 1954.

Understanding the Christian Faith. New York: Abingdon-Cokesbury Press, 1947.

Understanding the Kingdom of God. Nashville: Abingdon Press, 1974.

What Christians Believe. Nashville: Abingdon Press, 1965.

Women in Church and Society: A Historical and Theological Inquiry. Nashville: Abingdon Press, 1971.

Posthumously with Charles F. Kraft, *Biblical Backgrounds of the Middle East Conflict.* Nashville: Abingdon Press, 1976.

Articles Written by
Georgia Harkness

"The Abyss and The Given." *Christendom* (Autumn 1938).
"A Change for the Worse and Then for the Better." *The Junior Herald* (September 5, 1941).
"Achievements in Christian Unity." *The Pastor* (February 1956).
"Afflicted with Youth." *Sunday School Journal* (June 1925).
"All God's Children." *Christian Home* (January 1970).
"Americans' Thanksgiving Heritage." *Western Christian Advocate* (November 18, 1926).
"Are Pacifists Romantics?" *The Christian Century* (June 1, 1938).
"The Art of Public Prayer." *The Pulpit* (September 1943).
"By What Authority." *The Christian Advocate* (January 25, 1940).
"The Christian Woman: Of Women Ministers." *The Christian Advocate* (April 19, 1956).
"The Christian's Contribution to Peace." *Senior Quarterly* (January–March 1941).
"The Christian Dilemma." *The Christian Century* (August 6, 1941).
"Christians in an UnChristian World." *Accent On Youth* (March 1974).
"Christus Victor." *Report of World Conference of Christian Youth in Amsterdam* (August 17, 1939).
"The Church and Democracy." *Religion in Life* (1937).
"The Church and the Student." *The Christian Century* (January 26, 1938).
"The Church in a World at War." *The Christian Advocate* (August 22, 1940).

"The Church in a World at War." *Religious Digest* (October 1940).

"The Church in a World Gone Mad." *The Christian Advocate* (July 11, 1940).

"The Churches and Vietnam." *The Christian Century* (January 26, 1966).

"The Churches in This War." *The Christian Century* (November 18, 1942).

"Church Women and the New World." *Pulpit* (January 1945).

"The College Not a Faith-Wrecker." *Literary Digest* (December 6, 1924).

"Creative Insecurity." *Christian Home* (July 1965).

"A Crucial Issue." *The Union Signal* (April 3, 1943).

"Dare the Teacher Breathe?" *The American Scholar* (Summer 1935).

"The Dark Night of the Soul." *Religion in Life* (Summer 1944).

"De Senectute: Commend and Adenda on Growing Older." *The Christian Century* (October 18, 1967).

"The Discovery of God." *The Christian Century* (May 19, 1937).

"Divine Sovereignty and Human Freedom." *Personalism in Theology: A Symposium in Honor of Albert Cornelius Knudson.* Edited by Edgar Sheffield Brightman. (Boston: Boston University Press, 1943).

"Do We Need the Church?" *Accent On Youth* (September 1973).

"Does Science Disapprove of the Bible?" *Accent On Youth* (August 1973).

"Ecumenicity Marches On." *Zion's Herald* (August 9, 1939).

"Erasmus, Prophet of Peace." *The Methodist Review* (March 1929).

"The Ethical Approach to the Study of the Bible." *Journal of the National Association of Biblical Instructors.* (1933).

"Ethical Values in Economics." *Religion in Life* (Summer 1933).

"Faith and Other Requirements of Peace." *Current Religious Thought* (January 1944).

"Father Divine's Righteous Government." *The Christian Century* (October 13, 1965).

"The Fiery Furnace." *Christian Century Pulpit* (June 1941).

"For Such a Time as This." *The Christian Advocate* (July 18, 1940).

"For Such a Time as This." *The Church Woman* (1941).

"For the Spirit of Heaviness." *The Christian Century* (June 17, 1942).

"Germany and the War-Peace." *Zion's Herald* (January 7, 1925).

"Germany's Place in the Shadow." *The Christian Advocate* (January 22, 1925).

"Give Thanks Unto the Lord." *Child Guidance* (November 1948).

"Given to Hospitality." *World Outlook* (October 1965).

"God and the War." *The Christian Advocate* (September 7; September 14; September 21; October 5, 1944).

"God Is Alive in Our World." *Accent On Youth* (November 1969).

"The God Within Us." *The Christian Century* (November 22, 1972).

"A Goodly Heritage." *The Woman's Pulpit* (January–March 1971).

"The Gospel in the Churches." *The Christian Advocate* (October 27, 1949).

"The Greatest of These Is Love." *Accent on Youth* (December 1968).

"Helpful Counsel." *The Christian Century* (January 10, 1973).

"The 'Holy Catholic Church.' " *The Christian Advocate* (September 18, 1947).

"How Do We Find God?" *Accent On Youth* (March 1973).

"How Does One Commit Oneself to Christ?" *The Church School* (December 1968).

"How New Is the New Morality?" *The Pulpit* (November 1967).

"Humanitarian Activities of the League of Nations." *Zion's Herald* (April 15, 1925).

"I Walked Today Where Jesus Walked." *The Woman's Pulpit* (April–June 1963).

"If A Man Must Die." *The Link* (April 1945).

"If I Make My Bed in Hell." *The Christian Century* (January 14, 1942).

"If the Church Is to Be the Inclusive Body." *Nexus* (November 1963).

"Impressions of Oxford." *Journal of Bible and Religion* (October–December 1937).

"In a Crisis, They Will Stand." *Presbyterian Outlook* (April 10, 1967).

"Is Our Age of Anxiety a Post-Christian Era?" *Religion in Life* (Fall 1967).

"Is Pacifism Realism?" *The Christian Advocate* (March 13, 1941).

"Is the Church Meeting Our Needs Today?" *Accent On Youth* (February 1974).

"Jesus' Scale of Values." *The Christian Advocate* (September 1, 1938).

"John Wesley as Hymnologist." *Arkansas Methodist* (September 1, 1938).

"John Wesley as Hymnologist." *Zion's Herald* (May 18, 1938).

"The Layman's Faith." *The Christian Advocate* (January 29, 1948).

"The Layman's World." *The Christian Century* (December 24, 1947).

"The League of Nations—What is It?" *Zion's Herald* (April 1, 1925).

"Life on the Cross." *Motive* (December 1945).

"Life Beyond Death." *Accent On Youth* (December 1973).

"The Madras Conference and Church Unity." *World Outlook* (May 1939).

"Maneuvers in the Back Yard." *The Christian Century* (August 23, 1939).

"A Meditation for Peacemakers." *Classmate* (November 12, 1944).

"Methods of Private Prayer." *The Christian Advocate* (April 26; May 3; May 17, 1945).

"The Ministry as a Vocation for Women." *Religion in Life* (Autumn 1940).

"My Answer to This Question." *The Methodist Woman* (July–August 1951).

"The Nature and Reality of God." *Christian Students in a Changing World* (1937).

"The Nature and Reality of God." *The Intercollegian and Far Horizons* (February 1938).

"Nature as the Vehicle of Grace." *Religion in Life* (Autumn 1940).

"The New Morality and the Social Gospel." *The Pulpit* (December 1967).

"Notes on Christian Trends of Thought in the U.S.A." *The Student World* (1939).

"Nothing Burneth in Hell but Self-Will.' " *The Christian Century* (February 18, 1942).

"On Changing Patriarchy." *Comment* (Winter 1974).

"The One and the Many." *Zion's Herald* (February 25, 1925).

"'One in Christ Jesus.' " *The Christian Advocate* (May 9, 1940).

"'One in Christ Jesus.' " *The Daily Christian Advocate* (April 27, 1940).

"'One in Christ Jesus.' " *Religious Digest* (August 1940).

"Our Heritage." *The Christian Advocate* (January 2, 1941).

"Out of Diversity, Unity." *World Christianity* (Second Quarter 1939).

"Out of Diversity, Unity." *Zion's Herald* (February 15, 1939).

"A Pacifist Ecumenical Witness." *The Christian Century* (July 2, 1941).

"Parents—Keepers of the Faith." *The Christian Home* (January 1969).

"Peace Asks a Hearing." *Zion's Herald* (May 26, 1937).

"Peace—At Any Price?" *Elmira College Bulletin* (March 1937).

"'Perplexed But Not Unto Despair.' " *The Christian Century* (July 14, 1943).

"Pioneer Women in the Ministry." *Religion in Life* (Summer 1970).

"Pioneering in Women's Education." *The Presbyterian Tribune* (July 22, 1937).

"Plato's Philosophy of History." *Christendom* (Summer 1937).

"The Practice of the Presence of God." *The Christian Century* (January 26, 1944).

"Preaching and the Human Condition." *The Presbyterian Outlook* (August 19, 1970).

"Propageese." *Zion's Herald* (June 20, 1928).

"Protestants Plan World Strategy for Peace." *Fellowship* (September 1939).

"The Racial Issue and the Christian Church." *The Church and the New World Mind: The Drake Lectures for 1944.* (St. Louis: The Bethany Press, 1944).

"Redemption and Personal Destiny." *The Journal of Religious Thought* (Autumn–Winter 1946).

"The Relation of Social Ethics to the Curriculum as a Whole." *Journal of the National Association of Biblical Instructors* (1936).

"Religion in the Home." *Journal of Home Economics* (September 1945).

"Robert Elsmere and Thomas Hill Green." *The Personalist* (April 1926).

"Saints and Strategists." *The Christian Century* (July 3, 1935).

"The Second Coming." *Accent On Youth* (July 1973).

"A Second Look at the Dun Report." *The Christian Century* (October 17, 1951).

"Seed and Soil." *The American Baptist Publication Society* (September 14, 1947).

"Setting Your Goals." *Twelve/Fifteen* (November 28, 1965).

"The Seven Last Words from the Cross." *Twelve/Fifteen* (February 27, 1966).

"Shadows, Adjectives, and Brass Buttons." *The Christian Century* (May 31, 1928).

"Shall We Draft Out Women." *The Christian Advocate* (June 10, 1943).

"Shall Women Be Ordained?" *The Presbyterian* (March 15, 1947).

"A Spiritual Pilgrimage." *The Christian Century* (March 15, 1939).

"Spreading God's Love." *Accent On Youth* (March 1974).

"Strengthening the Spiritual Life." *The Pastor* (June 1951).

"Students and the Church." *The Christian Advocate* (February 14, 1935).

"The Symposium: Contemporary Issues in American Methodism." *Asbury Seminarian* (January 1966).

"A Symposium On Reinhold Niebuhr's *Nature and Destiny of Man*" *Christendom* (1941).

"T. H. Green as a Philosopher of Religion." *The Personalist* (July 1924).

"Take That Gun Off My Bible!" *The Christian Century* (January 21, 1926).

"Take That Gun Off My Bible!" *The Churchman* (November 7, 1925).

"The Task of Theology." *Religion in Life* (Winter 1961–1962).

"Teach Us to Pray." *Child Guidance in Christian Living* (June 1945).

"Teaching Content from a Philosophy of Religion." *Christian Education* (April 1930).

"The Theological Basis of the Missionary Message." *International Review of Missions* (October 1939).

"Theology and the Layman." *The Christian Century* (January 9, 1946).

"Theology for Babes." *The Christian Century* (July 29, 1936).

"Theology in Religious Education." *The Journal of Religion* (April 1941).

"The Theology of Dr. Rall." *Garrett Tower* (December 1962).

"Theology of Prayer." *Review and Expositor* (Summer 1974).

"Theology in Religious Education." *The Journal of Religion* (April 1941).

"The Things Which Belong Unto Peace." *Christian Foundations for Lasting Peace* (New York: General Department of United Church Women of the National Council of the Churches of Christ, 1951).

"The Things Which Belong Unto Peace." *The Church Woman* (March 1946).

"The Third World Conference on Faith and Order." *The Church Woman* (November 1952).

"Thy Will Be Done—Through Me." *Grand Rapids Presbyterian Woman* (May 1946).

"Toward a Theology of Social Change." *Religion in Life* (Winter 1967).

"Toward the Recovery of Discipline in Methodism." *The Christian Century* (July 17, 1963).

"Twenty Fateful Years." *The Christian Herald* (May 1963).

"Two Floods." *Zion's Herald* (October 19, 1938).

"Una Sancta: Impressions of the Oxford Conference." *Zion's Herald* (August 11, 1937).

"Vocation and Work in Protestant Perspective." *The United Church Herald* (May 1, 1964).

"Wanted—Prophets." *The Christian Century* (October 14, 1937).

"Was Madras Worth While?" *Garrett Tower* (April 1939).

"What Can Christians Do?" *The Christian Century* (May 29, 1940).

"What Can Prayer Mean to Me?" *Mature Years* (Summer 1974).

"What Is Christianity?" *The Christian Century* (April 2, 1941).

"What Is God Doing in This War?" *The Christian Century* (November 4, 1942).

"What Is Regeneration?" *The Christian Advocate* (July 24, 1952).

"What Is the Spirit of Jesus?" *The Christian Century* (January 21, 1926).

"What Is Your Picture of Jesus?" *Accent On Youth* (August 1973).

"What Prayer Means." *Accent On Youth* (October 1973).

"What Price Unity." *Zion's Herald* (June 7, 1939).

"What the War Has Done to France." *The Christian Advocate* (February 25, 1925).

"What, Then, Should Churches Do?" *The Christian Century* (August 14, 1940).

"When Is a Meeting One Too Many?" *The Christian Advocate* (September 1948).

"When the Christian Citizen Faces Conflict." *The Adult Bible Class Monthly* (July 1941).

"Who Will Show Us Any Good?" *The Presbyterian Tribune* (July–August 1950).

"Who Will Show Us Any Good?" *Chaplain* (July–August 1950).

"Why Peace-Making Is Hard." *Christian Advocate* (May 27, 1954).

"Will Protestantism Destroy Itself?" *The Christian Century* (November 4, 1926).

"Women and the Church." *The Christian Century* (June 2, 1937).

"Women and the Church." *World Call* (December 1938).

"Women . . . and the Ministry." *The Christian Advocate* (May 1, 1952).

"Women Confront a New Age." *The Methodist Woman* (June 1964).

"Women in a United Methodism: The Challenge of the Common Enterprise." *Zion's Herald* (July 17, 1940).

"Women Ministers." *The Christian Advocate* (November 2, 1939).

"Writing the Service for the World Day of Prayer." *The Church Woman* (1942).

"Young Women Leaders in the New Methodist Church." *World Outlook* (January 1939).

Index

Charles), 116
Harkness, Nehemiah, 34, 42, 46, 47-49, 63
Harkness, Thankful, 38, 46
Heck, Barbara, 43
Heilbrun, Carolyn, 37
Henderson, Arthur, 138
Hicks, Elias, 41
High, Stanley, 113
Hitler, 140, 204
Hocking, William Ernest, 119, 162, 173, 177, 270
Hodgkin, Henry T., 141
Hogue, Harland, 301
Hoover, Herbert, 213
Horton, Walter, 270
Hulslander, Paul, 297

Irwin, Paul, 300-301
Ives, Hilda, 236

John of the Cross, Saint, 29, 223, 225
Johnson, Pierce, 286, 299

Keller, Helen, 236
Kennedy, Gerald, 275
Keyes, President (of Skidmore School of Arts), 123
King, Martin Luther, Jr., 118
Knudson, Albert Cornelius, 20, 112, 119
Kolbe, Henry, 240, 242
Kraft, Charles F., 26, 289-90

Lagrange, Mr., 73-74, 77
Latourette, Kenneth Scott, 162
Lavely, John, 118
Lawrence, Brother, 227-28, 230
Leiffer, Murray and Dorothy, 18, 232, 240-41, 242, 243, 260
Lent, Frederick, 124, 132-33, 147, 148, 149
Lester, Muriel, 160
Lindbergh, Anne Morrow, 236

Luccock, Hal and Mary, 162
Luther, Martin, 225, 229
Lyell, Edna, 57
Lyman, Eugene, 164
Lyon, Mary, 79

MacArthur, Douglas, 250
McCoy, Charles, 266, 276-77, 278
McCulloh, Gerald, 240, 243
McDonald, Ramsay, 138
MacFarlane, 288
Macintosh, D. C., 162, 270
Marlatt, Earl, 113
Martin, Gertrude, 82
Maud, 70-71
Mead, Margaret, 35
Miller, Alexander, 265
Miller, Verna, 14, 20, 71, 232-35, 259, 261-62, 274, 276, 277-78, 281, 287-88, 298, 300-301
Moody, Dwight L., 90, 138
Moore, Mary Elizabeth, 293, 297
Morrison, Charles Clayton, 139
Mott, John R., 90-92, 138
Mould, E. W. K., 148, 172
Muelder, Walter, 118
Mueller, Reuben, 286
Murray, Pauli, 35

Niebuhr, Hulda, 35, 139
Niebuhr, Reinhold, 26, 139, 163, 164, 177, 183, 255, 267, 282-83
Niebuhr, Richard, 167
Northfelt, Merlyn, 18

O'Keefe, Georgia, 35
Overholt, John, 19, 300
Overholt, Peggy Harkness, 19, 89-90, 163, 171-72, 300

Page, Kirby, 138
Pak, Carmen, 275, 287